EXPLODING THE MYTHS

FRANK WATKINS

All correspondence to the publisher
Clockwork Print
PO Box 1144
West Perth 6872
WA Australia

© Copyright Frank Watkins 2008

First edition (revised) 2005
Vocational Education and Training Publications

Joshua Books edition first printed 2008

Clockwork Print edition first printed 2018

Pro Trader Pty Ltd
P.O. Box 756
Osborne Park WA 6916
Ph: 08 9202 3900 Fax: 08 9444 9705
www.protrader.com.au

ISBN 978 0 9804551 1 3

Category: Share Trading: Stock Market: Finance: Author: Title

Preface

This book is written by a trader. I have traded on various exchanges around the world and used most trading instruments, including stocks, futures contracts, nooners, options, warrants and CFD's. Whether trading futures contracts on the Winnipeg exchange or a stock on the New Zealand exchange, the set-up is the same – you need a trading plan with a set of rules that work for you. I have written this book for all traders – wherever you are - as a practical guide to cut through the industry jargon and set you on the path towards profitable trading and developing your plan.

It is not a compendium of technical and fundamental analysis mumbo jumbo. The methods I have described work for me. I hope they will work for you. It is my desire to see regular mum and dad investors become profitable traders rather than being among the millions of people who use the BHP (Buy, Hold and Pray) method of trading that is so prevalent among industry experts.

If you are serious about being a successful trader you will need to have some knowledge of technical analysis. I hope this book fills that void and you find much that is useful.

Dedicated to Lizzie Watkins

The author

With more than thirty years experience in trading, broking and educating, Frank Watkins is one of Australia's foremost technical analysts.

Prior to creating the Pro Trader software, Frank held a number of senior positions with some of the country's leading financial institutions.

His career has featured a heavy involvement in the equities, futures and currency markets. He has managed "night desks" with direct access to the floor of several international exchanges, including London, Chicago and New York.

Frank has advised a diverse range of clients at retail, corporate and institutional levels. He has been heavily involved in the rural sector, providing guidance to various state and national associations and commissions.

Frank has a very simple philosophy: buy stocks that are rising, use strict money management and risk management rules and the profits will flow during any market conditions.

His extensive experience at all levels of trading and broking has enabled him to identify and implement successful strategies. Frank details those successful methods in this book.

Frank currently holds the position of CEO of Pro Trader Pty Ltd, a company that specialises in software development, private retail client broking services and education. His primary role is in the education of those wishing to become better traders. He is a regular speaker at the Traders' Expos, the Australian Stock Exchange lunchtime lectures in each state, ATAA meetings throughout Australia and STANZ in New Zealand, as well as a speaker at private investment clubs.

Testimonials

"The most sensible book I have ever read ..."

Please thank Frank for his excellent book. It was the easiest and most sensible book I've ever read on technical analysis, and a most enjoyable read.

Barbara

"This will be the best I ever spent ..."

I've only had time to read the first chapter and flick through the rest of the book but it is very readable and informative. I believe this will be the best I ever spent. This should be regulation reading for anyone with money in superannuation funds and that, of course, is most of us. I believe this publication should be on the bookshelves of everyone in the general public.

Jude

"This is more than a book; it is a life changing experience ..."

I concur with the comments of the other readers. I have made many of the errors Frank highlights in his book, and concur with his conclusions. I come from a background that involved reading dozens of finance books written by the most highly qualified scholars and practitioners. My conclusion is that this is the most useful, logical and commonsensical book I have ever read. This is more than a book; it is a life changing experience.

Andrew

"Buy it, read it, use it! ..."

Frank Watkins book "Exploding the Myths" is a must read. Make it your first trade: Buy it, Read it, Use it!

Greg

"He puts his thoughts down so well ..."

Why did he not write this book two years ago?? Grrrrrrrr. It is hilarious to say the least, knowing how he talks; it is like having an audio book, not a written one. He puts his thoughts down so well.

Jackie

"His book software and business ethic is the most honest and practical I have encountered in my years as a professional ..."

As I mentioned last night, I attended the seminar last night primarily to meet the man in person as a matter of interest and to verify the perception I had of him which I had from reading his book "Exploding the Myths". I liked what I saw and got a sense of an honest individual who is making his best efforts to educate folk about the realities of trading the market. As I mentioned to Frank when I met him and shook his hand, I think his book, software and business ethic is the most honest and practical I have encountered in my years as a trader.

Craig

"Now if only I could get my husband to read it, we might not lose all our super ..."

I recommended your book to a member of a forum which I look at from time to time. This person, who is female, I believe, from her posts seems to be going through a similar difficult time that I did. Now if only I could get my husband to read it, we might not lose all our super!

Jackie

"Real sense ..."

I started by buying Frank's book, and from what I could understand it made sense. Real sense. I read it several times, gaining more knowledge each time. It was just so good.

K.M.H.

Contents

*"I always look at a chart of a company's price.
If the price is rising, the stock may be worth buying.
If, according to the last two quarterly reports,
the company has more cash this quarter
than it had at the end of the last quarter,
it is worth buying.
Cash is king!"*

1

What makes a successful trader?

Obviously you are interested in the share market. Perhaps you have never traded before and are looking to improve your knowledge before investing your hard earned nest egg. Perhaps you have traded in the past. If you have traded before, I can guess that you have lost some money and are now trying to rectify that situation and get your money back. Regardless of your particular situation, let me put you to the test.

Assume that a broker has phoned you with some advice on a particular share that he is recommending. The broker has given you a great rundown on this company and it sounds like a good trade. If you could ask the broker one question, what would that question be? Think about it. You are about to invest a reasonable amount of money into this company and you need to ask one question that will set your mind at ease and give you a strong chance of a profitable trade.

You might ask, "Does this company produce dividends?" but is this really relevant? Just because a company paid a dividend last year does not guarantee a dividend this year. It is also pretty pointless getting a dividend if the price of the share falls 50% over the course of the next year or two.

Or do you ask your broker, "Do you own any shares in this company?" A broker owning the stock is of little comfort and of no value. What is his motive for attempting to get you to buy a stock that he already owns? Perhaps he is trying to "talk the stock up". Perhaps there are no other buyers and he wants to sell his stock having made a bad investment choice himself?

Regardless of his motive, it is of no value knowing that the broker owns stock in this company. In fact it is usually detrimental. It is very difficult to give an unbiased assessment if you have a vested interest yourself.

Should you ask, "Who else is buying these shares?" If the broker answers this question I would find another broker. It is unethical to answer this question. It is also irrelevant. If you were given a prominent name it may not help. Look at the Packer and Murdoch investment in One-tel (they lost nearly one billion dollars in this failed Telco). Even great businessmen make mistakes.

Perhaps you've heard of net tangible assets and ask the broker, "What is the NTA?" (net tangible assets) This appears to be an astute question, but how can that information help you? NTA on its own is useless. The NTA may be falling due to poor performance and the company may be a heartbeat away from bankruptcy.

There are countless other questions you might ask regarding price earning ratios, dividend yield, rate of return and earnings per share, to name a few. I see little value in any of this information.

What is my question? When it comes to purchasing a stock, my philosophy is simple. There is only one issue - "Is the price of the stock rising?" Ask your broker this question and listen very carefully to the reply.

The best way to profit from your investment is if the price continues to rise. If prices are currently rising, there is a high probability that they will continue to rise for a little longer at least. The real issue is, "How can you tell whether or not a stock price is rising?" The answers are in this book.

When it comes to taking profits, my philosophy is just as simple. Let the market tell you when to get out of a stock. But where do you start?

Before we look at how to trade stocks, let's look briefly at some possible investment options.

Passive investing

You can be either a "passive" investor or you can take the bull by the horns and make your own direct investments. This involves handing your money to an "expert" and playing the waiting game.

Perhaps before you do that you might pick up the telephone, ring around the various fund managers and ask them for evidence of their average return over the last ten or even twenty years. Scrutinise the annual returns and see if the fund is outperforming the All Ordinaries Index. If the performance is below the Index each year I would not invest in the fund.

Why invest with someone who cannot outperform the market? If the performance is regularly below that of the All Ordinaries Index you would have to assume that you could do better by investing directly yourself. I would only invest with someone who could outperform the All Ordinaries.

Occasionally, you will find a fund that has a history of producing good returns; however, fund managers who create consistent profits are often poached by another fund, leading to poorer results in subsequent periods of time.

Managed funds

Until recently, Australians have been happy to hand over their spare investment dollars to professional fund managers. During the eighties most "passive" investors were pretty happy with the returns. With fixed interest of around 12% to 15% and very high inflation, everyone was getting what was perceived as a good return with reasonably little effort.

Returns during the nineties were still at acceptable levels despite the lower inflation and falling interest rates. Much of the higher return during the nineties can be attributed to the longest share market boom ever. This decade looks very different with declining markets, low inflation and low interest rates all contributing to lower fund returns.

Fund managers seem powerless to stem the flow, and lack any sort of plan to compensate for falling stock prices. Instead they hide behind the old catch-cry, "time in the market is more important than timing the market". Well, you can fool some of the people some of the time, but the truth is investors are uneasy and looking for better results.

Most people would find an average return of 10% per year acceptable. Unfortunately, few funds appear capable of producing these returns in the current economic climate. Many people are turning towards investing their own money, as they feel that they can do better than the fund managers and realise the need for higher returns with retirement looming.

Exploding the Myths

What a difference 3% makes!

The case for higher returns is best demonstrated in a case study conducted by investment giant MLC Investments. This study shows the incredible difference that a mere 3% per year can make over a working lifetime.

We have two investors, Anna and Ingrid. Both are 25 years old and each makes a regular contribution of $2000.00 per year to a managed fund. Anna invests in a unit trust share fund paying 10%. Ingrid chooses a more conservative fund with a 7% return.

Assuming they both contribute $2000 every year for 40 yrs, the results are incredibly different due to a paltry 3% per annum difference in returns.

SUMMARY		
	ANNA AT 10%	**INGRID AT 7%**
Amount invested	$80 000	$80 000
Years invested	40	40
Account value	**$973 704**	**$427 219**

Do you have what it takes to reach out and take that extra couple of percent? What could an extra 10% or 15% per annum do? A managed fund cannot

> *The main advantage a private trader has is the ability to move from stock to stock with a smaller amount of money.*

hope to achieve the returns that a private trader can achieve. There are many reasons why a fund finds it almost impossible to achieve the higher returns that a private investor can achieve. The main advantage a private trader has is the ability to move from stock to stock with a smaller amount of money.

Funds are simply too large to manoeuvre with any speed. Therefore they live in the hope that the compounding effect will do the job for them. Fund managers are often restricted to the top 200 stocks measured by market capitalisation. This is not necessarily where the big opportunities lie.

Fortunately, New Zealand has so far chosen not to follow Australia's lead and introduce compulsory superannuation. Perhaps it is only a matter of time, or maybe our Trans Tasman friends are simply too smart to allow a compulsory 10% super contribution on which the Government takes a 15% entry fee.

At the end of the day, you might invest in the same stocks as a fund manager, but you will not be paying all the fees, wages, advertising and other costs associated with running a fund. That difference alone might be the 3%, as shown in the previous example.

Superannuation

Your current superannuation scheme is unlikely to provide you with a satisfactory lifestyle after retirement. Negative returns on super funds are commonplace. Have you checked your fund lately? Have you ever had the feeling that you could do better?

Superannuation has failed in the past to provide retirees with satisfactory retirement benefits. I expect that failure to continue in the future despite the advent of compulsory super. Compulsory super has only served to provide Governments with another source of taxation revenue. We constantly see industry professionals "selling" superannuation as a very "tax effective" investment.

Tax effective for whom, you or the government? The 15% up-front tax or entry fee is the most insidious tax of all. A 15% up-front tax sets us back dramatically. A 15% loss requires more than a 19% profit to get back to break even. At an average return of 5% per year, it takes over 4 years to get your money back.

Meanwhile, more fees and charges have been taken on an annual basis. No wonder superannuation is "sold" to you as a long-term investment. There is no choice - a fund needs a long time to recover.

If I were a fund manager and told you that I would take 15% of your investment "up front" in fees, would you invest in my fund? I think not! Anyone who can read a newspaper will have had the opportunity to read the disturbing number of articles that suggest when the "baby boomers" retire, the funds available for pension payments will not be sufficient, nor will the superannuation be adequate.

And for the younger generation, don't be lulled into thinking you will be better off, thanks to compulsory super. A recent headline article entitled – "Black hole super alert" showed that:

- forty years of compulsory superannuation will leave the average Australian with less than $14 000 of personal retirement income each year
- women who on average spend just 21 years in full-time work but live an average of 5 years longer will generally be much worse off
- Australians are not saving enough!   (Herald Sun 3 June 2002)

Perhaps Australians are not saving enough, but the truth is a far cry from that simple suggestion. The truth is that:

- Australians pay more tax on super, and more often, than any other developed country
- superannuation returns are too low.
- the 15% up front tax is most insidious, as it reduces the base from which all earnings are generated.

According to expert actuary Wayne Walker, 56% of your contributions could be in Federal Government coffers by the time you see it at the other end.

I have another philosophical disagreement with compulsory super. There is no compulsion on the funds to actually perform. They can do virtually whatever they like and still charge annual fees. Imagine having no necessity to perform, but having an annual renewable supply of money. Give a child a million dollars every Christmas and see what effect that has on the child after a few years.

Why are we indoctrinated into accepting a fall in lifestyle after retirement? Super payouts are restricted to 80% of our retiring income. Why? Finally we retire and have the time to do all the things we wanted to do, but don't have enough money?

What a waste of a working life! But a successful trader can continue generating an income long after retirement.

Direct investing

There are many reasons for trading. You may wish to supplement your current income, or you may want to make investing a career. One of the most compelling reasons for people over forty is that very few have enough investments to see them through retirement.

What is the earning potential from the share market?

With the staggering amount of information that is available these days, it is difficult to know what is true and what is not. It is just as difficult to determine what is possible and what is not. Entrepreneurs promise staggering profits, but very astute people like Packer and Murdoch lost nearly a billion dollars in the One-tel fiasco. If successful businessmen like Packer and Murdoch lose such huge amounts of money, what chance do you have?

After more than thirty years trading experience, including ten years in the Futures and Stock broking industry, I am constantly bemused by the relationship between the exorbitant volumes of educational material available, detailing "How to make a living trading stocks" and the number of people who fail to make a cent, let alone live from the market.

> *Despite all the expert advice, the expert educators and numerous excellent books, the majority of people attracted to the stock market lose money. There is something badly amiss!*

Despite all the expert advice, the expert educators and numerous excellent books, the majority of people attracted to the stock market lose money. There is something badly amiss!

In the financial year ending June 2002, the average Australian Superannuation returns were negative 4.5%. In the same newspaper where this report appeared, an advertisement for a seminar invites the gullible to roll up and learn how to earn 69% per annum, while other advertisements infer earnings of over $3 500 per week as being an average sort of week for the average "mum and dad" investor.

So what is the truth? In the first place you need to remember that the media tend to focus on the negatives, and bad news travels faster and further than good news. Top performing stocks (and there are plenty of them) receive very little publicity and the people who make enormous profits receive even less.

From the failure of Poseidon during 1969, through the Bond and Quintex bankruptcies of 1987 and on to the failure of HIH insurance and One-tel following the Telco boom, you would assume that people should have learned to trade profitably by now.

Unfortunately this is not the case. People who lost money in the last boom appear to have learned nothing from the experience, so you won't learn much from them. Those who made money are too busy continuing to make money to bother passing on their winning methods.

Do you want to earn 25%, 50% or 100% each year?

The fact that you have picked up this book indicates that you want more than the traditional long-term investor's return of about 10% over any given decade. Hopefully, you have come to the conclusion that you want more than the offerings of fund managers.

This book will give you a different perspective on how the market works and on what is required for trading success. Hopefully, this will help you avoid many of the pitfalls of first time traders.

There are many "myths" and misconceptions that could prohibit you from attaining the success that you desire. The following chapters explain these myths and will help you avoid falling into the same old mistakes that newcomers make. Most of all, I hope to make you sit up and think and look before you leap. That alone will be an achievement because most newcomers to the market do not think and just jump on board the latest hot tip.

Observing the behaviour of hundreds of winners and thousands of losers has given me a few insights into the industry of which you may be unaware. I hope to impart the necessary "tricks of the trade" that might help you on the road to success. More importantly, I hope to show you what is required to keep your valuable capital intact. Survival is your first goal. The profits will follow.

What makes a good trader?

Wherever I go, people ask how I trade and can I teach them to trade. Of every hundred people I meet, ninety-nine admit to wanting to trade stocks for a living. My answer is always the same. Of course I can teach you how to trade and yes, you can trade for a living, but will *you* be able to learn how to trade profitably? Are you coachable? Do you have copious amounts of self-discipline? How do you react to stress?

Good trading skills are not inherited – they can be learned. Successful traders come from all walks of life: nurses, teachers, real estate agents, plumbers, sportspeople, builders and many other "ordinary" occupations. But what makes a good trader? Having watched thousands of people over the years, there are some common attributes that successful traders enjoy. Cultivate the attributes on page 18 and you will be well on your way to being a successful trader.

But be warned!

A high IQ is definitely no guarantee of success, nor is a large wallet or a fantastic education. Often these factors are hindrances when it comes to share trading. I have seen many extremely wealthy and intelligent people destroyed by the market.

Attributes of a successful trader

Establish self discipline	The book entitled *Market Wizards* presented a series of interviews with some of the world's great traders and fund managers. Each of these super traders achieved extraordinary profits, trading different markets with different plans, ideas and methods of analysis. The one common thread was their discipline. People employed in situations requiring discipline generally trade more profitably than others. These careers include the military, police and nurses.
Have an ability to learn	Are you coachable? You must be able to decipher and accept good advice when you hear it. When you read books and newspapers be able to interpret what is applicable to you and your method of trading. There is no single way to trade. To develop a personal trading plan, you must be able to listen, learn and accept guidance and coaching from various different sources until you find the ideal blend.
Develop perseverance	You need to stick at this business. There is no point jumping onto a hot tip from a friend, losing money and walking away. All this demonstrates is a lack of discipline and a greed orientation. Get serious. *I am not discouraged, because every wrong attempt discarded is another step forward.* Thomas Edison
Cultivate a desire to learn	The market changes every day, yet many aspects remain the same. It is rarely dull and boring. It will keep you constantly stimulated. Successful traders never stop learning. If you *do* stop learning, you will lose money. Read books on the subject, talk to other successful traders and attend any seminars where reputable speakers are involved. This will help you to find the method that works for you – then keep repeating that method.
Be passionate	Successful traders are passionate about what they do. Whatever your pursuit, you will not achieve at your greatest potential unless you are passionate about your cause. The best coaches, sportspeople, nurses, employees and employers are those who are passionate about their career and enjoy what they are doing.
Maintain a clear head	Clear your head of the clutter of preconceptions and share market myths. Much of what you already know will inhibit your growth as a trader. Many things you have learned over the years that stand you in good stead in other walks of life will not help in your share trading. You will need to clear your mind of some of your existing ideas.

My father told me of one certain way to make a small fortune - "*Start with a big one and whittle it down*". This tongue in cheek comment illustrates how difficult it is to build a decent sized nest egg. Some extremely intelligent people feel they are "smarter" than the market. Stepping into the market with this attitude can lead to disaster. I have watched one particular client blow away close to five million dollars over a two-month period. A bucket load of money is not the key to successful trading. Begin to cultivate personal attributes that build successful trading behaviour.

Where do you fit?

So you want to be a stock market trader? You may have a strong desire to build wealth and a lifestyle to match. Perhaps it's not only the wealth but also the excitement and intellectual challenge of finding hidden investment opportunities through successfully analysing and interpreting the market? You might also have a mental picture of a what a successful stock market trader is, but what is the reality?

First, don't give up your day job. You probably can't afford to. Many people visualise grabbing a stake of $10 000 and living from the proceeds. This is totally unrealistic. Let me give you an idea of reality.

Assume you want $50 000 each year for your living expenses and assume that you can achieve a constant 30% per annum return. Oh! And don't forget your contribution to Canberra. You will need a "gross" income of around $70 000. On this figure you will need to invest $210 000 and return 30% to achieve your required income.

But wait, there's more. You will also need your first year's income in a separate account, as you cannot afford to draw your first year of living expenses from the trading account. The total requirement is now $280 000. Also, you need to be free of any debt, including mortgage and car repayments. You will not trade successfully if you are depending on your next profitable trade to make a mortgage repayment.

Even with that sort of capital there are no guarantees. A fool and his money are soon parted! You need to become a very good trader to constantly achieve 30%. This does not mean trading is a full time occupation, unless that is what you choose. Analysis, order placement, money management and recording of transactions need not take up any more than one hour each day and the time involved could well be less.

Learning to trade successfully

Treat trading as you would any other career. Serve your apprenticeship, work and study hard and learn all the tricks of the trade. Read books and continuously upgrade your knowledge, attend courses and listen to other profitable traders. No other industry will reward hard work as much as the stock market!

Conclusions

- Any analysis proves that over the past fifty years, the stock market has outperformed all other asset classes.
- Superannuation returns will not provide an adequate retirement income.
- With a little help and a lot of work, you can outperform the market averages.
- A successful trader can work from anywhere in the world and produce an income long after retirement.
- When you read, research, or your broker makes a recommendation, check on one important detail - *"Is the price rising?"*

2

Investment Myths

Each stock market boom brings about a new wave of entrepreneurs and marketing gurus who will take advantage of the upswing using slick advertising and catch phrases to lure you into the latest investment. Dividend imputation funds, ethical investing, asset allocation, derivative trading and dollar-cost-averaging give the industry an exotic flavour. Money flows readily from our pockets into the latest managed fund. I have felt for some time that many of the advertising slogans are derived from old ideas that will not help you to be a profitable trader. These slogans along with other "old wives tales" are what I lump together as market myths.

As each new share market boom arrives, another generation of new investors is swept along on the crest of a wave that finally comes crashing down on them. Bewildered first timers are left holding worthless pieces of paper as companies enter bankruptcy and disappear off the face of the planet. Short-term trades entered for instant profit become long-term investments relegated to the bottom drawer.

Losing traders have no idea what went wrong. They are often too embarrassed to make an effort to analyse their mistakes, pass on their knowledge and ensure the next generation is more successful. Once bitten, twice shy!

Don't expect to get an education from the broking industry. It does not exist for that purpose. It is there to take a commission or a management fee from you. Don't expect your broker to make above average returns for you. Again, he is there to earn a commission. Each boom-time brings a new wave of investors being advised by a new wave of young advisers who have limited experience and lack the knowledge required to outperform the Index. Given that industry statistics show that 80% of newcomers lose, how good is the industry?

Many myths have been perpetuated over the years. You will be aware of them but will not understand how they affect your attempts to beat the averages. It is these Investment Myths that have led me to write this book. They are myths because they will not help you outperform the market index. I expect you want more than that. This book is all about exploding those myths and trying to set the newcomer on the road to financial independence through profitable trading.

1 | Myth one

Time in the market is important, not timing!

This is the biggest load of rubbish that I have ever heard. This saying is for those who are unable to get their timing right. For those who know better, it is a myth.

> *Wall Street's graveyards are filled with men who were right too soon.*
> William Hamilton

Waiting years and years for an investment to produce a higher than average return rates as the greatest fallacy of all. Is there any point buying shares in, say, Melbourne IT at $12.00 or $14.00 in March or April 2000 and watching for a couple of years as they go down to less than $1.00? Timing is of paramount importance! To suggest otherwise is absurd. Everything we do requires good timing.

Even the CEO of Telstra has learned the importance of correct timing. I can recall watching the CEO of Telstra on television following the release of the Telstra annual report in 2001. In this report Telstra had written off more than one billion dollars following some acquisitions in Asia. When questioned on the prudence of some of Telstras' expenditure during the Telco boom, his response was, *"There was nothing wrong with the business we invested in, but perhaps the timing could have been a little better".*

Timing is everything!

Do you still own Telstra? Do you plan your annual snow skiing trip to the Australian Alps in February? Can you imagine a wheat farmer in Southern Australia sowing his crop in December! Did you buy AMP at $35.00 on the day of the float, only to watch your capital halve a mere twelve months later?

Investing in stocks successfully means having the right stock at the right time. How many times have you heard someone saying, *"He's just lucky, he always seems to be in the right place at the right time."*

Accepting that time in the market is more important than timing is probably the greatest downfall of anyone who is trying to beat the market averages. Financial industry advertising patronisingly tells the public that time in the market is more important than timing the market. Could it be that the industry is after "sticky" money that stays in their coffers for five or ten years attracting the standard annual fee?

What can poor timing lead to?

How sensible was the timing of this broker recommendation on 18 August 1998 regarding HIH Insurance?

"This company recently announced an historic dividend of 6.6% (50% franked) and is one of Australia's largest general insurance companies – a company which has a strong market position and a demonstrated record of growth and profitability. Looks like a buy at this level".

At the time of this recommendation, HIH was trending down very sharply. The stock never, not even for one day, traded above the price at which it was recommended. As we all know, HIH insurance is now bankrupt. Unfortunately, bad timing of recommendations is commonplace. The previous recommendation is not an isolated case.

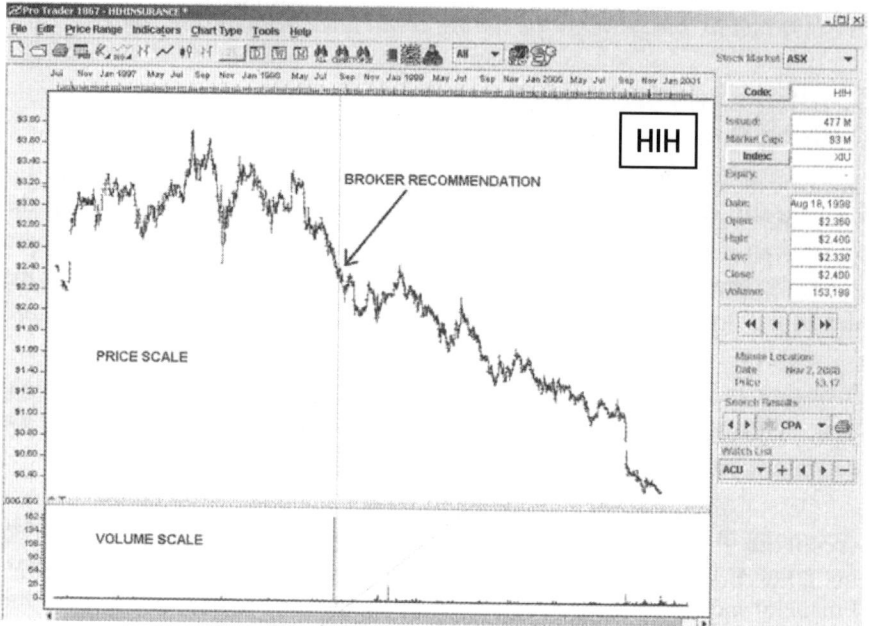

What can good timing do for you?

I was working in South Australia as an adviser in the futures market during the 1987 boom and subsequent crash. We advertised our broking services nationally. A young man from Perth responded and wanted to invest two and a half thousand dollars.

There's not much that can be done in futures with that sort of money. We recommended he purchase an S and P 500 put option that expired in December 1987. Without going into detail we were taking a position that would be profitable if the broad US market fell.

We were not anticipating the biggest fall in history. I'm sure the client had no idea what he was doing or what he had invested in. In October '87 the market crashed heavily. The phone call of the day came from the young guy in Perth. He was quite glum with his opening statement.

"I suppose I've lost all my money in the crash, havent I"?

Our response, *"No, a put option makes a profit when the market falls, your $2 500 option is currently worth $50 000 U.S. dollars, give or take a few bob".*

I cannot accurately relate his next response in this book; however, at the end of the conversation he gave us a very firm instruction to sell his option and post him a cheque. Regardless of whether this was luck, good advice or just good timing, the client will always remember turning $2 500 into $65 000 in about six weeks! I prefer to think that this was good timing!

> **It isn't as important to buy as cheap as possible as it is to buy at the right time.**
> Jesse Livermore

The small investor's advantage

Timing is where the small investor has a huge advantage over fund managers and brokers. The ability to move smaller amounts of equity from stock to stock cannot be under-estimated.

It does mean being a little more proactive than buying HIH insurance shares at two dollars, watching them for two years and waiting for a miracle as they slide into bankruptcy.

Those caught with losses in HIH are those who use the BHP method, Buying, Holding and Praying, for time to work in their favour.

How do we fine-tune our timing?

As we go through this book I will cover timing issues in more detail. It is generally accepted that technical analysis will assist in the timing of the purchase of a stock.

Getting your timing right will alleviate the problem of having your capital tied up for years on end in a stock that is not performing.

If 80% of traders lose, then I would suggest that the vast majority of those people have a timing problem. Get it right and you can trade from anywhere in the world and continue producing an income long after retirement.

2 Myth two
Diversify or perish

We are correctly led to believe that diversification reduces risk. Unfortunately, there is a heavy inference that diversification will also lead to handsome profits. That is the myth. Diversification is a method of investing that will almost ensure the standard 10% per annum average over any ten-year period.

> *Diversification is another word for risk minimisation, but has very little to do with making profits.*

Diversification within an overall investment philosophy makes a certain amount of sense, but diversification for the sake of being diversified achieves very little. To have funds in property, stocks, collectables or a business is practical, but ultimately many people over-diversify and lose sight of maximising profits. You can't have it both ways.

Managed funds and superannuation are incredibly diversified. A magical potion of cash, bonds, real estate, Australian equities and overseas equities are supposedly the key to investment success. But are they?

Anyone who has ever looked at the long-term returns on cash and bonds will be aware that they under-perform real estate and equities by a considerable margin. Cash and bonds hold down the overall performance of any fund. Quite apart from the poor returns on cash and bonds is the fact that if I want to invest in cash I am quite capable of doing that myself. I don't expect to give cash to a fund manager and have him invest in cash! The purpose of diversifying is to minimise overall risk in your share portfolio. The effect is to reduce profits.

Stock market diversification

As you begin to seek advice and invest intelligently, you will be told to have a spread of stocks in the various sectors of the market. Perhaps bank stocks, white goods, retail, resource, health and biotechnology, a building material stock, an engineering stock and a Telco. Sounds good! But does it work? Again, it is usually the recipe for the average 10% per year over any ten-year period. But why have funds tied up in the resource sector if commodity prices are falling and that sector is not performing?

Surely a concentration of funds in the best performing sector makes more sense? Over the last couple of years most of us have been alerted to the fact that the Australian market represents only 2% of the world markets. Campaigns are run suggesting that we should diversify into overseas equities. This suggestion amazes me. If you can't make money investing in the Australian market, how does buying overseas equities help you? More marketing baloney!

So how do we counter over-diversification? The scattergun approach of buying twenty or thirty stocks may ensure that you pick a couple of winners, but these will generally be outweighed by a number of poorly performing stocks. You need to learn to specialise and plan your approach. Part of the plan is to write down a maximum number of stocks that you will own according to the capital you have to invest. I will cover this in more detail in a later chapter.

Diversify your timing

Diversifying the timing of your entry into the market is something that is rarely considered. If you won lotto tonight and decided to invest $100 000 into equities, would you invest it all tomorrow? If you went to a broker with one hundred thousand dollars I'm pretty sure they would pull out a list of "Blue Chip" shares and have your funds fully invested within moments. If they are advocates of diversifying, why not diversify the timing of the entry into each stock and get the entry level right?

My mate Brian

Brian grew up with diversification. As a farmer thirty years ago he grew wheat, oats and barley and raised sheep, pigs, cattle and horses. That was about as diversified as you could get. He was always broke because either wool prices were low or maybe wheat prices had collapsed. There was always some aspect of his enterprise that held his profitability down.

These days he is far more specialised. The pigs and cattle have gone, the motorbike has replaced the horses, and he no longer grows oats and barley. His whole operation is leaner and meaner and highly specialised. Crops are planted faster and with better timing. Harvesting is a very slick operation minimising the potential for damage from summer rains. His enterprise is far more profitable than ever before. Brian's diversification now comes from off-farm investments.

There are examples of publicly listed companies on the Australian Stock Exchange that have over-diversified in the past. The share price has subsequently fallen. Action has then been taken to go back to their "core" business activity. When this happens prices stabilise and usually rally. Book after book, magazine after magazine will tell you to diversify. All I say is be careful, don't over do it, and you will find that specialising will produce higher results.

3 Myth three

Seek professional advice

Seeking professional advice would appear to be the wise path to choose, and for many people it is. It suits a large portion of the community to let others make investment decisions on their behalf. This is fine as long as you are prepared to wait years for the compounding effect to do the job that you could do. Many people do not have the time or knowledge to make their own decisions.

So why do I consider seeking professional advice to be a myth? The fact is that if the advice given was sound and profitable, why is it that 80% lose? Many of the 80% who lose have followed expert advice and lost large sums of money.

Before all the advisers out there start screaming, please consider the following. If we constantly received advice with satisfactory and profitable results, there would be a queue outside your door every payday and we could sit back and relax and enjoy the returns. Perhaps a broking firm would like to alter its structure and rather than take a fixed commission from each trade, consider working for a fee based on a percentage of profits.

We are seeing the beginning of what may be an avalanche of litigation against broking firms for over-trading, poor advice and even negligence.

Where are all the client's yachts?

A story told by Jake Bernstein goes along the following lines. A young Wall Street broker was wining and dining a wealthy potential client down at the New York Yacht club. As they strolled along the boardwalk, the broker was pointing out the brokers' yachts.

"There's Refcos' 200-footer, Shearson Leamans' 90-footer and Salomon Smith Barneys' 140-foot yacht," he told the prospect in an effort to impress.

The prospective client finally turned to the broker and asked quizzically, *"Where are all the clients' yachts?"* Hmmm, food for thought!

How do we get sound advice?

There is no such thing. There is simply advice that can lead to profits and advice that can lead to losses. You need to confirm which category the advice that you receive falls into. The easiest way to do this is by looking at the chart of the stock in conjunction with the advice. A chart of the prices of a stock shows at a glance whether or not the price is rising or falling. I have devoted a whole chapter to visual investing. (Chapter 4 – Investing is visual)

Exploding the Myths

Brian takes on a financial planner

Brian had a financial planner look after some of his spare capital. He was relating his experience to me just prior to the "Tech wreck" on the 17 April 2000. He had made the decision to use a financial planner, as he could not devote enough time to the investment process. For five years between 1995 and 2000 he had given the financial planner $10 000 each year to invest.

The local planner charged an annual fee of $2 000 to manage the portfolio. (This was, perhaps, Brian's first mistake, as a 20% up front fee is highway robbery.) Over the next five years Brian had deposited $50 000 with the financial planner, paying $10 000 in fees. And the portfolio balance after five years? A mere $30 000. This is a true story. Brian had lost $20 000. When approached, the financial planner was adamant that he just needed more time! More time for what? To lose even more? Unfortunately, this sort of story is not uncommon.

All advice is generally given with the best intent. Most people delivering advice believe in the story they are relaying to their client. Some people can receive good advice and still lose, perhaps because of poor timing or a lack of capital.

Using brokers

If you find that you rely on the advice of others, then at least go and meet the broker you are going to deal with. A face-to-face meeting will sort out some issues. Hopefully, you will find someone you feel that you can trust. Perhaps a mature broker who has been through the last crash. Ask if he trades his own account. How do you feel about that? Why doesn't he give advising away and trade his own account full time? Don't expect to become strong friends with this person. Keep the relationship professional. Remember, a good broker is rather like a good airline steward. They are there to ensure you have a good and safe journey, and to cater to your demands.

Myth four

4

Set up a "Blue Chip" portfolio

I have just been searching my trusty Oxford dictionary for the meaning of "Blue Chip" and was amused that Oxford gives no meaning. I'm inclined to agree with Oxford. There is no such thing! The term "Blue Chip" comes from the highest value chip in poker. A blue chip share is defined as a share in a company that is seen to be a solid and steady performer, delivering dividends in all market conditions.

Examples of "Blue Chip" companies today would include Commonwealth Bank, Western Mining, BHP-Billiton, Telstra, and AMP, to name a few. I dare say a list of "Blue Chip" shares from twenty years ago would be substantially different from today's list. This is exactly why buying and holding onto blue chip shares becomes a myth. Many blue chip shares can also be low yielding and expensive.

Perhaps on professional advice you have developed a "Blue Chip" portfolio or are exploring this possibility. There is a perception that expensive stocks are good stocks. However, a stock like BHP

> *Bear in mind that of the top 150 companies by market capitalisation twelve years ago, around 70 no longer exist!*

traded at approximately ten dollars per share (adjusted for a two-for-one split) in June 1997 and over four years later is still trading at around $10 per share. I see little point rejoicing over a dividend each year under these circumstances.

Friends of mine very proudly marched into a broking firm looking for advice on investing their life-time savings of $100 000. It was during November 1997. They left the broker's office that morning at 11.35 a.m. The broker advised a "diversified blue chip" portfolio and outlined the stocks that would be purchased. My friends were surprised that the whole $100 000 was invested that day.

The value of the portfolio declined from that moment on and six months later was worth $87 000. On a busy working day, how on earth does a broker make a $100 000 investment decision? Are there any checks and balances on the brokers' decision? It took a further three years before they had their account balance back over the original investment. So much for a choice selection of blue chip stocks!

Lets look at a portfolio of blue chip stocks over the last five years to see what sort of performance might be reasonable. We need to make some assumptions to complete this exercise. The stocks we will include are: ANZ Bank, Westpac, News Corporation, AMP Ltd, Commonwealth Bank, BHP Billiton, Woodside, Telstra, Western Mining and Lend Lease.

These are shown in the table on the following page, along with certain assumptions to demonstrate my point. I am quite sure that most experts across the country would have been recommending these stocks as blue chips five years ago. We also know that the banks have done well, so I have included three of them for the purpose of this exercise.

The return over this sample of stocks is 32.23%, an average of just over 6% per year. If we add an average of 4% per year as an allowance for dividends, we have the normal return of about 10% per annum. How much better would the returns have been if you had sold the worst four or five of these stocks when they failed to perform?

My whole point is that sensible 'pruning' would increase returns dramatically. Continually attempt to find strong rising stocks and get rid of the poor performing stocks. During the same five years you may have found the following hidden gems, Cochlear, up 700%, Woolworths, up 180%, Flight Centre, up 600% or Perpetual Trustees, up 350%.

How do we get the best return from a blue chip portfolio?

If you are going to set up a blue chip portfolio, then specialise in owning the ten best performing stocks. Please consider the following. If you have the ten best performing stocks in your portfolio and you buy another stock, you are automatically diluting the performance of the best ten.

Code	1 July 1997	Vol	Cost	30 June 2002	Profit/loss
ANZ	9.76	1000	9 840	19.29	9 370
CBA	15.84	1000	15 920	32.93	16 930
NAB	18.70	1000	18 780	35.40	16 540
AMP	18.92	1000	9 000	15.60	-3 480
LLC	13.88	1000	13	10.54	-3 500
WPL	11.33	1000	11 410	13.57	2 080
TLS	8.69	1000	8 770	4.66	-4 190
WMC	8.33	1000	8 410	9.09	600
BHP	8.62	1000	8 700	10.30	1 520
NCP	6.33	1000	6 410	9.68	3 190
			$121 200		$39 060

(Assume 1000 shares in each stock on 1 July 1997. AMP was added to the portfolio on 1 July 1998. Telstra was added on 1 July 1999, as this was the 1st July that they were " paid up". Assume $80.00 brokerage on entry and exit)

You will need to monitor your portfolio on a regular basis, selling off stocks that are not performing and replacing them with better stocks. It is incredibly unlikely that you will pick the best ten at any one time as conditions change. It is, however, an admirable goal. There is no point being a pilot and being satisfied with nine safe landings out of ten!

Once you have ten stocks that you are satisfied with, monitor them closely. If for some reason you need to purchase another stock, always sell the worst performing stock and replace it with the new purchase. Do not sell the best performing stock. If you continuously sell the best performing stock you will end up with ten stocks that are heading south. Only by selling the worst stock each time does your portfolio continually improve!

5 Myth five

Beware October

October suffers the stigma of being a bad month in the share market, following the October 1929 crash and the October 1987 crash. There have been other hiccups in October, but to suggest it is "the worst month" is a myth. The following article appeared in the press during October 1998.

Exploding the Myths

A Much Maligned Month

The 42% crash in the All Ordinaries Index in October '87 and the 11% slide last year have built fears about the month. This month the index has dipped 1.5%.

How bad is October? Financial planning group Godfrey Pembroke visited the records for 19½ years to June this year and found 1987 and 1997 were the only two Octobers on the list of 20 worst months.

Three of the best months were October. This put it alongside March and July as the month appearing most often in the top 20. February appeared four times in the 20 worst months; and January, March, May, September, October and November twice each. December did not appear on the worst list for the period.

The West Australian, October 1998

I haven't bothered checking these statistics. There is no doubt that the two biggest crashes of all time occurred in October. There were severe corrections during October 1997 and October 1999. Despite these occurrences it is not particularly intelligent to suggest getting out of all stocks during October, just in case the market falls.

Interestingly, while the average return for October is roughly negative 1%, there have been more positive Octobers than negative ones since 1980. It's just that when October has a bad month, it can really be a downer!

Far better to use October as an opportunity to buy stock at a discount. The media perpetuates this myth each year with reminders during September that we should all "beware October". Each September there seems to be a journalist somewhere who writes an article suggesting investors be very cautious during October, such as in the following extracts from the Financial Review.

—— Exploding the Myths ——

Markets fall with the autumn leaves

"... Mr Montgomery also tracks even more esoteric "non-rational" (his words) relationships, among them the change in the seasons. Markets tend to top around September 22 more than any other date, he says, or roughly around the beginning of autumn.

That leads to the familiar October stockmarket plunges, as Mr Montgomery recalls in 1979, 1987 and 1989. Global capital markets also were thrown into tizzies by the Asian crisis in 1997 and the collapse of long term capital markets in 1998. And, of course, there was last year's post September 11 plunge."

Aust Financial Review, Mon 16 September 2002

My view is that October is just another month in the calendar. If you are in stocks that are rising, and have your risk management rules in place, you will not be hurt much by a severe correction. If there is a decent correction at any time, not only October, I would view it as an opportunity to buy shares rather than approach each October with trepidation.

6 Myth six

You can't make money in a bear market

There is no doubt that a seasoned trader can make substantial profits in a bear market. Profits can be generated with the same trading methodology as that used in a bull market. In other words, *just keep buying stocks that are rising*. It is the simplest way of generating significant returns.

While values do not tend to rise as rapidly as they will in a bull market, there are still plenty of opportunities. Bear market or not, if a company strikes oil or gold or makes a medical breakthrough it will perform well.

Some refer to these as "situation stocks", as the focus is on a particular situation or event that occurs even in a bearish market.

This chart shows the performance of Woolworths (WOW) shares since the Telco crash in April 2000. There will always be "situation stocks" that will rise when the general trend of the market is down.

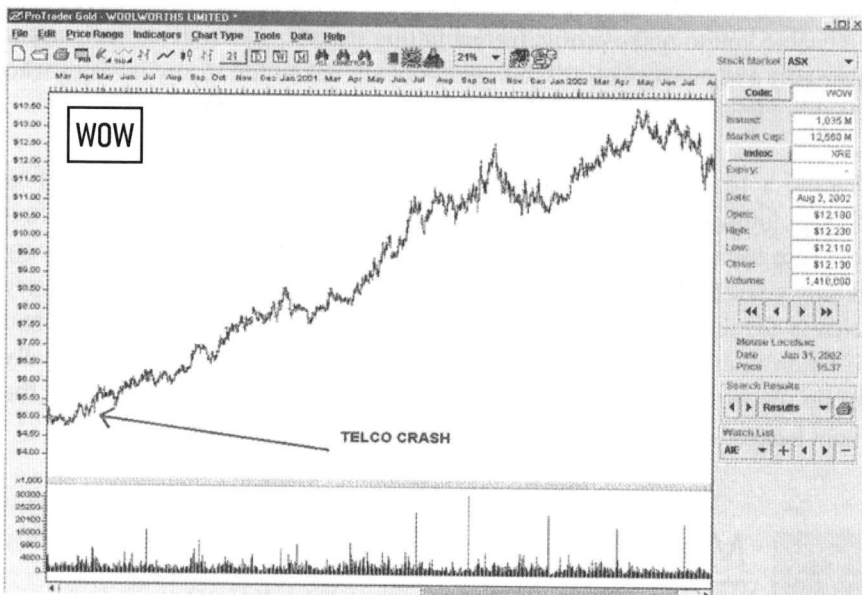

Similarly, Ion Carbide, Flight Centre, Cochlear, Sirtex, Patrick Corporation and many others have had a very good run since the Telco crash. There are many stocks that will rise because of their particular "situation" in terms of their individual prospects, new markets, new inventions, new contracts and the like.

These days, there are plenty of trading instruments available that are designed to enable you to make profits from a falling market. Derivatives, such as put warrants and put options fill this need, but are not suited to any investor who does not have an exceptional understanding of these instruments.

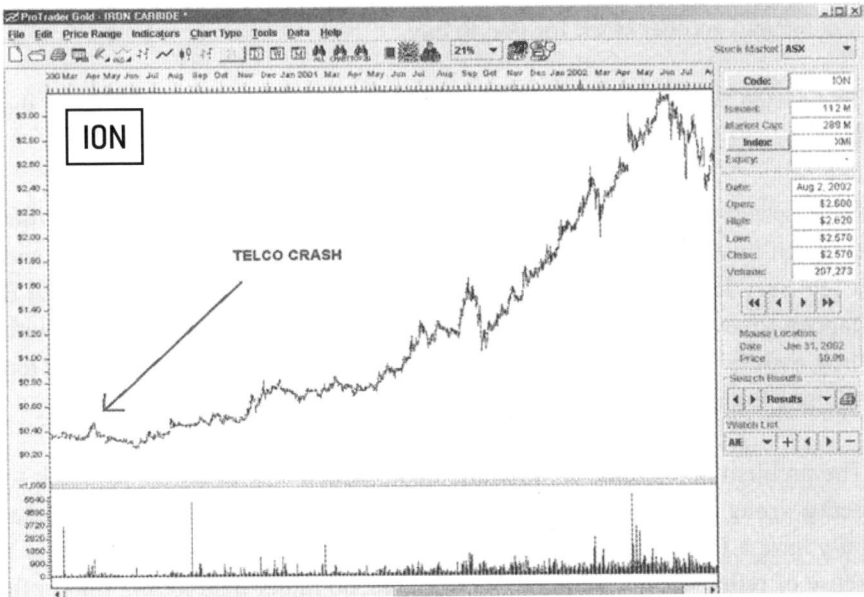

During a bear market many newcomers search for a method of profiting from a falling market. Invariably, they will turn to "derivatives", in the first instance, usually a warrant, or possibly an "exchange traded option". My very strong advice is to stay away from these trading instruments. They are very clearly for the professional trader. Warrants are particularly dangerous and if I didn't know better I would have a feeling they were designed specifically to rip the money from your hip pocket. Derivatives generally are not for the faint-hearted or the novice trader.

7 | Myth seven
You can't go broke taking a profit

You can't go broke taking a profit. That is such an obvious statement you must be wondering why I have included this as a market myth. Next time you have a profitable stock, ring your broker and ask if you should take a profit. Of course he will say yes. That simple answer will bring in a further two commissions. One for the sale and another because the broker will recommend another stock for you to buy.

The advice "you can't go broke taking a profit" sounds good, but is it? If the stock is still rising, why are you selling it?

Most newcomers are so relieved when a stock is in a profitable situation, that they can't wait to take a profit. This usually leads to lots of small profits and a few very large losses. You *can* go broke taking profits! I have seen it happen time and time again while broking. Clients have come to me with their trading advices and shown where they have had six or seven out of ten winning trades, but their account is still well below the starting capital.

The problem is twofold. It generally starts with a lack of ability to admit to being wrong about a stock and taking a small loss. So the clients' statements only have a few losses but they are huge. After the first huge loss there is a sense of relief when a trade turns profitable, so rather than letting the profit extend its run, the client will take a small profit just for the sake of being right. The end result is seven small profits and three huge losses. All of which boils down to a lack of planning.

Most books will make a point of suggesting that a trader need only "win" four of each ten trades and they can still be profitable if they cut the losses short and let the profits run. The problem seems to be that newcomers only observe the first part of this advice. They win four out of ten trades, but forget to cut the losses short and let the profits run their full extent.

Plan for profits

I tend to think that a trading plan that results in four out of ten profitable trades is a trading plan that needs more work done on it. Seven out of ten winning trades is achievable, but the target should be to develop a plan that gives you the best opportunity of winning ten out of ten trades. Constant revision and, when necessary, fine-tuning your trading plan is the only method of getting close to this goal.

8 | Myth eight

Buy cheap

Oxford Dictionary: cheap *adj.* 1. low in price, worth more than it cost; charging low prices, offering good value; 2. poor in quality, of low value; showy but worthless, silly.

> *When a stock becomes a screaming buy because it cannot possibly drop further, try to buy it thirty cents lower.*
>
> Al Rizzo

There are two meanings mentioned in the Oxford. Most people love a good bargain, buying something that is low in price but worth more than it cost. We are taught to seek a "bargain" and to buy cheaply. This is fine when we are at the local supermarket. But have you ever been caught out with a cheap second-hand car or a cheap computer or, dare I say it, a cheap stock? Is it then a bargain?

Beware the advice of the broker who rings you and suggests the purchase of a stock because it is cheap.

At some stage of your trading career, your broker will ring you and suggests buying a stock "because it is cheap". When applying the word cheap to stocks, we are generally describing something that is poor in quality, of low value; showy but worthless and silly. Buying cheap in the stock market is a myth that can cost a small fortune. Cheap in comparison to what? Recent prices? If a stock is cheap compared to recent prices, it must follow that those prices are falling. If prices are falling, why buy the stock? Surely the purpose of investing is to buy a stock that is rising in price.

Anyone buying a stock that is cheap, but still falling in price, is gambling on a recovery at some stage. It could be a very long and costly wait.

This is the chart of Resolute (RSG) in July 1998. Despite a recent rally, *the price is still in a downward trend.* I have drawn a line across the chart to show the sideways movement and the fact that the price seems to be unable to move above the level indicated by the line. There is price resistance at this level.

Now here is a stock that is cheap and trading at a discount, according to the broker. Is Resolute a bargain and worth more than it costs, or is it poor in quality and silly? Was it cheap, meaning that recent prices had been falling? This type of research and recommendation is commonplace.

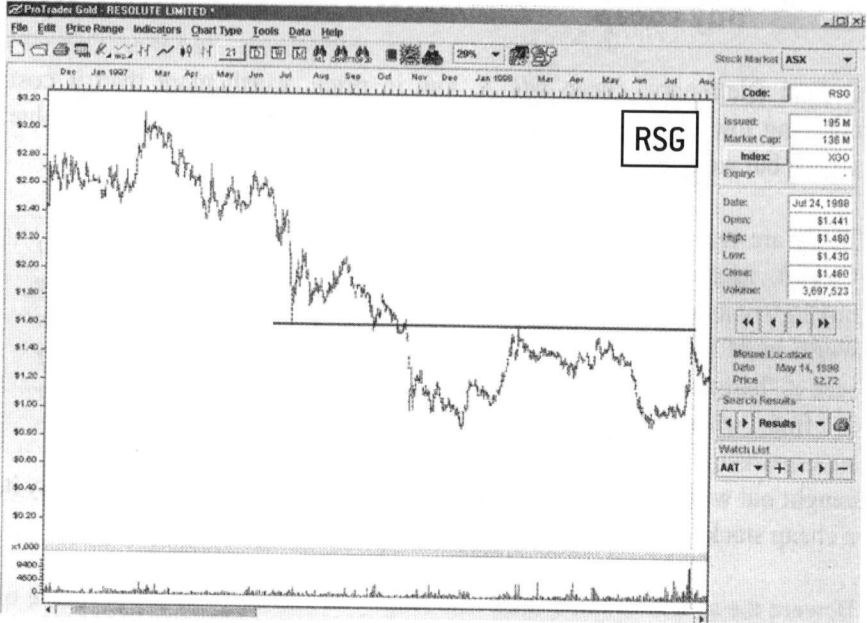

Exploding the Myths

Be resolute - don't buy falling stocks!

We expect Resolute will be re-rated upwards, as the stock is trading at a massive 38% discount to our NPV of $2.35. The sale of Bulong enables Resolute to focus on the growth of its' gold business through the development of emerging projects and acquisitions. Resolute's objective is to increase annual gold production to at least 750 000 oz within the next five years at a cash cost of below US$200/oz. We believe this is wholly achievable given the company's excellent exploration portfolio. In addition, Resolute proposes a share buy back scheme for up to 10% of it's stock, along with a new dividend policy, paying approximately 50% of after tax profits." STRONG BUY.

(Broker recommendation 24 July 1998 – Resolute gold)

The up to date chart which follows tells all! The price continues its downward path! Buying cheap in this market is fraught with danger. This is not shopping at the local supermarket! These myths are my observations after a lifetime trading and broking, watching the professionals take money from the newcomers each boom-time.

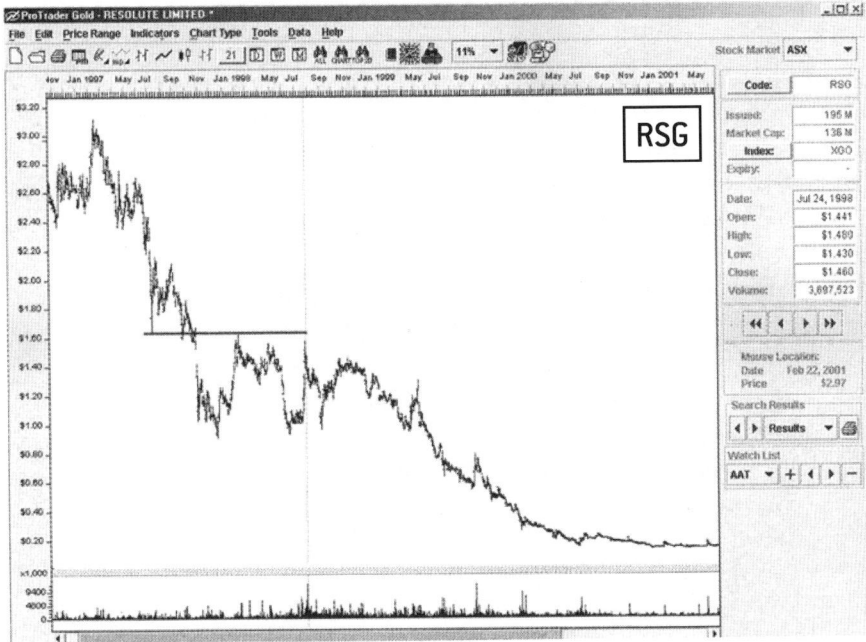

My message is simple: learn to see through the marketing hype, make intelligent decisions based on evidence, not stories, and above all, buy stocks that are rising in price.

The main thrust of my book was to expose old market adages and new marketing ploys as "Market Myths" that do not help the general public when they come to invest their own funds. I am lucky to be in a position where I have not only written the book on these myths, but now have the opportunity to review what has transpired in the two years following the first release of "Exploding the Myths".

Has public perception changed in the last two years?

There is little doubt in my mind that the vast majority of private investors understand that much of the so called professional advice is not conducive to helping outperform the market indicies.

Let's look at what I labeled as myths.

Myth one: Time in the market is more important than timing the market
Let's face it – time in the market is rarely the cure for a bad investment.

The following is the promo blurb from the February 2005 edition of the "Personal Investor" magazine published in Australia.

> "Healthy gains eluded most of us in 2001 and 2002, but they have come back over the last 18 months, rewarding patient fund members. From June 2003 to June 2004, the average superannuation fund added 13.2%, and the rampaging returns continued over the six months to the end of December 2004, with an average gain of 7.2%. That is a mighty 20% return on your savings over 18 months, but it is also a savage reminder that there is no point in starting to contribute selectively in a strong year."

The average return of 13.2% for FY2004 may sound fantastic after the negative returns of 2001 and 2002, but let's face it, the All Ordinaries Index rose over 16 percent that year. The "rampaging returns" of 7.2% for the six months to the end of 2004 is hardly worth shouting about when the Index rose over 14 percent in the same time.

I believe that the investing public is far more attuned to getting their timing right. Timing is paramount and while the small investor acknowledges this – the fund managers cannot change course. Despite growing public awareness, there will always be a small group of novice uneducated investors who will buy in the boom and sell in the gloom.

Myth two: Diversify or perish
Despite the fund management industry still using and advocating diversification, the private investing public has become very aware that

diversification alone will not bring about above average returns. There is enough statistical evidence to show you that any more than twelve stocks in a portfolio will dilute your return. In fact, the returns from the super funds shown in Myth one are enough evidence to show that a diversified fund will under perform the market averages.

Myth three: Seek professional advice

My views here have not changed at all. There is no doubt that more and more private investors are seeking to trade on a do it yourself basis using the Internet, rather than seeking the traditional full service broker. Most investors would prefer to have their funds managed professionally, but having tried this and had little success, feel they, at least, cannot do any worse than their ex-broker. I do wonder what percentage of new D.I.Y. investors will at some stage hand the reigns back to a broker when they realise that trading your own money can be tough.

Myth four: Set up a "Blue Chip" portfolio

I think I will let the numbers do the talking. In the first edition of "Exploding the Myths" I put together a fictitious portfolio of 10 "Blue Chip" stocks. These are shown on the following page.

Let's look at an update of this portfolio and see what another two and a half years has done to the performance.

Between 1 July 1997 and 30 June 2002, this portfolio had averaged around 6% per annum. Some 2 + years further on, the annual average return is now – you guessed it - 5.94%.

Points of interest here are the $6 500 decline in NAB profits, and further losses of over $8 000 in the AMP investment. The performance of these two companies neutralises the effect of the good performance by Woodside Petroleum (WPL), News Corp (NCP) and the terrific result from the restructuring of Western Mining Corporation (WMC). My point is that even a "Blue Chip" portfolio needs to be actively managed.

43

Code	1 July	Vol	Cost	30 /6/02 Price	Profit/ Loss	31/12/04 Price	P/L
ANZ	9.76	1000	9 840	19.29	9 370	20.59	10 670
CBA	15.84	1000	15 920	32.93	16 930	32.10	16 100
NAB	18.70	1000	18 780	35.40	16 540	28.82	9 960
AMP	18.92	1000	19 000	15.60	-3 480	7.26	11820
LLC	13.88	1000	13 960	10.54	-3 500	13.25	–790
WPL	11.33	1000	11 410	13.57	2 080	20.10	8 610
TLS	8.69	1000	8 770	4.66	-4 190	4.91	–3 940
WMC	8.33	1000	8 410	9.09	600		
WMR		1000				7.22	7 140
AWC		1000				5.94	5 860
BHP	8.62	1000	8 700	10.30	1 520	15.34	6 560
NCP	6.33	1000	6 410	9.68	3 190	12.25	5 760
			$121 200		$39 060		$54 110

Myth five: Beware October

Again, let the numbers tell the story.

October 2002	the All Ordinaries Index rose 45 points or 0.15%
October 2003	the All Ordinaries Index rose 118 points or 0.3%
October 2004	the All Ordinaries Index rose 117 points or .3%
February 2003	the All Ordinaries fell 157 points or 0.5%
February 2004	the All Ordinaries rose 85 points or 0.2%

This simply adds to the fact that October is not the shocker that it is supposed to be – and February still shows up as the poorest month on average.

Myth six: You can't make money in a bear market

While I believe this to be a myth – the performance of most fund managers during 2001/2002 would suggest that indeed it is true – you can't make money in a bear market. The private professional trader can make money in any market and many did just that. Perhaps you should seek out these people and try to find out how they manage. There is no doubt that it is much tougher, but it is possible.

In "Myth six: You can't make money in a bear market" I used Ion Carbide (ION) as an example of a stock that performed admirably during the bear market of 2001/2002. ION rose from lows of 40 cents at the time of the Telco crash in April 2000, to the dizzy heights of $3.20 only 14 months later. This is a great return in any portfolio at any time, let alone a bear market.

The great irony is that 2004 was a great market – not a bull market, but very strong, nonetheless - with the All Ordinaries Index rising 22 percent and, at the end of this great run, ION entered liquidation.

So here is a stock that rose 800 percent in a bear market and went broke in a bull market.

Myth seven: You can't go broke taking a profit

I have very little to add here, other than this is still an expression used by some brokers who seem unable to allow a small profit to turn into a large profit.

Myth eight: Buy cheap

Myth eight discusses the consequences of buying a stock just because it is cheap. In revising this book, it is interesting to note that a stock like Telstra is as cheap today as it was two or three years ago.

In concluding this review of chapter two and the investment myths, it is evident that most educated investors concur with these myths. Any portfolio must be actively managed and, in particular, diversification is not the answer for those wanting to beat the market averages.

3

Traps for beginners and the unwary

In this chapter, I will summarise the main errors that newcomers typically make when they begin trading – the traps that gobble up their precious nest eggs and leave them disillusioned and worse off for the experience. These errors recur boom after boom, and no doubt will occur during and after the next boom. It is only by studying past mistakes that we can improve and become proficient in our trading. In every walk of life we are taught to go back, analyse our mistakes, improve and learn from the experience. When it comes to a losing trade we simply blame the broker or adviser for bad advice.

Newcomers make the same mistakes year after year, boom after boom, making it clear that at least in this market, we do not learn from our mistakes or the mistakes of past generations. Nor do we analyse why these mistakes are so common. Greed rules the brain! For now, I want to put these traps down on paper, in one place, just so you can't miss the message!

This chapter is a compilation of the common mistakes that I have seen newcomers make during and after the 1980, 1987 and 2000 boom. They are the same mistakes that I made during the 1969 boom.

1 Trap one

Entering near or at the peak of a bull market

While I doubt that any statistics exist on this subject, I think it would be fair to say that at least 80% of newcomers make their first trade during a boom. Many within six months of the end of a boom, usually buying overvalued stocks near their peak. Many normally conservative people finally succumb to the temptation of easy money as the media report the booming conditions and carry stories of the latest new breed of millionaires.

Readers misinterpret reports and come to the conclusion that there is easy money to be made, probably with little effort. Newcomers flock to the market like moths to a flame. When prices decline at the end of the bull market, they have no idea how to handle the situation. They have not considered, let alone prepared for, the possibility of falling prices. Good advice at this stage is as scarce as hen's teeth. Most advisers have never seen anything like this. They are as green as many of the investors whom they advise.

As the bubble bursts, newcomers react like rabbits frozen in the spotlight, almost paralysed with the fear of losing. Many will ring their broker to seek an "expert" opinion, but unfortunately many brokers have no idea what to do. Few brokers have been through a market downturn so they, too, are frozen like rabbits in the spotlight. More often than not a broker will suggest that you "hold on" and "wait for the recovery". Many companies opt for bankruptcy rather than recovery. Other stocks take years to recover.

Entering the market at or near a peak is not the end of the world, if you have appropriate risk management measures in place. There are many "signs of a top" and I will summarise these at a later stage. While it is not too difficult to see the signs of a top, it is difficult to withdraw from the market at this stage. The fear of missing out on easy profits blurs the judgement.

The trap is not necessarily entering at the top of a bull market; it is not having contingency plans to avoid the damage associated with a sharp decline. A well-planned trading strategy incorporating risk management rules will help overcome this trap.

2   Trap two
The hot tip syndrome

Trap one is generally caused by trap two; that is, you get a hot tip from a friend or work colleague and rush out to invest in something you have probably never heard of before. When this happens the market is generally very close to a peak.

At some stage, I'll bet you know someone who knows a geologist who works for a company that has made a significant mineral find. Of course no one else knows about this discovery yet. Give me a break! By the time you are told, the whole market knows! I have seen people put up to $50 000 on a story like this.

Most new entrants act on a tip from a friend or colleague. Often the story told is little more than Chinese whispers. During a stock market boom, most social conversations at some stage turn to the market. Whether the conversation takes place at a dinner party or in the local hotel or at work, invariably, someone is spouting about his or her latest foray into the market. You turn green with envy as they tell how easy it is to double your money in a week or two.

Greed takes over and the next morning you find a broker who will open an account and buy the shares for you. Perhaps you question the broker to see if there is any truth in the story you heard.

> *Every decade has its characteristic folly, but the basic cause is the same people persist in believing that what has happened in the recent past will go on happening into the indefinite future, even while the ground is shifting under their feet.*
>
> George J Church

Your new adviser will put his spin on the story and tell you that he has just received the inside word from the company director's wife's cousin's scientist's uncle, that the company is about to come out with a new medical wonder drug. He mentions that it's highly confidential information at this stage and not generally known by the market.

The hot tip syndrome is directly responsible for enormous losses. Brokers are just as guilty as the taxi driver. This is not just a recent or one-off phenomenon. It has happened in the four booms I have witnessed since 1969.

When the hot tip syndrome is running riot, it is a sure fire signal to professional traders that the boom is about to end. During a boom, some of these tips will no doubt be profitable, but you must watch for the signs that the market is overheated. My advice to you? Never think that your ears are an analytical tool. Cut your ears off!

3 Trap three
Accepting poor advice

At the risk of being repetitious, accepting poor advice is tied in closely with the hot tip syndrome. Poor advice comes from all directions; whether it is the taxi driver, the publican or the broker. Most of the time, the broker you are dealing with is a new kid on the block who has never seen boom times before, let alone a bear market.

He is just as excited and naïve as you are. Unfortunately, you think you are dealing with an expert who has some wisdom and knowledge that you don't possess. Each year the media approaches various brokers and asks the question, "What is your one stock pick for the next twelve months?"

The following table shows the stocks that were chosen by various brokers in November 1997 as "the best 10 picks for 1998". Let's assume that you had been given fifty thousand dollars to invest and choose to accept this free advice from some leading brokers. With your $50 000 you decide to invest $5 000 in each company. The following table shows the results.

Company	Nov 97 Price	Investment	Volume	31 Dec 1998 Price
China Construction	0.85	5000	5882	0.22
Normandy	1.76	5000	2841	1.51
MIM Holdings	1.61	5000	3106	0.72
CIO	1.64	5000	3049	0.29
Davids	0.81	5000	6173	0.50
Crown	1.63	5000	3067	0.78
QBE Insurance	8.50	5000	588	6.75
North Broken Hill	4.75	5000	1053	2.66
Tathong Holding	1.18	5000	4237	0.72
ICI	12.71	5000	393	8.23
		$50000		**$27249**

What a disaster! Not one of the ten stocks was profitable at the end of the twelve-month period. In fact, your capital would have been almost halved. This particular portfolio has never recovered and never been in profit at any stage in the ensuing five years.

Fortunately, there have been other occasions where the "brokers tips for the next twelve months" have fared a little better than this.

> *Stockbroking is the amazing industry where clients in Jaguars and Rollers drive into the CBD to get advice from people who caught the train to work.*
>
> Shares Magazine November 1997

The disaster above is evidence that you cannot blindly follow expert advice, buy shares and walk away from them in the hope that they will rise. As with any investment, it needs to be constantly reviewed and massaged to keep it in shape.

Despite these stocks being chosen as the brokers pick for 1998, I thought it would be interesting to see whether or not time in the market could cure the problems associated with poor stock selection. We can see that Davids (now trading as Metcash) has gone from strength to strength and has clearly been a winner. In fact, if it were not for Davids/Metcash, these "Tips" would have shown a sad and sorry tale. What was a disastrous portfolio of tips from day one has recovered to a certain extent by being lucky enough to pick one decent stock from ten.

Company	Volume held	Price 31/12/04	Value 31/12/04	Cash
China Construction	xx		0	
Normandy	xx			1 420
Newmont	1 093		6 241	
MIM Holdings	xx			8 600
CIO	3 049	0.07	213	0.29
Davids	6 173	3.35	20 680	
Crown	278	17.5	4 865	
QBE Insurance	588	15.35	9 026	
North Broken Hill				5 001
Tathong Holding	10 592	0.295	3 215	
ICI	xx		2 161	
			$46 310	**$15 021**

$61 331

(i)   China Construction was delisted in March 2001.
(ii) Normany was taken over by Newmont for payment of 50 cents cash and 38.5 Newmont shares for each Normandy share owned.
(iii) MIM holding was taken over by Xtrata for a cash payment of $1.72
(iv) CIO changed code to AGY.
(v)   Davids changed names to Metcash.
(vi) Crown merged with PBL on a 1:11 basis.
(vii) North Broken Hill shareholders received a cash payment of $4.75 following a buyout from Rio Tinto (RIO).
(viii) ICI shareholders received a cash payout of $5.50 from following a cash buyout.

The final "success" of this portfolio would to a large degree depend on how well you invested the cash from the various buyouts.

QBE Insurance (QBE) is also in the positive column despite the events surrounding the World Trade Center attack, the Bali bombing and the Asian Tsunami. Time has improved what was a disastrous start with these stocks, but again we can clearly see that these selections have hardly been a success. However you look at this result, it must be clear to all that to really outperform the market, you have to constantly review your stocks, culling those that are not performing and adding rising stocks.

4 Trap four

Not looking at the picture! Seeing is believing

One way of overcoming the first three traps is to look at a chart of the prices of any company that you are about to invest in. The same instinct that makes you look at a car before you purchase should be applied to the purchase of shares. You must look at any stock before you buy it. Fair enough, you say, but how do you "look at a stock"? By looking at a price chart! The chart conveys the "health" of a company.

A chart represents the consensus of thousands of analysts who buy and sell shares each day. If a company is being poorly managed, or has any problem, these analysts will not buy the stock. Prices will fall until management gets its house back in order.

If you look at old charts of all those disasters you have heard of, from Bond Corporation and Quintex, to One-tel, Compass and HIH, they all had one thing in common. The price was declining for months prior to their ultimate demise. This showed up very clearly in the charts. At seminars all over the country I show people the HIH chart and, without fail, the audience is unanimous in its opinion that prices were falling from early 1998, more than three years prior to the ultimate bankruptcy.

Why are we silly enough to invest fortunes on someone's story? Do you believe a story from a car salesman? "Pssst, I've got a really good second hand Commodore, last year's model, one owner, low kilometres, good body, really clean car." Would you buy this car or any other car without looking at it? To even suggest this is ridiculous.

Yet most new investors will hand over their hard earned funds to a broker on the basis of a story. The story may have no foundation in truth. We have (or used to have) an implicit belief in brokers and their research. That unquestioned trust is in grave danger of disappearing.

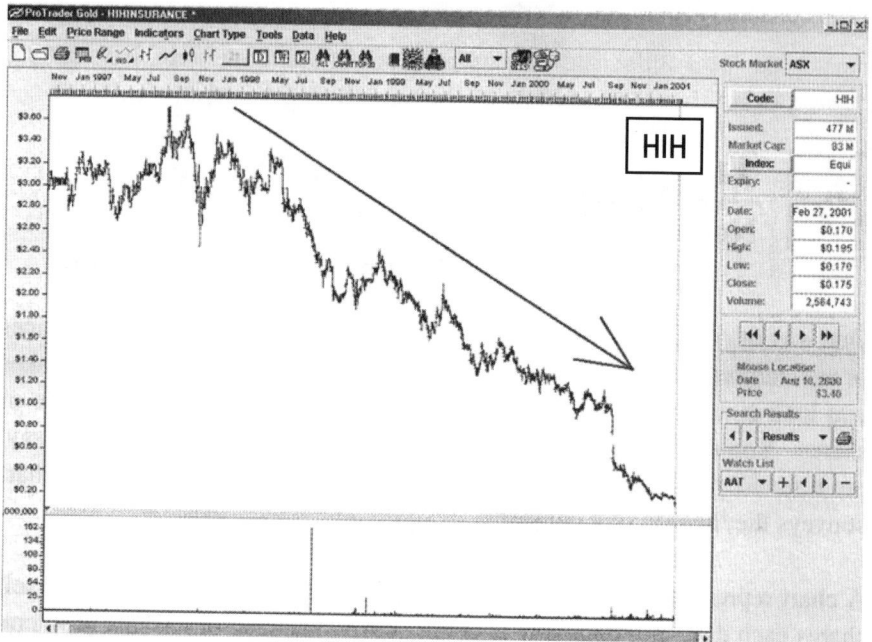

This is what I call "visual investing"

Look at the chart of a stock before you invest in that company. This is visual investing and is so basic – and so frequently overlooked – that I have devoted a whole chapter to it. This error is one of the most common causes of substantial losses in share trading, and newcomers are the most vulnerable of all traders to this oversight.

5 | Trap five
Plunging

Plunging simply means investing all your capital into one stock. While I have warned of the ramifications of over-diversification, plunging all your capital into one stock is just as dangerous. Mind you, plunging seems to be "the Australian way". Just look at our annual plunge on the Melbourne Cup. Australians plunge millions of dollars on one horse, one race, once a year in much the same way that newcomers plunge on one stock, once every five to ten years, during boom-time.

No wonder the market is seen as a "bit of a gamble". Too many newcomers approach the market with a gambler's attitude. On the other hand, a professional gambler may not bet on the Melbourne Cup unless a horse meets his selection criteria. You can bet that the professional gambler will have a set of rules, or some other selection criteria; otherwise, he will not be a professional gambler for long.

Newcomers plunge their whole nest egg on one stock, based on a very limited set of information, usually just a tip. As with any other gambler, if that plunge wins, they will re-invest all the capital, plunging again and again until the inevitable downturn that wipes out most, if not all, the capital.

Can you imagine putting $5 000 on a horse at the races, based on a hot tip? Or placing $10 000 on the number 17 on the roulette table because you've had a feeling that number would win? If you can contemplate that without shuddering, then you're probably a gambler. I haven't written this book for you. I've written it for non-gamblers who have a nest egg that they want to look after and build into a bigger nest egg.

The antidote to plunging is to have a plan that incorporates more than one stock and to have a strategy that takes account of appropriate information – usually technical analysis – and ignores inappropriate information. There is plenty more about this approach throughout this book.

If you have stayed away from share trading because you thought it was too much like gambling, then I hope you will gain confidence and I can help you turn the share market into an intelligent investment.

6 | Trap six
Risk without insurance

Newcomers typically make their first share purchases without any thought to protecting their stake. What if there is a sudden overnight drop in price? What could you do about it?

Most newcomers who are caught in this situation are frozen with fear - feeling sick at the money they've lost, feeling frustrated that they can't work out what to do about it and, ultimately, walking away from the loss pretending it didn't happen.

Isn't it a shame to lose money when a little insurance might have made a difference? And isn't it a pity that newcomers should have bad experiences and be turned off trading when there is clearly money to be made? So what to do?

Newcomers make stock purchases for additional income, so they do not have the time to watch stock movements hour by hour. There are simple strategies that can insure any trader against losses. Insurance for share traders encompasses a couple of different strategies covered in this book.

The stop loss is the most important of the safety valves to which I look. It enables you to leave a standing order with your broker to sell the stock if certain conditions are met. Simple in concept, stop losses are quite complicated in practice; therefore, I have spent considerable time explaining them. Also, in later chapters, is more detail about the kind of risks you are exposed to in share trading.

> *The stop loss is the most important of the safety valves. It is a major aspect of insurance against extended losses.*

Having a plan in place will also help to guide you through the decisions you have to make, sets profit objectives and, just as importantly, help you to define the size of the risk you are prepared to take; in other words, how much are you prepared to lose on the transaction. This then helps you to determine at what point to pull out of the stock, especially if there is a downturn in the price.

7 Trap seven

False expectations

Newcomers in boom-time expect a ten-cent stock to run up to a dollar. Greed takes over all other emotions. Rational people become irrational, brimming with false expectations.

It always amuses me when a broker, or some research, says that a share will rise to a particular level. It is generally fundamental nonsense pumped out by tip sheet writers and brokers. Crystal ball gazing does not work in this market; careful analysis does.

I bumped into a young couple in July 1999. They were both university students without a dollar to their name. They had borrowed $1 000 from their parents and bought 10 000 Sydney Gas shares at 11 cents per share on the back of a hot tip.

At the time of purchase, the broker had confirmed the hot tip by saying that SGC would go to $5.00 per share. When we met, SGC were trading at $1.00 per share, so they had done very well. I suggested selling two or three thousand shares to repay the debt, pay some bills and have a little fun.

They flatly refused, as they had implicit faith in the brokers' profit target of $5.00. The shares peaked at $1.40 two weeks later and are now trading at 35 cents. The young couple is still in front on their investment, and hopefully a little wiser. In my opinion, however, they have turned twelve to fourteen thousand dollars into three and a half thousand.

Forget about profits - you have two main considerations when investing in the market:

* What are my risks?
* How can I protect myself against that risk?

The returns are irrelevant in your early days. Survival and preservation of capital is paramount. How on earth can anyone know with any certainty what price a stock is going to rally to?

8 | Trap eight

Counting your chickens before they hatch

I have heard countless people telling others that they have ten or twenty or thirty thousand dollars profit in a particular stock. This borders on being another sign of the top of a market. As with any other investment, you have not made a cent until you have realised your profit. Don't count your chickens before they hatch!

During my futures broking years, I ran an advertisement looking for new clients. One potential client responded asking what sort of returns I could help him achieve. I was naturally vague with my answer – there are too many variables. He proceeded to tell me he had bought a sizeable parcel of shares in a small diamond exploration company at about 15 cents each. As we spoke, the shares were trading at $1.00 (and worth $300 000).

He asked if I could make those sorts of returns. I told him that he had not made a return at all. A month later, my company placed another advertisement that drew another phone call from the same person. He didn't ask about the futures market, but began to brag about his diamond exploration stock that was now trading at around $2.50. He was now worth $750 000. I congratulated him and asked why he didn't take some profit. He responded with a derisive snort, and a sound argument about the stock going to $10.00.

His shares peaked at $4.80 one night during London trading. I heard about this on the news. It was the first time I had ever heard mention of a spec stock that was trading on the London exchange during a news bulletin. I rang the person involved and told him to sell at least the major part of his holding, as all the good news was in the market. The value of his parcel was $1.4 million. He laughed again. The company finally went broke and the client was left holding worthless stock. He lost his initial $30 000 investment, as well as the $1.4 million profit. You may smile when you read this and think it will never happen to you, but I have seen this on occasions. Another "couldabeen" champion.

Just remember that you have not made one cent until the tax man has ripped out his share!

9 Trap nine

Fighting the market

Go with the market and it will reward you. Fight the market and you will lose again and again. If you find yourself walking around mumbling, "But it's not logical, the market should be higher", or thinking that a particular stock should be trading at a certain level, it is *you* who is out of step with the market. Remember, the market is always right – you are either in step and making money from the market, or you are out of step and losing.

This does not change between a bull and a bear market. Even in a bear market, the easiest way to make money is to buy into a stock that is rising and sell when it starts to fall.

> *The worst mistake investors make is taking their profits too soon and their losses too late.*
>
> Michael Price

I think that at the end of the day, Michael Price sums up the most common failing of all market participants, not only newcomers. Fund managers, brokers, traders and newcomers alike have difficulty with timing entry and exits levels. Learn this art and you will be rewarded time and time again. Ignore timing at your peril.

Timing does not need to be a split second requirement, within a day or two is pretty good, within a month or two may suffice on most occasions. I can assure you that one way or another, timing the market is a critical issue.

Exploding the Myths

Do not over-commit during a bull market
Avoid hot tips, even from your broker
Be wary of ANY advice
Look at a chart before buying
Do not plunge all your capital into one stock
Consider all risks and insure your investment
Be realistic
Don't count your chickens before they hatch
Listen to the market, don't fight it

'The major three factors that stop people from being successful traders is lack of capital, lack of patience and lack of a plan."

4

Investing is visual

In recent years we have seen a major surge in public interest in the share market. The advent of the global economy, and global communications networks has allowed us to watch the machinations of share markets all over the world. Since the 1986 Chernobyl incident and the 1987 crash, we have watched the Gulf War, the Asian Crisis and the Hi-Tech market downturn reverberate on markets around the globe.

The pervasiveness of the home computer and Internet access has led to the development of an online broking industry with inexpensive fees that have shaken the foundations of the traditional broker. This has led to an unprecedented number of first time traders accessing the markets. The "Dick Tracy" generation has arrived and they trade with the speed of light!

In Australia, the public share market floats of companies, such as Commonwealth Bank, Telstra and AMP, have helped introduce hundreds of thousands of ordinary people to share ownership. Unfortunately, the experiences of these first-time shareholders have not always been positive. Very few of these investors have actually "looked" at the companies they have invested in; rather, they have been told a pretty convincing story which may or may not prove to be profitable.

There is one tool that is available to all parties who invest in the stock market. That tool is a chart. A chart is a visual representation showing the health of a company, as reflected by the company's price.

What is visual investing?

Visual investing is probably the simplest, most direct way to decide which stocks to buy, which stocks not to buy and when to sell. By visual investing, I mean *looking* – looking at a chart that shows the movement of prices for the particular stock. The chart of a stock's price movement is the most basic tool for successful investing. It plots the day-by-day price movements of a stock and can be used in lots of different ways to make decisions about buying and selling. The first and most basic thing that a chart will tell you is whether or not the price is rising.

Everyone has been exposed to charts at some stage, at company presentations, sales meetings and in newspapers. There is no mystique.

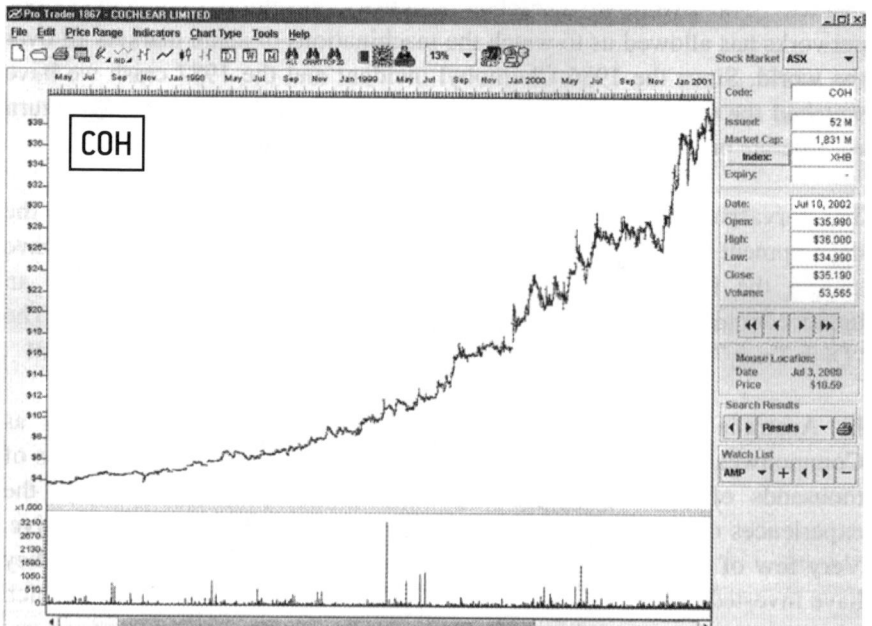

Charts have been used for a long time in all sorts of situations to help us visualiSe data that shows past performance in a realistic attempt to predict future performance.

Take a look for yourself! You'll notice in both stocks there are short- term fluctuations up and down. But you can see that overall there is a clear trend in one direction or the other. The purchase of one stock will make you money, and the purchase of the other stock will lose money. The choice is yours!

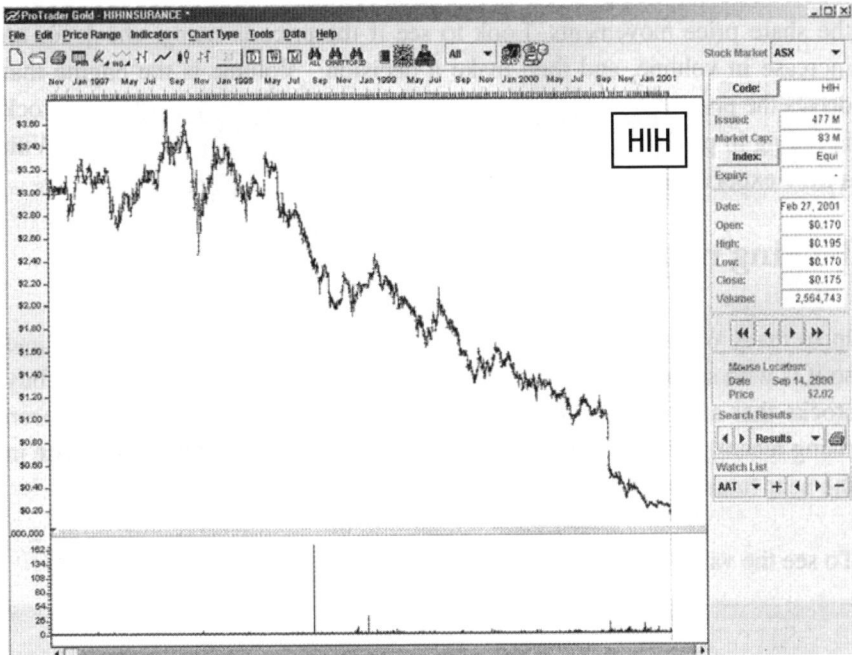

ProTrader Gold - HIHINSURANCE

File Edit Price Range Indicators Chart Type Tools Data Help

Stock Market ASX

HIH

Code:	HIH
Issued:	477 M
Market Cap:	83 M
Index:	Equi
Expiry:	-
Date:	Feb 27, 2001
Open:	$0.170
High:	$0.195
Low:	$0.170
Close:	$0.175
Volume:	2,564,743

Mouse Location
Date Sep 14, 2000
Price $2.02

Search Results
Results

Watch List
AAT

Why use a chart in share trading?

Everywhere you look you will get tips on which stocks to buy: on television, in newspapers, from a friend, a newsletter or from a broker. If the majority of these stories or tips were profitable, we would have been wealthy decades ago. You will be bombarded with ideas about stocks to trade in. So how do you choose which ones to act on?

Have you ever looked at a glossy brochure for an expensive sports car –

perhaps the latest Alfa, or how about a nice BMW? If you had the money and needed a new vehicle, would you rush to the telephone and buy it on the strength of that brochure and the specification sheet? I doubt it. You would make the trek to the car yard, kick the tyres, sniff the new upholstery and take the vehicle for a test drive. You would look at the car, not just believe the brochure. In share trading, you don't have to be a mechanic, you simply need to be able to interpret the price action shown on a chart. The chart is the equivalent of the test drive.

A visual check of the chart will confirm or deny the validity of the fundamental information you have picked up. The chart will tell the story of the share price movements. Look to see if the price is rising, check for an increase in volume, and then make a decision. Volume is the engine that drives the price. If your information is suggesting higher prices but the stock is falling in price, your information is either incorrect or poorly timed. With a little experience, a chart will tell you what you to do.

Picking rising stocks

In so many walks of life, it is often the simplest method that is the best, and so it is with share trading. To make money trading, all you have to do is buy stocks that are rising, then sell them at a higher price. If a price has been rising recently, there is a very strong likelihood that it will continue to rise in the near future.

We will see the value of a chart by examining a few examples.

What is this chart telling you?

Are the prices rising or falling? What is your first instinct? Now go and ask a ten-year old what he or she thinks. If you are not sure, you have a fallback position: "IF IN DOUBT – STAY OUT"! Hopefully, your first thought is that the price of this stock is falling.

Now, what if I give you a brokers' research story? Will it change your mind, or can you believe what you see?

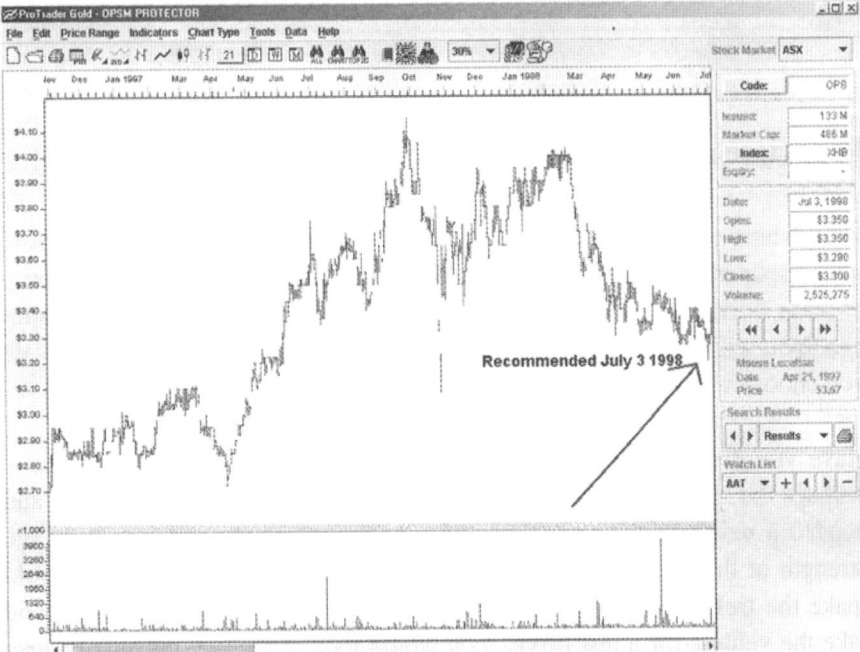

ProTrader Gold - OPSM PROTECTOR chart showing price history with annotation "Recommended July 3 1998"

Exploding the Myths

OPSM Protector - a buy?

"Each of OPSM's three business units generates strong returns on equity. In the Financial year of '98 the return on equity for the entire group is forecast to be 26%. Despite the fact that OPSM has invested consistently above its depreciation, return on equity, return on assets and return on tangible capital have all risen since 1992. The company is the beneficiary of an ageing population and increasingly high standards of workplace safety.

Growth will come from acquisitions (Dunlop Industrial Footwear and the Optical Shop), new business initiatives (new lens grinding laboratory, Pro Safe Direct, OPSM Face It, OPSM Next and OPSM's NZ operations) and cost reductions (changes to the logistics in Protector, initiatives in Protector Technologies). The stock is defensive in a difficult market. Low debt levels, high market share businesses and identifiable sources of growth make the stock a core holding." BUY.

Research document dated 3 July 1998.

This broker research sounds great, doesn't it! Low debt, high market share, defensive, a forecast 26% return on equity. This is a stock for core holding in a balanced portfolio.

Does this story change your mind? Are your ears a better analysis tool than your eyes?

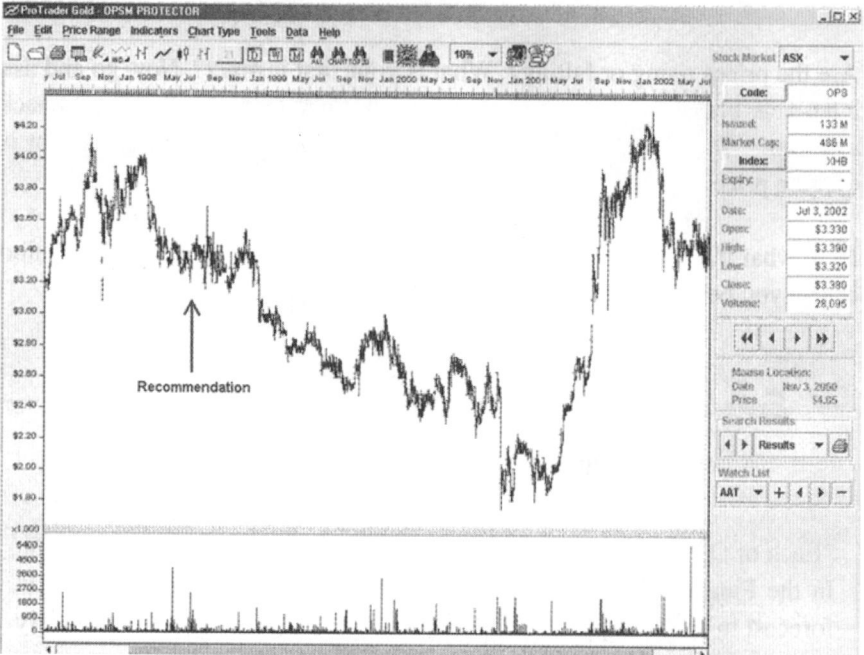

The end result?

OPSM Protector spent the best part of the next three years going down before beginning a strong recovery in June 2001. Exactly four years later, it was eight cents above the recommended purchase level. What a waste of time! And surely looking at the chart you could have picked your timing a little better?

Lets try again ...

What is this next chart telling you?

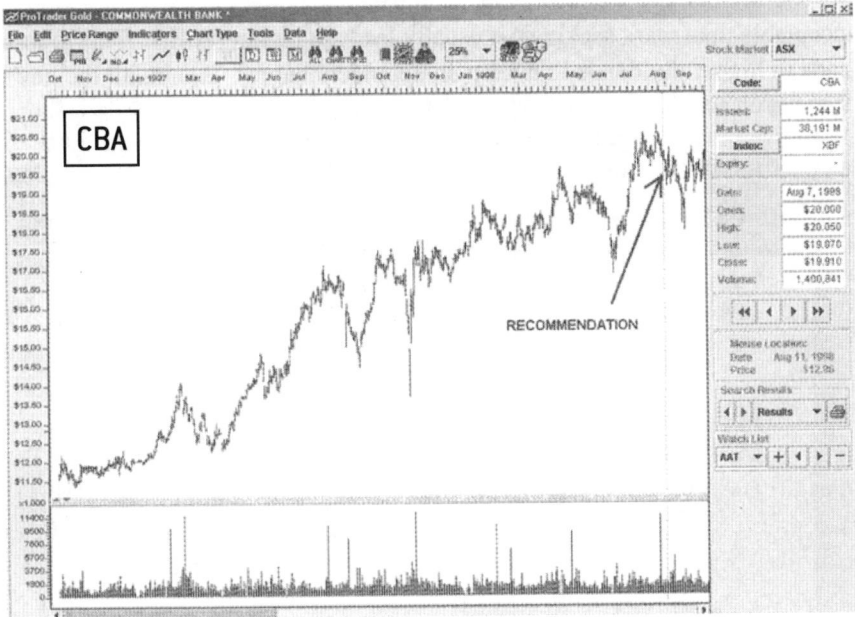

Are the prices rising or falling? What is your first instinct? Don't look for hidden traps or tricks. That chart represents the consensus of thousands of investors, traders, brokers and research analysts.

> *A chart represents the consensus of thousands of investors, traders, brokers and research analysts - ignore it at your own peril!*

You would have to agree that the prices appear to be in an upward trend.

The only issue that would bother a newcomer is the feeling that this stock has risen from twelve dollars in October 1996 to the current recommended level of nearly twenty dollars and you may be feeling that you have "missed out" on the best part of the rise. Look at the following research and then the following chart.

Exploding the Myths

Which Bank ...?

"CBA has announced a pre-tax restructuring charge of $200m ($128m after tax) for the financial year 1998. The change includes 1000 staff redundancies in FY98 and a further 2000 positions in FY99 to EDS and other outsourcing arrangements, rationalisation of processing and admin functions and the reconfiguration of delivery systems.

A further $35 million net abnormal charge will be taken to move to dynamic positioning. We regard the restructuring charge as positive, demonstrating a long-term commitment to cost cutting and efficiency gains and accelerating market expectations of the pace of change. CBA will announce its full year result (our forecast $1232 million) on 12 August.

Research document dated 7 August 1998.

Despite the outrage we feel when people are made redundant (sounds more acceptable than mass sacking), it usually leads to higher profits. This, in turn, leads to higher dividends that keep shareholders happy. Again, all the news or research sounds positive.

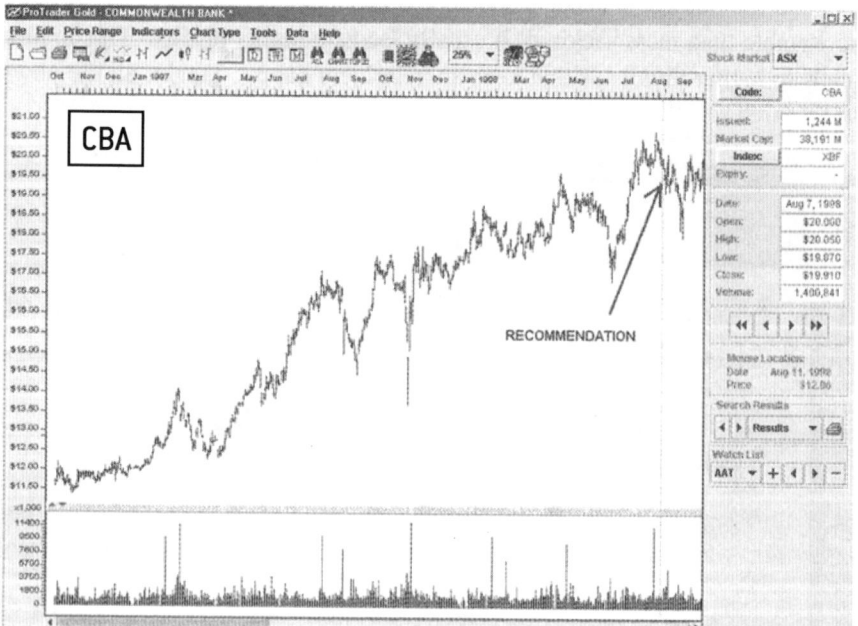

And what was the end result?

A good trade results with the Commonwealth Bank (CBA) rising over the next four years. The question is, "Was this good research?" At the end of the day, any research is good if the result is a profitable trade. Research is lousy if the result is a loss. The problem is that research is inconsistent.

Buy stocks that are rising!

The only absolute truth about stocks is represented at the end of each day in the form of the price and volume of shares traded. The truth is the open, high, low, close and volume. You do need software and a computer to be able to see clearly what is happening. The chart is a representation of the financial health and the managerial capability of a company. It measures past performance and can be a guide to future performance. Next time you pick up any form of research or recommendation, have a look at the chart and see whether the price is rising or falling. If, after looking at a chart, you are still doubtful, don't buy the stock.

Let me show you another scenario. You are sitting around and, for some reason, you suddenly decide to invest in shares. Rather than listen to a tip, you choose to get some research from a broker. You ring a broker and receive the following research.

Exploding the Myths

Queensland Cotton Holdings Ltd (QCH) $5.10   BUY

"At QCH's AGM, the chairman announced a reduction in the groups' profitability of up to 25% in the financial year 1999 following difficult operating conditions in the U.S. due to a poor Californian cotton crop (down 40%) and the under performance of the U.S. cotton seed milling business. Despite the profit warning, we are confident that QCH is making the right strategic moves in becoming a global supply chain manager to the cotton industry. The move into the U.S. has enabled the company to become the foremost year-round supplier of premium cotton to the world market. Management is confident in earnings returning to previous record levels and the maintenance of dividends at 28 cents per share should provide limited downside from the five dollar level".   Broker research document 17 July 1998

The chart below accompanied this recommendation for QCH. Look at this chart! Two days before this broker recommendation was written, the price fell 90 cents per share. It has just traded at a thirteen month low! Why on earth would you recommend this stock? The analyst involved in this research must go bungee jumping on the weekend! Seeing is believing! The result of this recommendation is also shown in a subsequent chart. The main issue is how much of your capital will you risk in an effort to find out if the research is going to be profitable or not? If, for some reason, you find you have to follow a recommendation like this one, you need to set a risk level. If you do not calculate your risk before entering a stock, you are gambling.

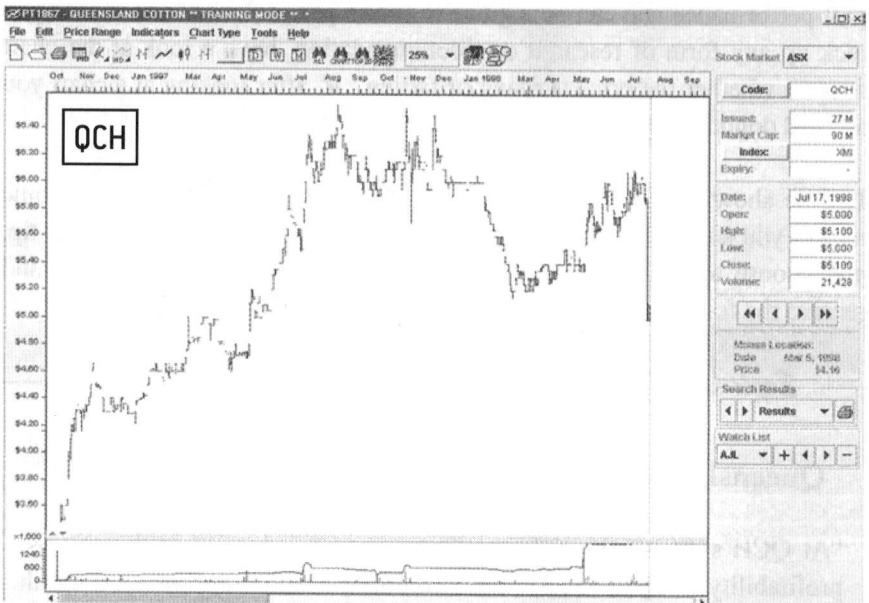

There is always a certain risk involved in any investment. The educated trader will minimise this risk. In other words, if you are wrong, sell the stock. This is not like the Melbourne Cup. You can withdraw your bet during the race! "You can change your mind, you cannot change the market".

Follow-up chart and comment

Two years after commenting on the stupidity of the recommendation on Queensland Cotton, we can finally see the emergence of an upward trend. A series of higher highs and higher lows could make this an attractive investment at last, regardless of any news, Chairman's address or broker recommendation. You still need to work out how much you would risk on this stock before any purchase.

We have looked at several charts that show a clear picture of a stock. These charts are known as daily bar charts. Over the centuries, various different methods of displaying price data have been used. The following pages display some of these methods.

What are some of the types of charts available?

There are various different ways of presenting prices. The most common is the "daily bar chart", where each day of trading is represented by what is called a daily bar. This bar represents the open, high, low and closing price. The volume is shown on a separate scale underneath the prices (see below). The high and low for the day are shown by the vertical line. The small horizontal line to the left shows the opening price. The small horizontal line to the right shows the closing price.

In the sample below, we can see two day's data. The daily bar on the left shows a stock that opened near the low and closed near the high. This clearly indicates that the buyers were stronger than the sellers during the day. The daily bar on the right shows a stock that opened near the high and traded down to close near the low, showing the sellers were in control.

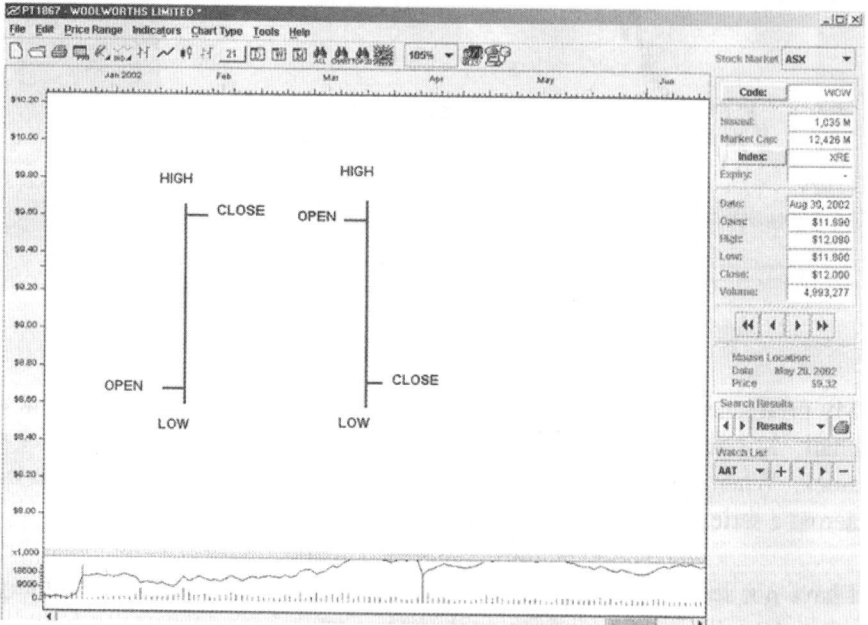

Daily bar chart

A daily bar chart reflects the daily trading range. This is the most commonly used charting format. With most computer packages the date appears above the prices and the price scale is shown on the left axis. Volume is a separate scale below the prices.

It is generally accepted that the closing price is the most important price of the day. The open can be quite volatile, as traders react to overnight news from international markets. The high and the low are simply the extremes reached during the trading day.

My preference is to use a daily bar chart at all times for my first look at a chart. My reasoning is that I want to see the intra-day highs and lows for a stock. When drawing trend-lines, I draw my lines across a series of highs or across a series of lows, in the case of a support line.

I have not seen any evidence that "proves" any one chart is better than any other chart; it is a matter of personal preference.

Daily line chart

A continuous line drawn through the closing price of each day represents a line chart. A line chart eliminates much of the "noise" in the market (particularly day traders) because the high and low are ignored.

It is potentially easier to visualise the prevailing trend.

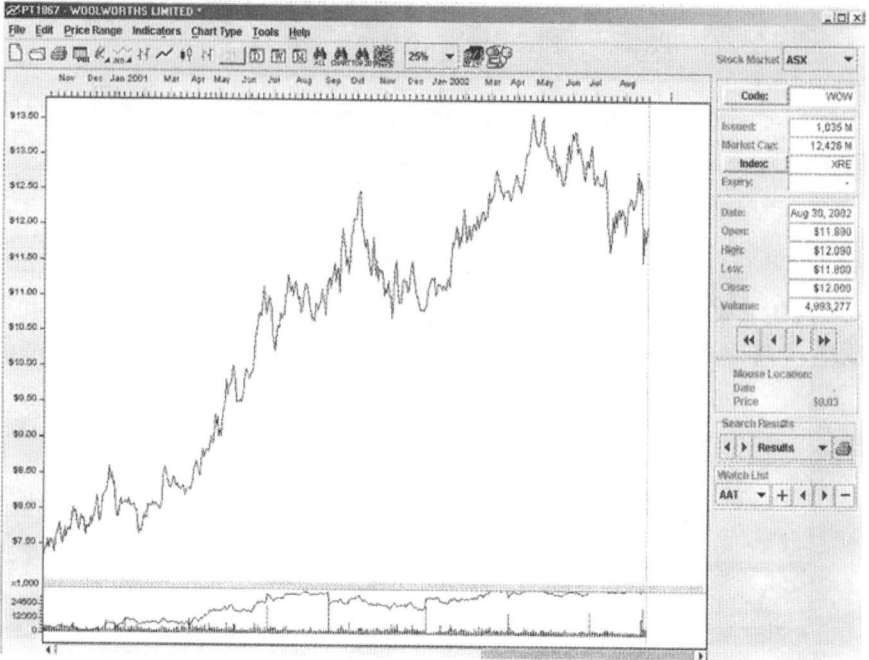

Because a line chart is a continuous line drawn through closing prices, it conveys some important information. It is important to focus on *closing* prices, rather than opening prices or intra day prices.

The closing price reflects only those participants who are prepared to hold a position overnight and, more particularly, over a weekend. These people are more likely to be in tune with the prevailing trend.

With the overwhelming number of day traders playing the very risky side of the market, the line chart is possibly more relevant these days than in the past. Again, it is a matter of personal preference.

Daily candlestick chart

Candlestick charting evolved in Japan around 1750 AD. Each days trading is represented by a candle shape rather than a line. More emphasis is placed on the open and close. The candle body is filled in or black, if the close is below the open, and if the close is above the open, the candle is empty or white. The high and low ranges above and below the candle are referred to as the wick or shadow.

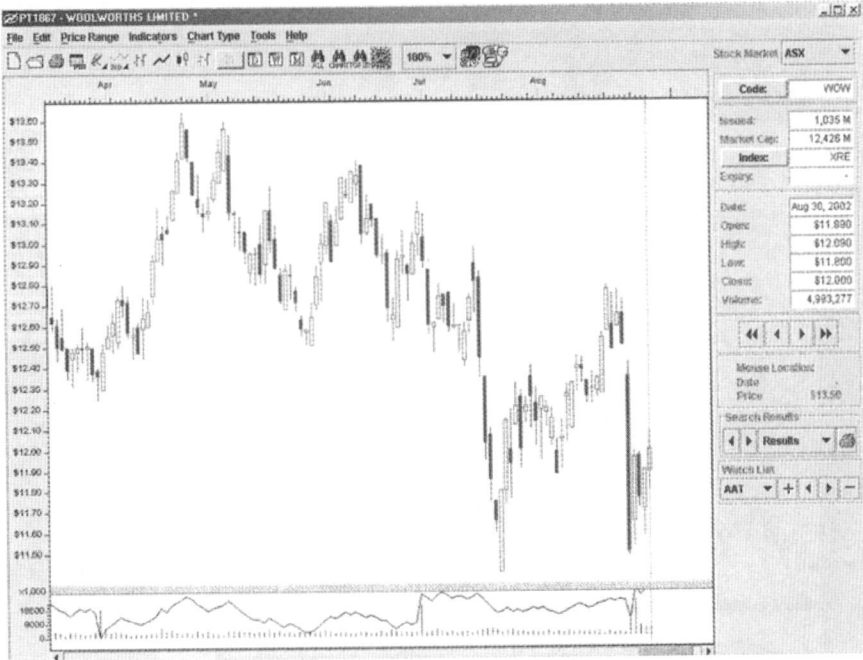

We are bombarded with research and analysis from brokers, magazines and tip sheets. Regardless of the source of this information, or the speed with which you receive it, there are two fundamental problems - the information may be totally wrong, or it may be too late to be of any advantage.

The only way to satisfactorily check the validity of the information is to look at the chart. All the fundamental information is already reflected in the price. If you only take one message from this book, make it this one - *always look at a chart for confirmation of the story before you purchase shares in the company.*

Put more bluntly - cut your ears off and use your eyes!

5

Practical technical analysis

Learning technical analysis can be rather like learning a new language. You may pick it up easily or it may take some hard work and practice. You can learn enough to get by, or you can attempt to master all the intricacies of a new language. It is not my intention to cover every aspect of this topic: there are hundreds of other books out there that will go into far greater detail than I care to. My purpose is to give you a very simple understanding of what works and what doesn't work.

Jack Schwager interviewed Marty Schwartz in his classic book "The Market Wizards". Schwartz racked up enormous percentage gains every year since he became a full time trader in 1979, and did so without ever losing more than 3% of his equity on a monthly basis.

> *I always laugh at people who say, "I've never met a rich technician" I love that! It is such an arrogant, nonsensical response. I used fundamentals for nine years and got rich as a technical analyst.*
>
> Marty Schwartz

Technical analysis is the study of a chart. The average Australian investor has become more aware of technical analysis over the past five years or so. The use of the home personal computer has accelerated the use and acceptance of technical analysis as a plausible method of analysis in Australia. The pure technical analyst believes that all the research conducted by the fundamentalist is represented by the price and reflected in the chart. There must be an element of truth in this attitude.

Charts have been in use one way or another for many decades. Remember the charts at the foot of a hospital bed, charting the health of a patient? It is also reasonable to use a chart to measure the health of a company. After all, the price of a stock at any time reflects the value attributed to that stock by all the market participants, both amateur and professional, during the course of the trading day. If you can "read" those prices correctly, in conjunction with the volume traded each day, you have unlocked the door to consistent profitable trades.

Chartists are cheaters!

"Chartists are cheaters. Why? Because charting is a shortcut form of fundamental analysis. It enables a chartist to analyse a stock or an industry without doing all the work of a fundamental analyst. How does it do that? Simply by telling the chartist whether the fundamentals of a stock are bullish or bearish by the direction its price is moving. If the market perceives the fundamentals are bullish, the stock will be rewarded with a higher price."

(John J Murphy from his book "The Visual Investor")

Arguably, those who study the patterns contained within charts get an "advance notice" on the health or fundamentals of a particular stock without having to do all the hard work usually associated with fundamental analysis.

This book deals primarily with what really works in the realm of successful trading, not wishful fantasies. I have, however, included an appendix to this chapter that outlines the main aspects of fundamental analysis for those of you who are unfamiliar with the traditional "value" analysis. It includes price earning ratios, earnings per share, net tangible assets, dividends per share and other common fundamental measures of a stocks historical performance.

What can a chart do for you?

If you pass a petrol station on the same route every day, plot a graph of the petrol price each day. After a while, you will begin to notice some patterns emerge. Perhaps, as has been suggested to me, you may find prices a little higher on a Friday than on a Tuesday. Could this be because the fuel companies know that we top up the tank for a weekend drive and need to refill for work on Monday? You may already think this, but you need to plot the figures to prove whether you are right or wrong.

Many suggest that prices rise on Government pension day. Keeping a chart will either prove or dispel this notion. Not only will the chart prove your suspicions, it will also predict when you should buy petrol in the future. The patterns that you will recognise in price charts are what we technical analysts label pattern recognition. Different patterns are given different names, such as "ascending triangles" and "head and shoulder" patterns. An understanding of these patterns and the psychology behind their formation will give you an edge over other traders and help make you a profitable investor.

Exploding the Myths

"Technical analysis has been shown to generate statistically significant profits, despite its incompatibility with most economists' notions of efficient markets"

(Federal Reserve Bank of New York, C.L. Osler and P.H. Kevin Chang, Staff Report, No 4 August 1995. This report followed the successful Central Bank intervention to support the U.S. dollar in 1995. The financial press attributed a part of the successful intervention as being due to the fact that central bankers had actually employed some technical trading methods on the markets)

Much of this book is about pattern recognition, not a new concept by any means, but a form of analysis that I have found to have a profound and beneficial effect on my trading.

Consider this: there are analysts all over the county right now working out whether to buy or sell a stock. Each day, the ASX holds what amounts to a daily auction of shares in all publicly listed companies. All these analysts are buying and selling all day long. So surely the analysis is done for you, all you need do is look at the price. The psychology of the other investors is reflected in the price action.

The technical analyst accepts that the only "true" information that comes from the market each day is the Open, High, Low, Close and Volume. From these numbers and charts, he or she will make a buy or sell decision. The technician accepts that the market has little to do with value; it is more to do with perception of value, both current and future, and the psychology of the market participants.

Trends and trend-lines

A trend is any general direction of movement. For example, there is an upward trend in banking stocks, or there is a trend towards ownership of 4 wheel drive vehicles. A trend-line allows us to determine which way shares prices are moving: up, down, or sideways. This may sound elementary but it is a crucial factor and one overlooked by many. There is an old market adage, "the trend is your friend". You would do well to observe this as trading against the trend is like swimming upstream. Go with the flow! Trends are quite easy to spot, and are the building blocks of trading.

A trend-line is a line that is drawn on a chart connecting several price points with one straight line. Drawing a trend-line is a very effective method of determining the direction of stock prices. The importance of a trend-line depends on three factors:

1. The length of the line. (The longer the trend-line, the stronger the trend)

2. The number of times it has been touched or approached.

3. The angle or slope of the trend-line. (A trend-line that is extremely steep will not be maintained for too long).

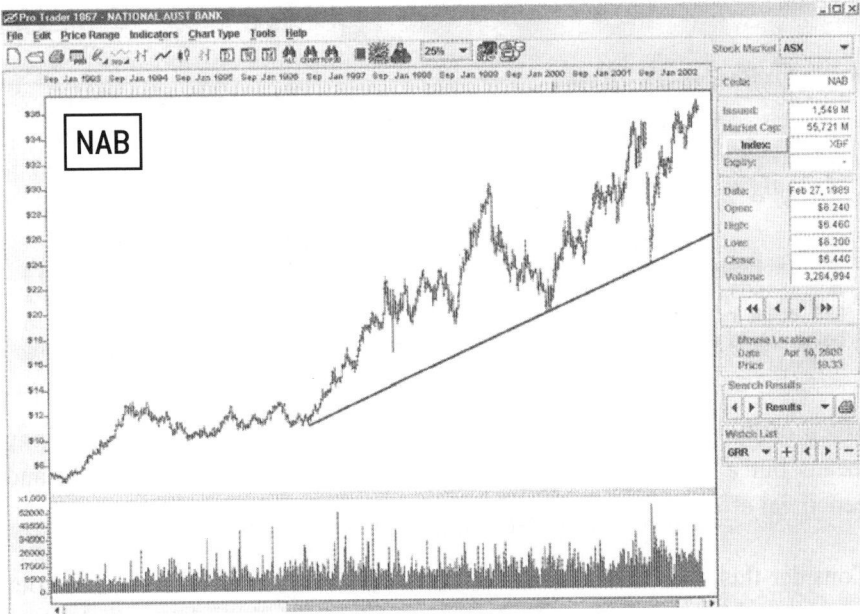

The above chart of the National Australia Bank (NAB) clearly shows a strong upward trend shown by a trend-line. Once a trend is established it normally continues for some time. Most banking stocks in Australia, after a sideways move from 1993 to 1996, trended upwards for the next six years.

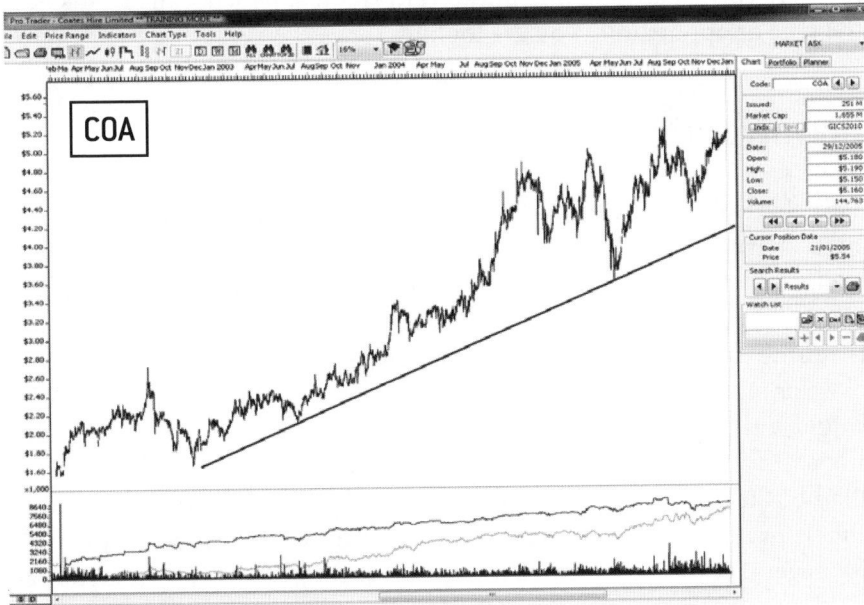

In the past two years, Coates Hire (COA) has moved from $1.80 to $4.40 with hardly a hiccup. This is a better than 50% per annum rise, just for drawing a trend line and buying a rising stock. The issue now is, "What do we do next?" You can adopt the buy, hold and pray industry attitude and wait for the price to go all the way down again (and I can assure you – it will), or you can take profits now and perhaps miss out on another 50% next year, or you can plan an intelligent method of selling this stock when the sell signals emerge.

These sell signals could be as simple as selling when the price falls below a 100 day moving average, or perhaps a 34 and a 55 day dual moving average crossover. Either way, you need to plan your exit now!

If you are ever in doubt as to the direction of a stock's price, print out a chart and stick it on a wall. Go and find a ten-year-old and stand against the opposite wall. Ask the ten-year-old if the price on the chart is going up or down. If they don't know, stay out of the stock. If the ten-year-old says that the price is going up, you would do well to consider buying the stock.

A trend-line is one of the best weapons in a trader's toolbox. The visual effect is obvious from the chart of Coates Hire. As you can see, after a few years of poor performance with downward trending prices, the company's fortunes turned around and an upward trend emerged. This is precisely the type of opportunity you are looking for.

Downward trend

This chart of Ridley Corporation (RIC) clearly shows a downward trend. This chart is almost a photocopy of the previous chart. It shows a prolonged downward trend, followed by a good strong upward trend.

If, during the downward trend, you see any research suggesting that a stock like this is a "good buy", you must question the sanity of the author. Why would you buy this prior to the trend turning up?

Blame "the Asian crisis", blame a downturn in commodity prices, blame the economic climate or anyone else who comes along. It doesn't matter. Management has a choice, "get your act together, or go broke". As you can see, this company decided to get its act together.

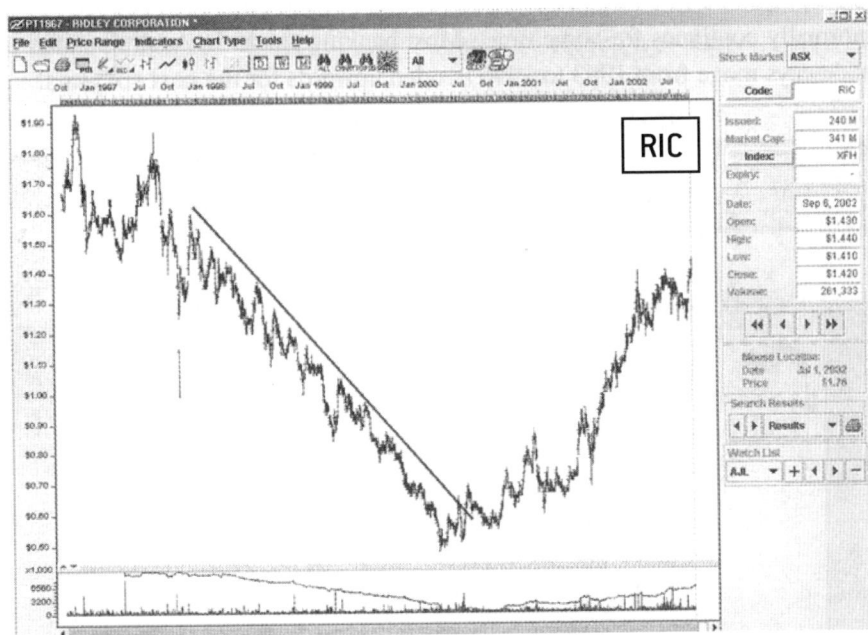

Trend-lines can be drawn above the prices or below the prices. Lines drawn underneath prices are support lines and those drawn above prices act as resistance lines. Every successful technical analyst will draw trend-lines to show levels of price support and resistance. These lines are important for the analyst, leading to potential buy and sell signals. Trend-lines are often drawn at a level that reflects the intrinsic value of a stock, explaining why these levels act like magnets.

Support

The concept of support is very simple and something that everyone is familiar with. For a technical analyst, the recognition of a price support level is crucial. It is a price level where buyers begin to out-number sellers, then become willing to pay higher and higher prices for the stock. Support is the low price in a cycle of peaks and troughs. As the price drops, more buyers begin to see the stock as attractive and start to buy, slowly halting and eventually reversing the downward trend. It is like a price barrier beyond which prices are unlikely to fall.

Horizontal support

Coles-Myer (CML) shares showed support for many years at the $6.00 level. This price support was evident from July 1998 after three attempts to penetrate below that level. There were several strong rebounds from this level before the support broke nearly four years later.

Upward Support

Support can slope upwards or sideways. The chart of Woolworths (WOW), below, shows upward support. (support obviously cannot slope downwards) There is a point at which a stock moves from a downward trend to an upward trend.

Many analysts will wait for prices to fall, and buy as the prices approach a strong support level. Most people concerned with saving a dollar or two will apply the same principle when it comes to filling the car with petrol.

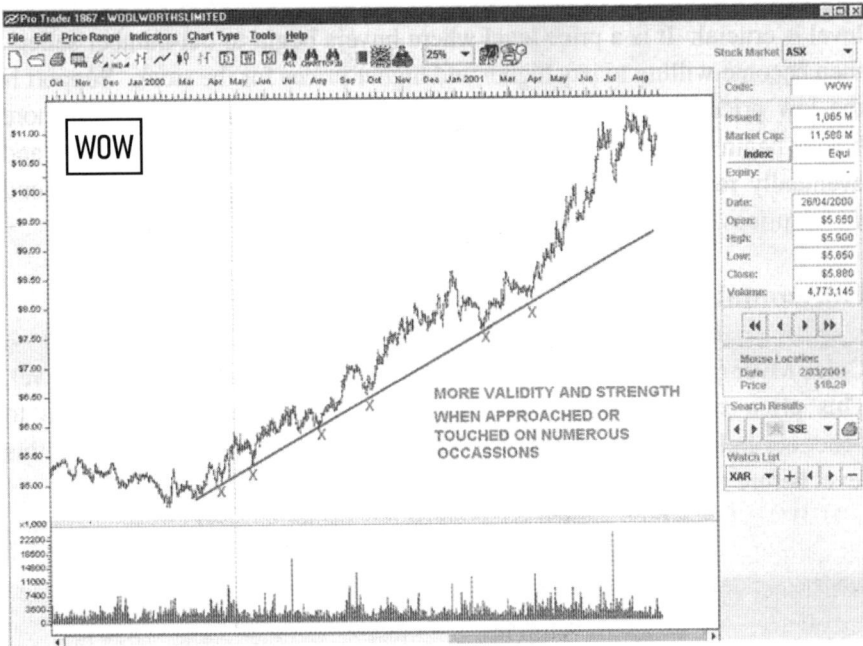

Resistance

As we have seen in earlier examples, share prices move in a series of peaks and troughs. The peaks are called *resistance* because they indicate a price range where sellers outweigh the buyers. This change reverses the trend. You could think of resistance as being like a price barrier – a price level that is difficult to break through. Resistance is the reverse of *support*. Whereas *support* is like the lower price barrier on a product or share, *resistance* is the top price barrier.

On a graph of the stock prices over a particular period, we can mark price peaks and draw a line connecting them. That's the *resistance line* – it marks the price barrier for that stock during that particular period.

Horizontal resistance

Following an upward move in a stock, there is a point where the stock becomes too expensive, or overvalued, and the buyers pull out. Resistance levels form.

85

Sloping resistance

Resistance can be either downward sloping or horizontal. A common error for novices is to draw upward sloping resistance lines. Just as shares have a support price where buyers outnumber sellers, they also have *resistance* levels, where sellers dominate buyers who are not willing to pay higher prices. The next chart of Pacific Dunlop shows a clear resistance line. When prices penetrate above a downward sloping resistance line, the trend has changed, giving us a very good buy signal. This is one of the signals I use for entering stocks, and I have written more about this method in the chapter specifically covering buy signals.

The chart, below, of Telstra (TLS) clearly demonstrates two resistance levels, the first being horizontal resistance at a touch over $9.00. Since those highs at around $9.00 were made in late 1999, we now have a trend-line showing downward sloping resistance.

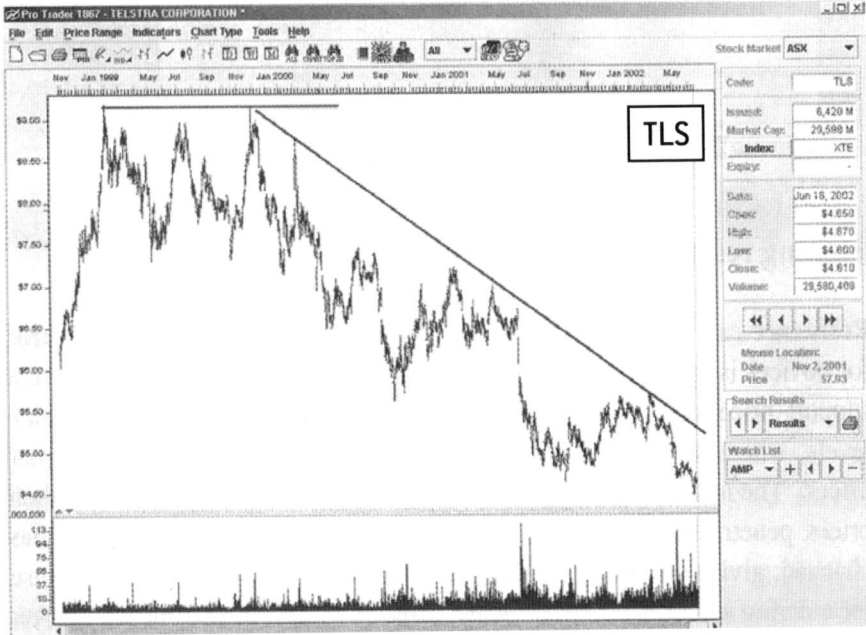

Channels

What are channels? Often you get shares that are caught in a very distinctive channel; that is, bouncing between a support and resistance level.

Channels are market phases where buyers and sellers are undecided about market direction. There are different types of channels.

Accumulation channel

Let's look at the chart on the following page. For a period of 18 months, Western Mining Corporation (WMC) traded in a channel between a low of around $4.20 and a high of $5.60.

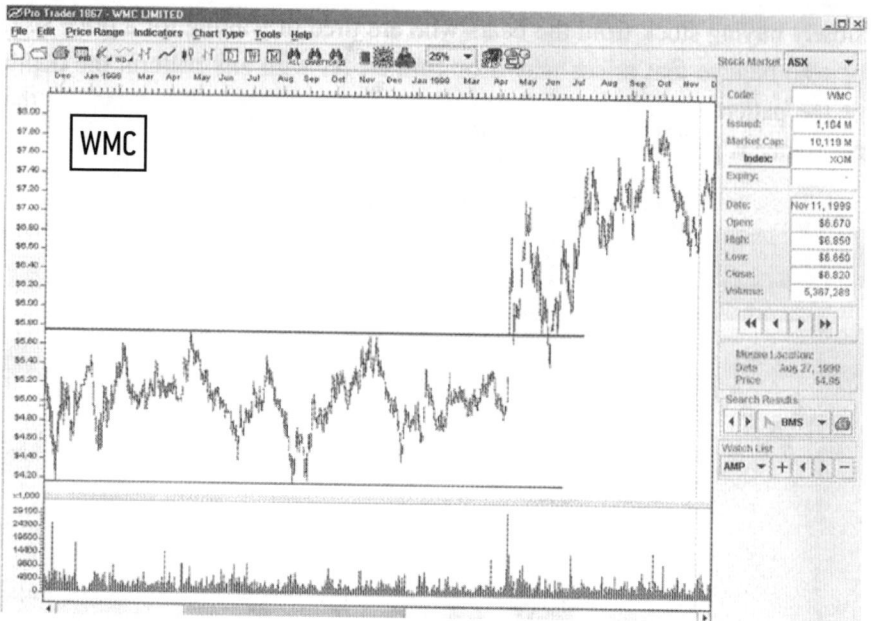

In this case, the trend channel occurred at an historically low price range. We call this channel an "accumulation phase". It is an area where the "smart money" slowly enters the market and accumulates stock. The bulls are slowly buying stock from the bears who are tired of waiting for a price rise, or who believe that prices may drop further. As with any pattern, the depth of the pattern gives us an indication of how far prices will move once the resistance is penetrated.

Trading an accumulation channel

There are two methods of trading a channel. The first method is to *buy on support* (place a stop loss below the support level) and sell as the resistance level is approached. In the case of WMC, there were two chances in August and September 1998 to buy near the support level of $4.20. There were two chances to take profits near the $5.60 resistance level in November 1998, a return of over 20% in four months.

The second method (and the safest) arises when the resistance level is penetrated. The experienced trader will place an order to purchase stock as the resistance level is penetrated (say, $5.70 in the case of WMC) and look for a profit target equal to the depth of the pattern, the depth being the price difference between support and resistance. In the case of WMC, the depth or height of the pattern is $1.40 (subtract $4.20 from $5.60). If resistance is broken we can expect the price to move to $7.00. ($5.60 plus $1.40)

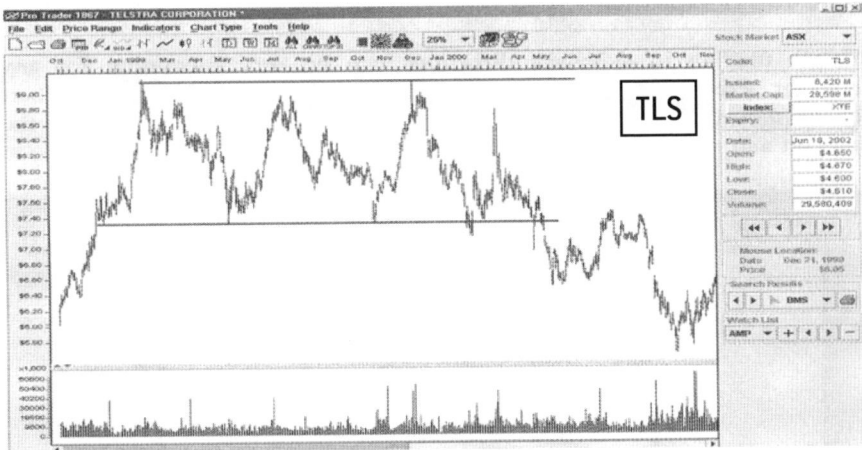

When we see a trend channel form after a run upwards in a stock, we can start to look for signs of a market top. When we can finally recognise a clear channel at a top, we know that we have what is called a "distribution phase" (distribution channel). The stronger, more educated traders are slowly selling out to the weaker, less educated traders. This was certainly the case with Telstra, as shown on the next chart.

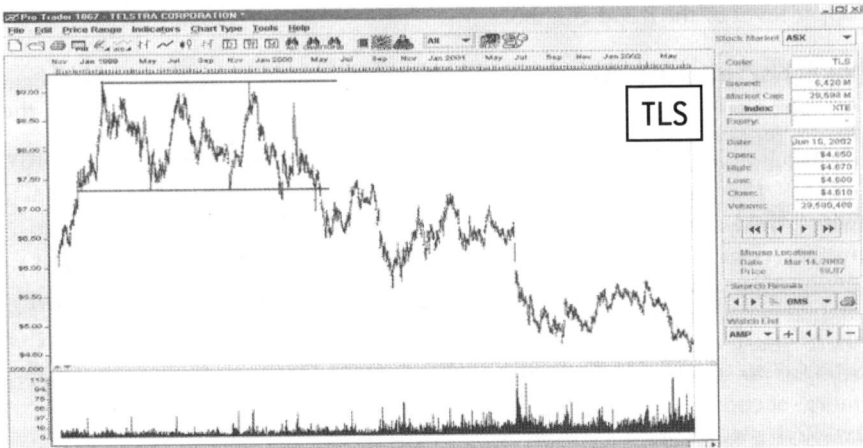

Trading a distribution channel

Get out! Sell! As soon as the support level fails, sell your stock; you can always get back in if the stock rallies and gives you appropriate buy signals. There is absolutely no point holding onto a stock like this, waiting ... waiting for what? If you purchase a stock and wait and watch as it trades lower and lower, you are gambling.

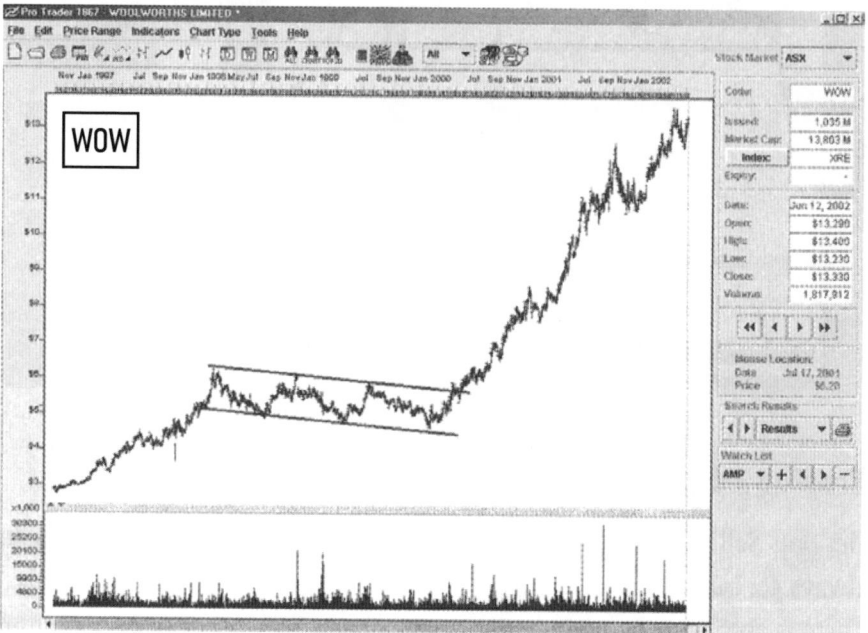

Mid-range channel

Shares moving in sideways directions can be very frustrating for any investor. Precious capital is non productive in a sideways market. The chart, below, shows the price movement of Woolworths' shares. Again, once the support and resistance lines can be drawn (remember, we need to be able to connect three prices with a straight line) we may see some trading opportunities. The real opportunity comes when the prices penetrate the upper level of the trend channel.

"Woolies" has been a marvellous trade for the technical analyst, the recent upward channel proving to be most profitable. If prices break below the lower support line in this channel, the technical analyst will sell the stock. The "long term" investor will "hold on", waiting for a further rise. That rise may be many years away, eroding the annual percentage return.

Drawing these lines on a chart allow an analyst to time the market far more accurately than traditional research methods.

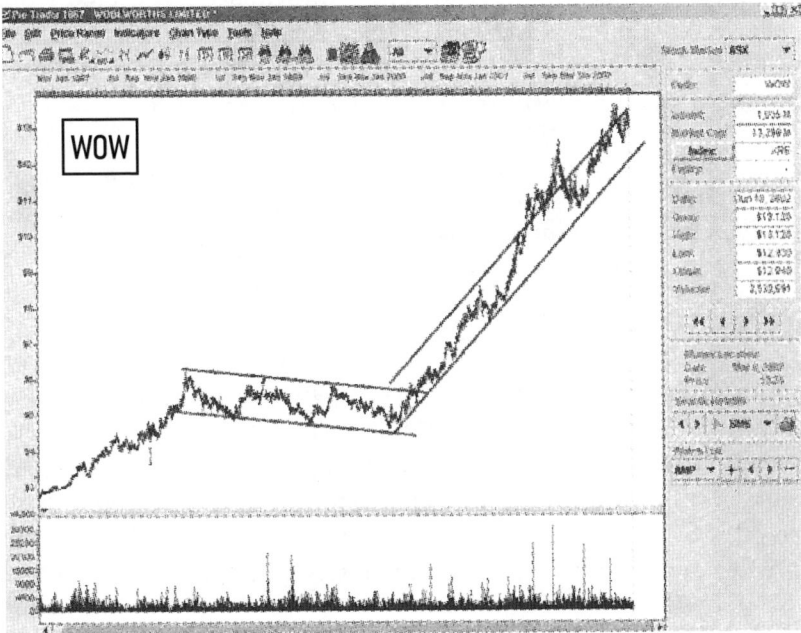

Appendix

Fundamental analysis - an overview

Virtually everyone commences trading unwittingly as a fundamental analyst. New traders will study any readily available information in an attempt to gain a better understanding of a particular company. This may be the latest company report, or other information gathered from a newsletter, broker's research, newspaper or a magazine. The company report will divulge such information as net tangible assets, dividends, earnings per share and other relevant financial information.

> *With enough information and a million dollars you can go broke in a year.*
> Warren Buffet

There is a danger in accepting the written word as the truth. Broker's research is a classic example. While it may be the truth at the time of writing, the story often does not unfold as suggested. When brokers' research is accompanied with a disclaimer stating that the author or the broking firm may own shares in the company that is covered in the document, you need to be ultra-careful. Clearly, if the author owns shares in the company being researched, the author is biased. I have often felt the industry would be better off banning trading by brokers and their research staff. (I can hear them screaming now!)

Company reports often disguise bad news. In recent years there have been a few high profile bankruptcies in Australia, and even as the liquidators are walking through the front door, company directors are denying any financial problems exist. If we look at the American example, company reports have been falsified by literally billions of dollars.

Most of the fundamental information you receive will be available to the rest of the market as well. Whether the information comes via a fax or email or printed newsletter, it is often too late. It is very rare that you will receive genuine information about a stock that is not already known by the market. The broad currency of the information will usually be reflected in the price action or volume traded figures on the chart of that stock.

What is fundamental analysis?

A fundamentalist analyses historical company data. This includes auditor's reports, profit and loss statements, sales data, production capacity, dividend records, cash flow and managerial capability, just to name a few. The fundamentalist will probably be an avid reader of daily papers, financial magazines, broker's research papers and various tip sheets. Finally, he or she evaluates a stock and concludes that the current price is above or below that valuation and a decision to buy or sell is made. Unfortunately, a strong history and a highly favourable track record is no guarantee of future success.

Most stockbrokers are fundamental analysts. If you ask a broker's advice, you can expect a long story about why a particular stock price will rise. Only too often, these stories do not unfold according to plan.

> *There is no such thing as being right or beating the market. If you make money, it is because you understand the same thing the market did. If you lose, it is simply because you got it wrong. There is no other way of looking at it.*
>
> Musawer Mansoon Iiaz

If you dig deeper into fundamental analysis you will discover the company reports, price earnings ratios, dividends, earnings per share and a range of other statistical information designed to assist in your analysis.

There are some problems with fundamental analysis. As mentioned, the data you are analysing may be flawed. Companies often hide the bad news from their shareholders. Meanwhile, good news may be released to a select few in the form of a "corporate briefing". The price of the stock may have risen considerably before this news is released to the public.

The last half of the nineties has brought about many changes. Personal computers and the Internet have changed the way we think, analyse and invest. While fundamental analysis has its merits, it is impossible to analyse and track the progress of well over a thousand publicly listed companies.

Broking firms may have a team of analysts and still not research more than fifty or a hundred companies. There is so much information available it is impossible to read it all, let alone conduct in-depth analysis.

Most professional traders accept that fundamental analysis will indicate the potential direction of the company's price, while technical analysis will give you better timing of purchase and subsequent sale of stock.

I have a bias towards technical analysis, but believe that a combination of technical and fundamental gives you the best of both worlds. With that in mind, let's look at some of the more common areas of fundamental analysis.

Price earnings ratio (PER)

A PER is the share price divided by the earnings per share.

So, a company trading at $2.00 per share with earnings of ten cents per share is said to have a PER of 20 (or twenty times). This means that it would take this particular company 20 years at the current rate of earnings to pay the shareholder back the cost of the shares.

There is a recent perception among the uninformed public that a low PER shows that a stock is undervalued, and all you need do is buy a stock with a low PER and wait for the profits to roll in.

Unfortunately, a low PER may mean that company profits are in decline and the company may be one step away from liquidation. Look for the reasons for a low PER. The other problem with an over-reliance on the PER is that you are looking at an historic snapshot of company performance.

Use your common sense. If successful investing was simply buying a low PER and getting rich, we would have been investing in that manner years ago. There is nothing new in this market. More often than not, if a stock is trading at a low PER there is a good reason for it.

Earnings per share (EPS)

EPS is the net profit divided by the number of shares. For example, if a company earns a net profit of 20 million dollars and has 100 million shares issued, the EPS is 20 cents.

Earnings per share is the amount of net profit that has been earned for each ordinary share on issue and is expressed in cents per share. There is a correlation between a company's share price and the EPS.

Net tangible assets (NTA)

Net tangible assets are a measure of what each share is worth if the company was liquidated. This assumes a theoretical price the assets may be worth if the company was liquidated. Intangible assets are excluded from the NTA calculation because they are difficult to value. These intangibles include goodwill, brand names and intellectual property. Often these are the main assets of a company.

Dividend per share (DPS)

The dividend per share is the dividend paid divided by the number of ordinary shares on issue. DPS is the amount paid to shareholders from net profits and is expressed in cents per share. It is the return that a shareholder receives for investing in that company.

Annual reports

All listed companies are required to lodge an annual report. These sometimes glossy and very costly publications are full of an endless amount of numbers and figures that appear to be designed to confuse. The main facts are among the list below:

- Net profit
- Franking credits (tax)

- Profit and loss account
- Balance sheet, including a statement of assets and liabilities
- Dividend
- Cash-flow statement

> *I'm always turned off by an overly optimistic letter from the President in the annual report. If his letter is mildly pessimistic, to me that's a good sign.*
>
> Philip Carret

There is also a Director's report and an auditor's report. The auditor's report should ensure the integrity of the annual report. This is not necessarily true. We have seen in the US recently where annual reports have been fudged by literally billions of dollars. Again, by the time you get to read and analyse an annual report, it is already ancient history as far as the market is concerned.

Company announcements

> *News on stocks is not important. How the stock reacts to it is important.*
>
> Michael Burke

When you first begin to trade you will notice occasions where the release of good news is met by a fall in the price of a stock. A couple of years ago, the National Australia Bank announced one of Australia's largest ever corporate profits, and fell $2.00 per share in the following 48 hours. A couple of years later, the National Australia Bank announced one of Australia's largest corporate write-offs.

This was met with a strong price rise over subsequent weeks as the public lapped up the news. You may ask, "What is going on here?" Why are so many apparently favorable announcements met with a fall in price, and vice versa?

This is a phenomenon that is very difficult for a newcomer to rationalize. A broker rings them and suggests the purchase of a stock because the company involved is making an announcement next week. You charge in and buy, then either the announcement does not eventuate, the announcement was a very moderated version of what you were told, or the expected announcement came and the stock price fell immediately.

It is quite clear to even a casual observer that the news is "already in the market". So many announcements are factored into the price prior to the announcement. These are the dilemmas that face the fundamental analyst. Lets look at one of the problems associated with fundamental analysis. A seemingly very balanced article in the "Shares Magazine" January 1999 begins as follows.

Exploding the Myths

"When a company is the subject of takeover speculation, it is usually a dangerous time to buy the stock for the longer term – obviously you win if the rumours are right, but if they're wrong the shares will take some time to make up the lost ground. Pasminco is in that category, but at $1.40 the shares are still good value for longer term investors. It may make sense for longer term investors wanting a position in the world zinc market to buy some Pasminco now with the intention of picking up more should no takeover eventuate..."

Here is the first buy at $1.40.

In July 2000 "Shares Magazine" follows up with an article.

"According to some stockbrokers, Pasminco is trading at a whopping 50% discount to net present value."

This time Pasminco was trading at the 90c level.
In March 2001 there was a broker research article.

Exploding the Myths

Pasminco —risk takers can BUY

"As if Pasminco hadn't had enough to go through lately, the stock has just been hit by the latest half yearly report. In the six months to 31 December, despite rising sales, the company was in the red, losing $37 million after abnormals. The share price hasn't been badly hit, down only 7%, the market realising that without this hassle operating profit was actually 57% better at $88 million, thanks to Century zinc mines great performance. The hedge problems seem temporary to us.

The shares were trading at 67 cents at this stage.

This is an interesting situation. All the news seems bad, but we have a buy recommendation, albeit for "risk takers". This can be pretty confusing for a newcomer to the market, as well as potentially costly. To buy or not to buy? What would you do? The chart will tell you. Is the price going up or down?

Already we know that prices have fallen from $1.40 at the time of the first recommendation to current levels of 67 cents. Methinks the trend is down! This is a recommendation *for the suicidal, not just the risk takers*. I do question the motive of a recommendation like this. The broker could have written the same research up to the last line. Substitute "risk takers can buy" with "we would prefer to see our clients on the sideline until there is evidence that Pasminco has returned to profitability and the share price is on the rise"!

In July 2001, a tip sheet recommends buying as the price heads lower and lower, the current price now down to 32 cents.

And finally, in August 2001, the last word (and the most intelligent) came from a writer in the shares magazine in the August 2001 edition.

Exploding the Myths

Pasminco - don't catch a falling knife

"Some brokers, principally CIBC and Hartley Poynton, have tipped Pasminco as a buy despite the slide. They argue that the Zinc market will recover and the company's flagship Centenary mine is a world class asset. Perhaps it is, but there's no denying the danger of trying to catch a falling knife."

Shares Magazine, August 2001

In September 2001, Pasminco entered bankruptcy!

The Pasminco story shown above is common and, unfortunately, has a human side. At a presentation I was making last year, a young married couple told the audience they had placed an inheritance into Pasminco on the basis of one of these recommendations. There was never any follow up from the broker, never any suggestion of an error in judgment, and never a sell recommendation.

Spin-doctors

My experience would suggest that of all recommendations that you will receive, whether from a broker, a newsletter or a hot tip, 90% of them are buys;

> *I have never known the price of a stock to be in a clear upward trend as the company enters bankruptcy!*

no-one gives you a hot tip on when to sell a stock! I never cease to be amazed by the reaction of people when they look at a chart of stocks that they are holding. Once they see a picture, they often wonder why they bought the stock in the first place. Obviously, they fell for the spin-doctor's story rather than checking the chart for the truth.

6

Five effective buy signals

This is where it all begins. Buying your first share is usually tinged with a little apprehension. You probably already have thoughts of how to spend the profits and hope that the tip or research proves to be profitable. Rarely is the risk considered. We will cover risks later on.

In this chapter, we look at some of the entry methods that I use, and that have stood the test of time. These methods are designed to get you into a profitable trade as painlessly as possible. There is nothing worse than buying a stock

> *As a general tip for you, I would strongly suggest that you replace the old saying "buy low sell high" with a new saying, "buy dear and sell dearer!"*

and watching prices fall from that moment onwards. There are obviously many ways to enter the market, but I have restricted my trading plan to incorporate only four principle methods. Given my belief that timing is critical in any investment, I must have precise rules for timing my entry into a stock.

If you want to make money share trading, you will have to learn the basic building blocks. Four core elements are -

- Buy the right stock at the right time and price.
- Confirm the buy signal is heavily weighted towards success.
- Put in place some risk insurance measures to limit damage.
- Sell at the right time and price.

This chapter covers the first element - how to choose the right time and price to buy a stock. All buy signals are based on technical data, that is, trading volume, open, high, low and the closing price.

We look for changes (or breaks) in patterns in the price movement of a stock. This is a mostly technical chapter, building on some concepts already presented in earlier chapters, and introducing new analytical tools and terms.

> *Successful trading is all about investing when all the odds are in your favour.*

Interestingly, the subject of buying the right stock at the right time is not something that is discussed, let alone taught. I have attended countless professional development days where "experts" stand and pontificate on a variety of subjects. I have studied and sat for many exams prior to, during, and after my broking career. I cannot recall ever being asked a question relating to whether or not I could make money trading shares. Surely this is the very essence of either broking or advising or teaching.

1 | Buy signal one
Higher highs and higher lows

After a prolonged downturn, a stock may flatten out and accumulation may begin. Wait for a stock to make consecutive higher highs and higher lows over a period of several weeks.

A consecutive run of rising prices (both high and low) would intuitively suggest an upward trend. This pattern – bottoming out, followed by a steady climb in highs and lows – is generally considered to be the first sign of a bull market.

Ion Carbide (ION) shows a classic opportunity for a trader. Following a prolonged two-year downward trend, prices clearly changed direction and started to rise. From this moment on, it is a case of waiting for the prices to make consecutive higher highs and higher lows. The buy signal is generated when the prices penetrate the second higher high.

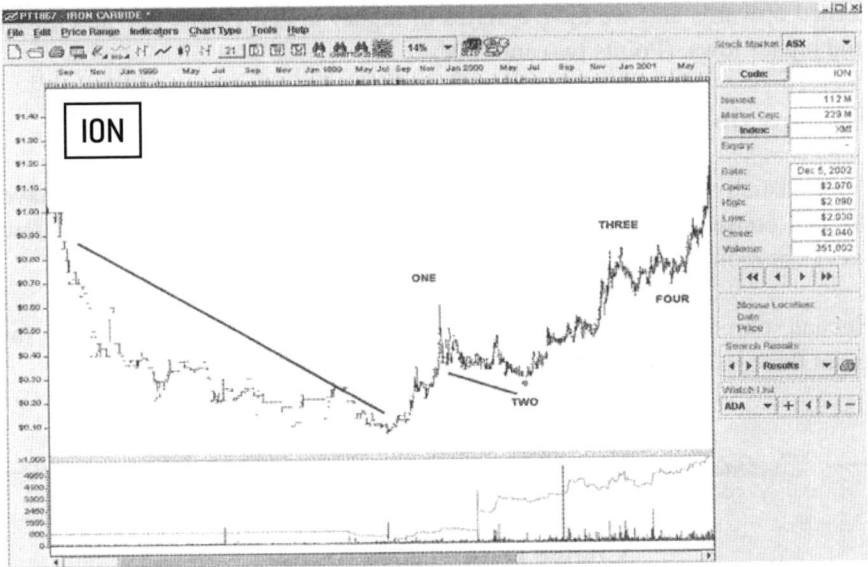

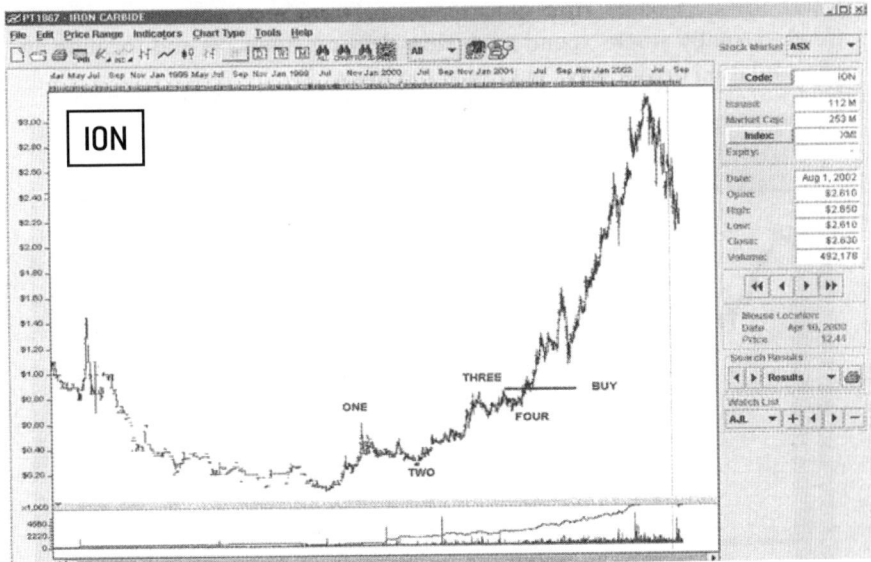

We can see in the first instance (from the previous charts) that this stock was making lower highs and lower lows as prices trended downwards. The prices finally turned upwards and we have a series of higher highs (Points one and three) and higher lows. (Points two and four)

So, how do you apply buy signal one?

First, visually check to see that you have found a stock where prices have formed consecutive higher highs and higher lows over a period of a few weeks or months.

Second, purchase shares when the prices break above the second high (at point three in the chart), after the second higher low (at point four).

Exploding the Myths

Coates Hire - goes higher?

Although not as distinct, this chart shows a pattern of higher highs and lower lows. Coates Hire (COA) quickly turned from a downtrend to an up-trend. Usually, stocks spend more time drifting sideways and forming an accumulation or sideways pattern at the lows.

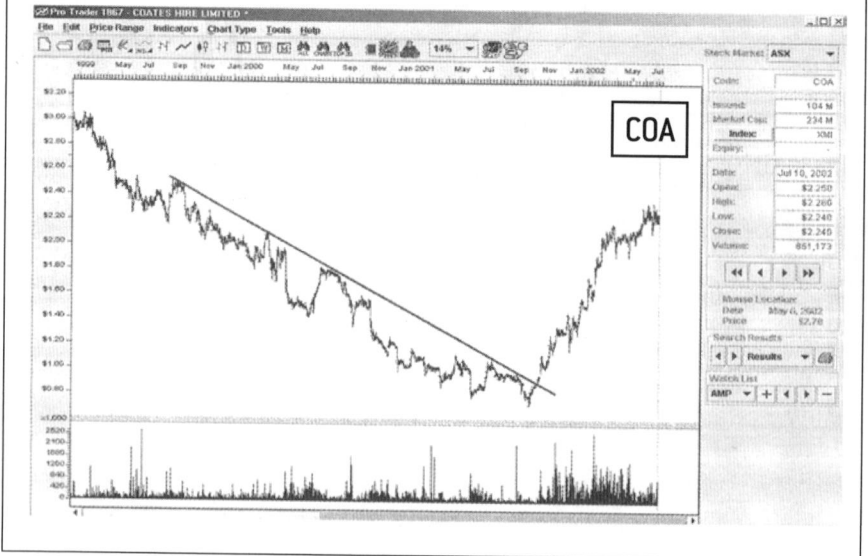

Consider the psychology behind this stock. The Coates Hire chart shows a prolonged downtrend for the best part of four years with prices falling from $3.80 to 80 cents. Regardless of what you want to blame for the falling prices; from "the Asian Crisis" and falling commodity prices, to low interest rates and poor market conditions or any other factor, management has not been particularly efficient and was rather tardy in addressing the problem. Management ultimately faced a serious threat, "Get your act together or go broke". When prices start to rise you have to assume they chose the former course of action. It is fair to assume that prices will probably continue to rise for some considerable length of time (perhaps as much as two to four years). If a stock spends a long period of time in decline, then it is likely to also have a longer and more sustained upswing when it finally does reverse the trend. To reverse out of such a "habitual" downtrend would have required a considerable change in sentiment and/or financial fundamentals, so this change is likely to be more sustained over a period of time.

2 Buy signal two
Key reversal bottom

A key reversal bottom sometimes forms at the end of a downward trend. It is possibly the only way to intelligently try to "pick a bottom", that is, buy the low price.

When a stock has been in a prolonged downtrend, there may be a final heavy sell-off as speculators finally give up on the stock. This final selling is accompanied by high volume as the last wave of panic selling hits the stock.

On the key reversal day, prices open lower than the previous day, and recover during the day to finally close higher than the previous day's close.

The software I use scans the total ASX database in a matter of moments and finds key reversal days for me. This is virtually impossible to do without the appropriate software.

Key Reversal Bottom

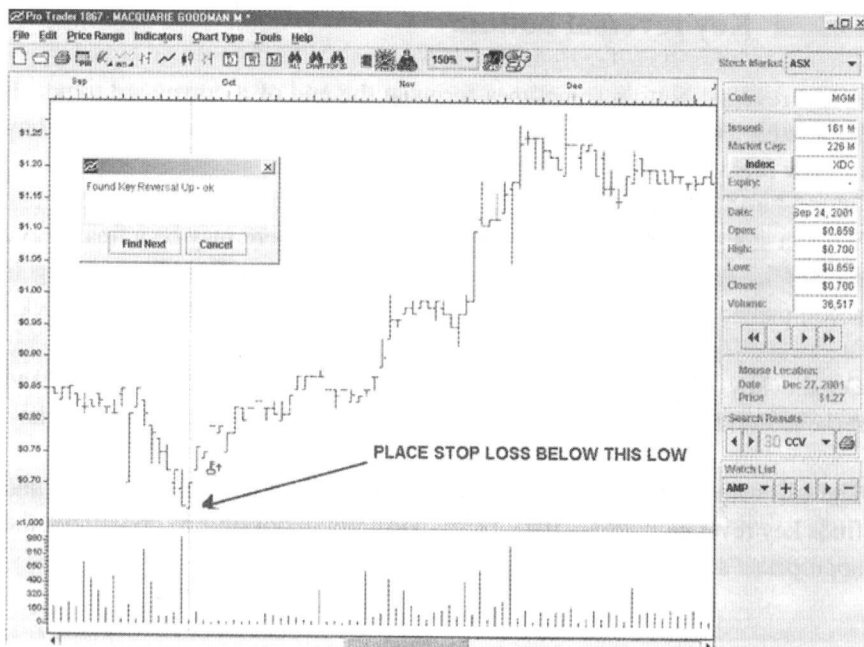

Found Key Reversal Up - ok

Find Next   Cancel

PLACE STOP LOSS BELOW THIS LOW

So, how do you apply buy signal two?

First, use a charting software package to scan the total ASX list of stocks and identify key reversal bottoms in a matter of seconds. This is one of the key reasons that drove me to have my own software developed.

Second, purchase shares at the "open" (the commencement of trading) the day after a key reversal is found.

Finally, place a stop at a price point below the low of the reversal day; that is, below the low of the lowest day! It is especially important to place a stop loss when you are attempting to pick a turning point in a stock. Preserve capital and avoid any unnecessary risk.

3 Buy signal three
Resistance breakouts

When resistance lines are broken, it shows a willingness of traders to pay higher prices. I have found that "buying a break" of a resistance line generally gives a safe entry point. The longer it takes for the resistance to form, the better the chances for a very profitable trade.

If you are looking for resistance as a buy signal, then consider the following:

- The more a stock trades at a particular level, the stronger the resistance becomes and generally the stronger the breakout is when it comes.

- Often, resistance price levels are at significant round numbers, for example $1.00, $10.00. This is due to sellers not thinking intelligently. A person who is looking to take a profit will virtually always place a sell at a "big" number. A profit taker will sell at $2.00, a smart profit taker will sell at $1.97 or $1.98, before the big mass of unthinking sellers.

- Price resistance can be horizontal or sloping downwards.

- When prices break through resistance after a consolidation phase, they can advance rapidly.

Short-term resistance

The critical period for buying is as resistance levels are broken – as prices move beyond the price barrier. It's as though, having broken through the barrier, prices take off. This breakout is often followed by a news event that propels the stock even higher. The prices will generally react long before you get to see the news item that caused the price break.

The trick is to determine your trading time frame before you begin. A short-term outlook is from one day to six weeks. I have shown some short-term trend lines on the chart, below. Each time prices penetrate these trend-lines, a short-term trader may choose to buy stock.

In the chart, below, Patrick Corporation (PRK) shows several short-term resistance lines.

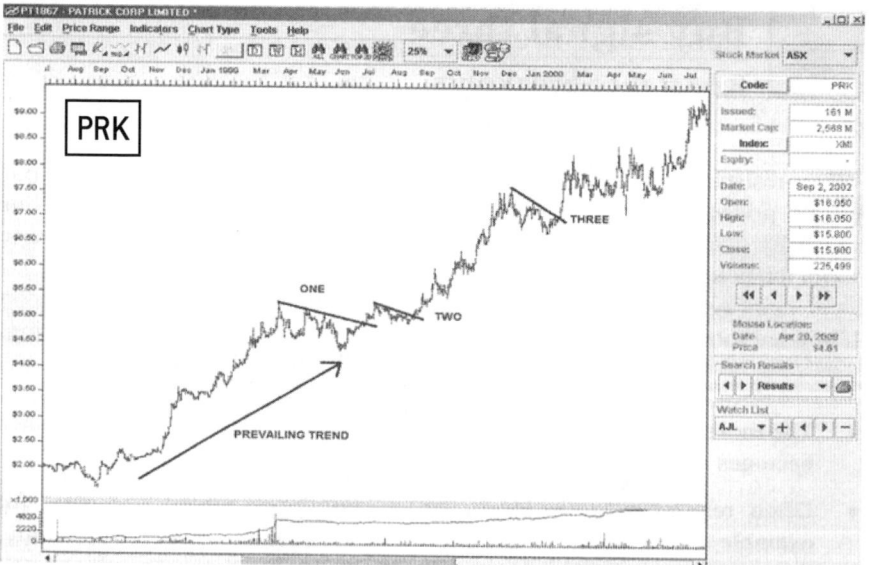

Medium-term resistance

My definition of medium-term is from six weeks to nine months. The same chart of Patrick Corporation shows a medium-term resistance line. In this case, the resistance line formed over a period of six months and happens to engulf two of the previously shown short-term resistance lines.

Buy stocks as they trade above any medium-term resistance lines.

Long-term resistance

The following chart of Ridley Corporation (RIC) shows a long downward trend on the resistance line, followed by a new upward trend established when prices turned up. I consider long-term as being a period greater than nine months.

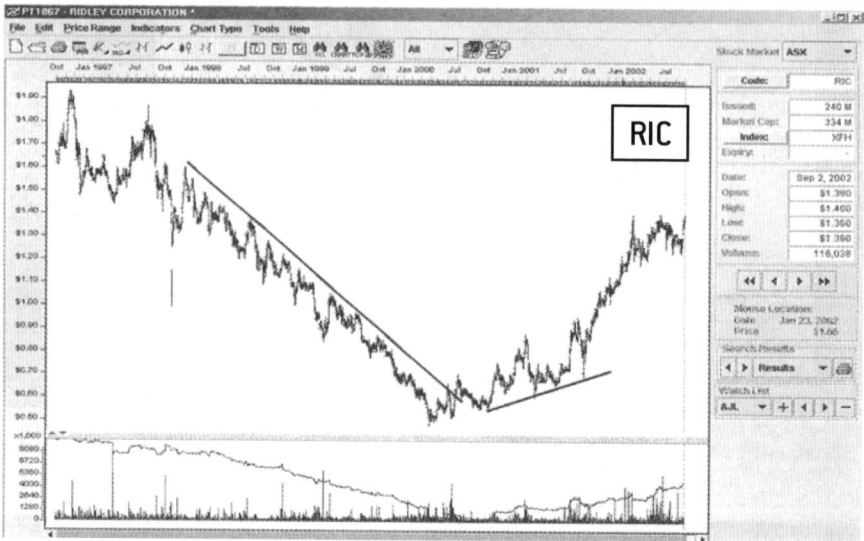

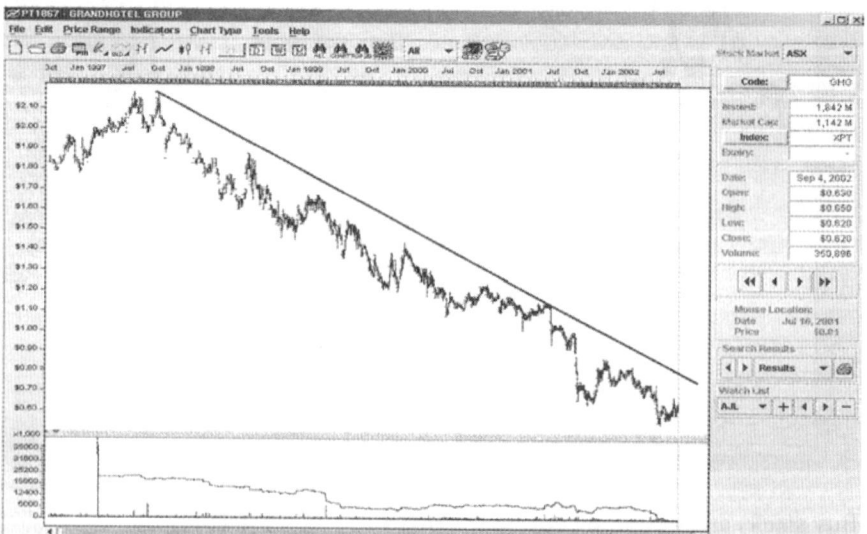

This updated chart shows that the trend-line that was drawn in September 2002 was finally penetrated in August 2003. Prices have since exhibited a classic bull market structure with higher highs and higher lows being evident.

4 | Buy signal four

Buying on support

The chart on the following page is a chart of the National Australia Bank (NAB) with a long-term support line drawn underneath the data.

What is support?

Basically, a support level is a point on a chart where the probabilities favour a temporary halt in the prevailing trend.

This may be very temporary or it may be more sustained as prices "bounce"

off these support levels. A support acts more or less as a "floor" in which sellers become less enthusiastic or less willing to sell their existing stock.

Price support levels are either horizontal or sloping upward.

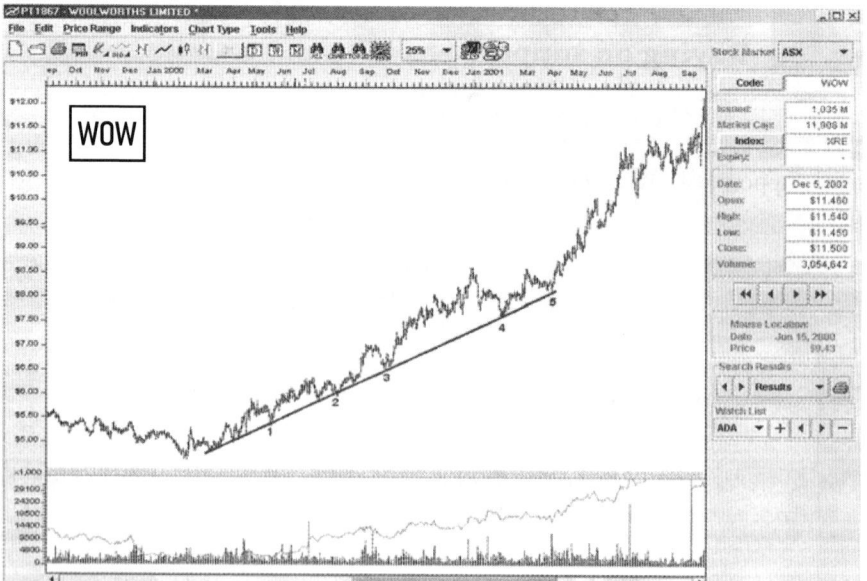

Buying on support

The Woolworths' (WOW) chart has given us plenty of opportunity to "buy on support".

If you are looking for support as a buy signal, consider the following:

- The longer and more often a stock trades at a support level, the stronger that support is. As shown on the Woolies chart, our trendline is drawn at a very strong support level.

- If support levels are horizontal, they will often be at significant round numbers, for example, 20 cents, 50 cents, $1.00, $10.00.

- The critical time to buy a stock is when support levels are being tested.

- In an up-trend, if previous resistance is broken, that resistance becomes a new support level.

- Support is a price level that traders judge to be "fair value".

Exploding the Myths

Say cheese please ...

A supermarket analogy is helpful in understanding the concept of support, because normal perishable goods often show a similar pattern of peaks and troughs. Anyone who does the weekly shopping will be aware of price support levels, even though they may not know the terminology.

A one-kilogram block of cheese at my local supermarket is normally priced at $5.99. Periodically, the same cheese sells at the "special" price of $3.99. If you go to my fridge and find two or three blocks of cheese, you will know that there has been a "special". After looking at the same product for a while, I have come to recognise a low price for cheese and, like many other shoppers, will buy at this low price. Hence, $3.99 is the support level. I have the opportunity to apply this principle to share trading.

If I run out of cheese and the price is too high, I go without. Other less cautious people will pay the high price without any thought. The same applies in trading.

As well as a price barrier, you can also think of support as a safety net. As prices drop, they eventually reach a point where people think it is worth buying. The stock is supported – prevented from dropping further.

5 Buy signal five

Multiple moving averages

Many traders combine two or more moving averages: a fast moving average and a slower moving average. A dual moving average generates buy and sell signals in its own right, when the fast moving average line on the graph crosses the slower moving average line.

Given that the moving average is based on past prices, moving averages in a rising market will generally be below the current price.

Dual moving averages are used successfully to give buy and sell signals. Below is a chart of Metcash (MTT) with 2 exponential moving averages overlaid, in this case, a 34 and a 55-day.

We can see the initial crossover buy signal, and further on is the sell signal as the averages cross again.

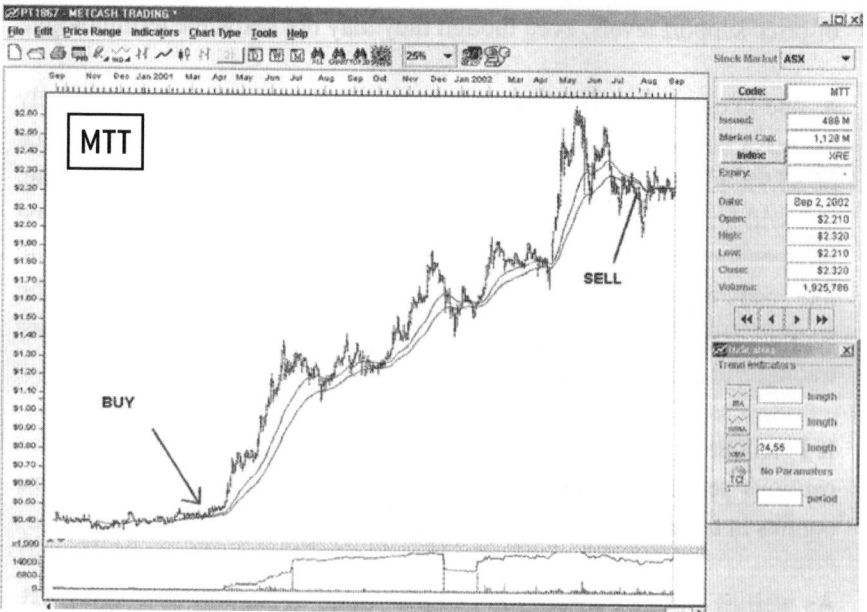

There are other variations on this theme. All variations can be categorised as trend following systems. Given this definition, trend following systems will never buy at the bottom or sell at the top.

A 3 and a 10 day moving average crossover will respond faster than a 15 and a 45 day crossover. The three and ten-day will also give more false buy and sell signals. This can be costly as brokerage becomes a major factor in short term trading systems.

Dual moving averages and patterns

In the case of ION Carbide (ION), we have an entry signal generated by the dual moving average crossover, then the prices move into an ascending triangle pattern. If I had used the moving average crossover as my entry, I would use the moving average crossover as my sell, but this would not stop me from trading the ascending triangle as well.

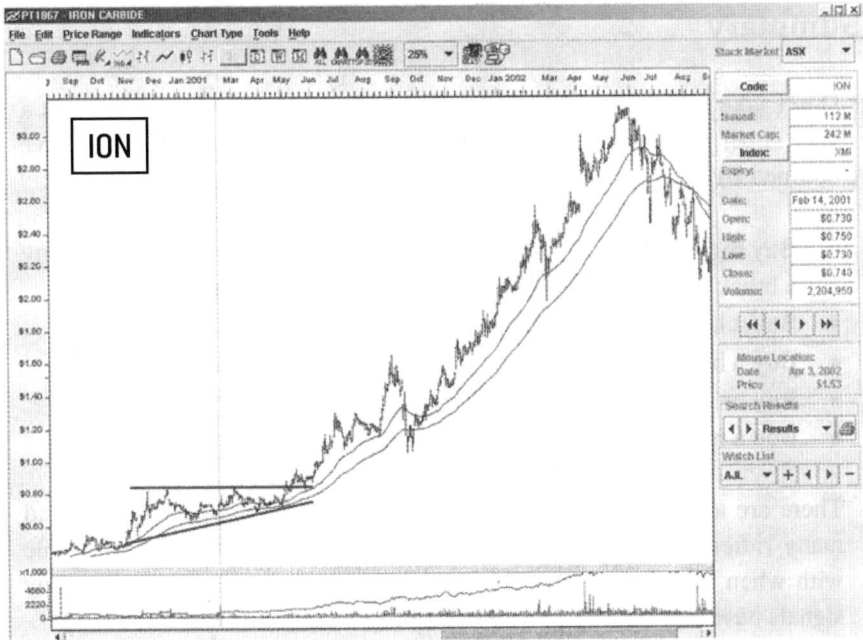

In this case, it is entirely possible to have two trades on the one stock at the same time. If you do this at any stage, keep the trades separate from each other.

But how do you find these stocks?

This was my great dilemma when I gave away my broking career to trade my own account. Obviously, software is required. It is impossible to keep hundreds of charts manually. Given my trading and broking background, I began to search the hundreds of available software programs.

I needed a piece of software that would scan the total ASX data base in a matter of moments and give me a short list of stocks that met my buying criteria. There was no such software commercially available, so I set about having my own developed. I have included a brief overview of this software, for those of you who may not yet own a suitable system, in the appendix to this chapter. All of the charts in this book are taken from this software package. ("Pro Trader 1867".)

Summary

Don't take a deep breath and rush out to buy a stock, yet. Buying is a very small piece of a rather large and complex jig-saw puzzle. I have outlined five buy signals that I use repetitively in all market conditions:

- Buy higher highs and higher lows. (After a major low is in place, buy a break of the second high after a second low is clear.)
- Buy a key reversal bottom.
- Buy a break of resistance.
- Buy on support.
- Buy a multiple moving average crossover.

There are a multitude of other ways to buy shares, some successful and many ridiculous. While entry is important, more people have trouble with when to sell. But prior to the sale, we need to ensure that our buy signals have a good chance of success.

As Martin Pring, the well known American technical analyist and author once told me, you need the "weight of evidence" in your favour. We need to confirm the validity and strength of the buy signal. To achieve this, we need a clear picture of what constitutes a buy signal, and what constitutes a confirmation factor.

7

Trading patterns

In the previous chapter we looked at buy signals based on support and resistance, picking a potential bottom, and the visual effect of seeing a series of higher highs and higher lows. The purpose of this chapter is to introduce buy signals based on technical analysis, and the patterns that appear in chart prices.

Why look for patterns?

- Trading patterns are something that professional traders have used profitably for nearly two hundred years, long before computers invaded our lives.
- Patterns in stock prices are as recognisable as the low price for petrol in the middle of the week.
- Patterns give you a reliable profit target.
- With a little experience (and a lot of hard work) you should be able to trade seven out of ten patterns profitably.
- All orders, the buy, the protective stop loss, and the profit target, can be placed simultaneously, at the time of entering the stock, leaving you free to go about your work.

Many people are already trading patterns without knowing it. As previously mentioned, if you notice over a period of several weeks, or preferably several months, that your local petrol station sells petrol at a lower price each Wednesday than any other day of the week, you will soon find yourself filling your car each Wednesday. You may also notice that fuel prices are at their highest on the weekend. Wouldn't it be nice to be able to sell fuel on those days?

> *Patterns answer the age-old problem of timing - they tell us when we can enter and exit the market with the odds of success in our favour.*

Just as patterns tell you the best day to buy petrol, they can tell us the best time to buy stocks. Furthermore, patterns give us precise levels at which to buy and sell stocks, and they do it in advance! Patterns answer the age-old problem of timing - they tell us when we can enter and exit the market with the odds of success in our favour.

It is not my intention to cover all patterns in this book. Again, there are plenty of books on the shelf that go into great detail on pattern recognition. It is, however, my intention to give you a better insight into the easiest patterns to identify and enough patterns for the reader to be able to go and trade them with success.

Pattern recognition

Stock prices can only move up, down or sideways. As buyers and sellers jostle their way into and out of the market, their movements are recorded and plotted on a chart. We often see patterns emerge in these charts, and learning to read charts and interpret chart patterns is the very foundation of technical analysis.

The sideways movement can be the most frustrating. Holders of stock during a sideways movement that may last for several months are uncertain whether to stay in the stock or whether to get out. Potential buyers are hesitant to enter. How can you know what to do in a situation like this? Often the clue is in the pattern that emerges during this sideways movement. Sideways movement and consolidation may well form a recognisable trading pattern. These recognisable patterns include the triangle family, flags, pennants and saucers.

The Triangle family

On occasions, you will find that support and resistance lines on a chart will intersect each other and the resultant shape forms a triangle. There is no magic or mystery here; the triangles referred to in technical analysis are shapes that we saw in elementary mathematics at primary school. Triangles usually form during an upward move in prices. Triangular shapes that form during an upward move are referred to as "continuation patterns". That is, a triangular shape that forms after an upward move, it is most likely to continue its way upwards when prices break out of the triangle.

While there are several triangular shapes, it is my intention to deal with the one that I have found to be profitable time and time again over many years and in all kinds of market conditions: it is the ascending triangle. While they are generally easy to identify, the trick is to look at the right chart at the right time. The software I have developed was specifically written to do that job for me.

1 | Buy signal one
Ascending triangles

An ascending triangle forms when a horizontal resistance line is intersected by an upward sloping support line.

Ascending triangles are, in my opinion, the most reliable pattern for a trader. They are easy to recognise, and the psychology behind their formation is logical.

You can define the entry price, profit target and stop loss levels prior to entering the market. This makes trading ascending triangles stress free. An ascending triangle can appear as a bottom formation, but is better traded as a continuation pattern.

Recognising an ascending triangle

An ascending triangle has a distinctly horizontal resistance line and an upward sloping support line. From this pattern, two conclusions can be drawn. First, there are more buyers in the market than sellers, hence the upward sloping support line.

Secondly, and the major factor, is the horizontal resistance line. This is, generally, evidence that a major shareholder has a large block of shares to sell at a specific price. Each time the price gets to that level, this large block of shares appears for sale, knocking prices down again.

Ultimately, if the buyers prove to be stronger than the seller, they will absorb the large parcel from the seller and prices are then free to continue upwards.

The chart, above, clearly shows an ascending triangle formation in the price of Ion Carbide (ION). Ascending triangles are perhaps the most reliable form of predictable pattern for the investor. My software scans the data that I download daily from the ASX, and finds them for me.

How do you trade an ascending triangle?

- In effect, you are buying a break of a resistance line. Always wait for prices to break the resistance line with increased volume before buying the stock.

- Place your profit target and, preferably, a stop loss at the time of entry. The stop loss should be below the support line at the point where prices break through the resistance line.

The following chart shows more clearly and visually (and aren't we on about this?) the resistance, support and "height" of the triangle, and what could reasonably be expected as a profit target.

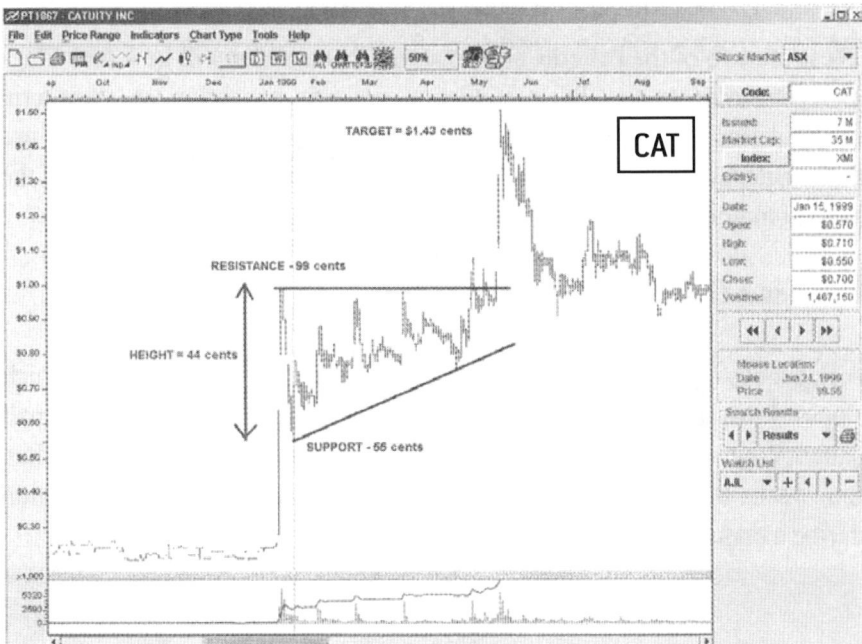

My first experience with ascending triangles was in 1981. I was reading a book on technical analysis at the time. The book was first published in 1948 and most of the examples related to charts of stocks from 1936 to 1945.

The patterns that were shown on those stocks were appearing on charts that I was trading during the gold boom. I was stunned!

I had discovered that what was profitable in the forties was just as profitable and applicable in the eighties. Now, some twenty years on, I still trade patterns, particularly ascending triangles.

2 Buy signal two

Flags and pennants

Turn on the television next time there is a sporting event being shown. Whether it's the formula one grand prix, Aussie rules football, rugby, soccer or cricket, you will see spectators madly waving flags. Take a closer look and you will see that in actual fact some of them are waving flags and some are waving pennants. The only difference is the shape.

These are two of the patterns or formations that a trader will look for. Flags and pennants are usually continuation patterns appearing as short-term consolidation periods in a trending market. A short-term trader may use these patterns as short-term entry signals. Flags and pennants are two of the more common patterns that appear regularly in charts.

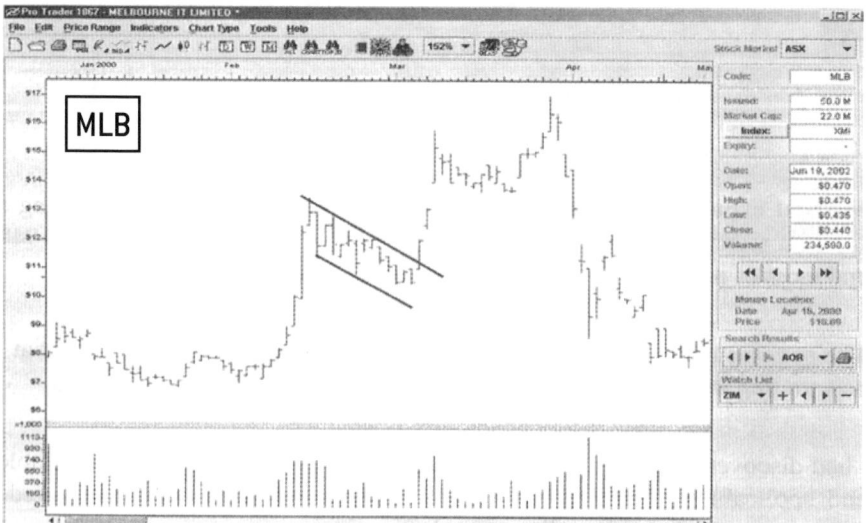

What is a flag?

A flag looks like a flag. In an up-trend, a flag is a small parallelogram, which slopes down against the stocks prevailing trend (see opposite). It is a small pattern confined within two parallel trend-lines that usually takes less than four weeks to form. It generally represents a small period of consolidation during a major trend.

What is a pennant?

A pennant, or pointed flag, is a small, compact, sloping triangle. A pennant is very similar to a flag in most respects. The only real difference is that the support and resistance lines converge. A pennant will slant downwards in an up-trend, and upwards in a down-trend. A pennant will generally form in two to three weeks, slightly faster than a flag. A pennant may look like a triangle but the triangle has a much longer duration.

Flags and pennants must have a "flagpole". For us, the flagpole is three to four very strong days upward, accompanied by high volume. The flag or

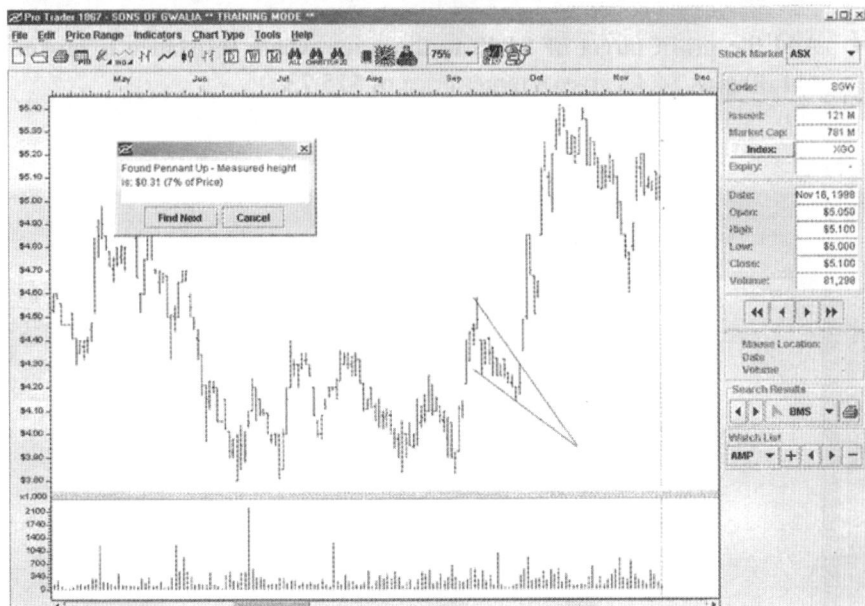

pennant appears at the top of a "flagpole" and slopes downward in an uptrend in much the same way as is does for the sports-mad fan waving the flag for his team.

Volume is important when assessing whether to trade the flag or pennant. While volume should decline as the pennant or flag is forming, it must increase as prices break through the resistance.

When prices break through the resistance, it can be seen as confirmation that the trend will continue. Similarly, should prices penetrate the pennant or flag in the opposite direction, this is evidence of a trend reversal.

This current chart of the ANZ shows a classic pennant formation. The price at the support level (1) is $19.23, and the price at the resistance level (1) is $20.95, giving us a depth of $1.72. When the price of the ANZ penetrates the resistance we should see a move to the $22.67 level. (add $1.72 – the depth, to the breakout point - $20.95)

This anticipated move could be traded using either the stock, Exchange Traded Options, CFD's or Warrants.

Trading flags and pennants

- Draw the support and resistance lines as you would any other trend-line.

- Measure the height of the flagpole. (The low in Melbourne I.T. Ltd (MLB) is $9.02 and the high is $13.45 – therefore, the height of the flagpole is $4.43).

- The height of the flagpole ($4.43) becomes your profit objective.

- Buy when prices break through the resistance ($11.30) level.

- Add the profit target of $4.43 to the price where resistance is broken, $11.30 plus $4.43 gives a target price of $15.73.

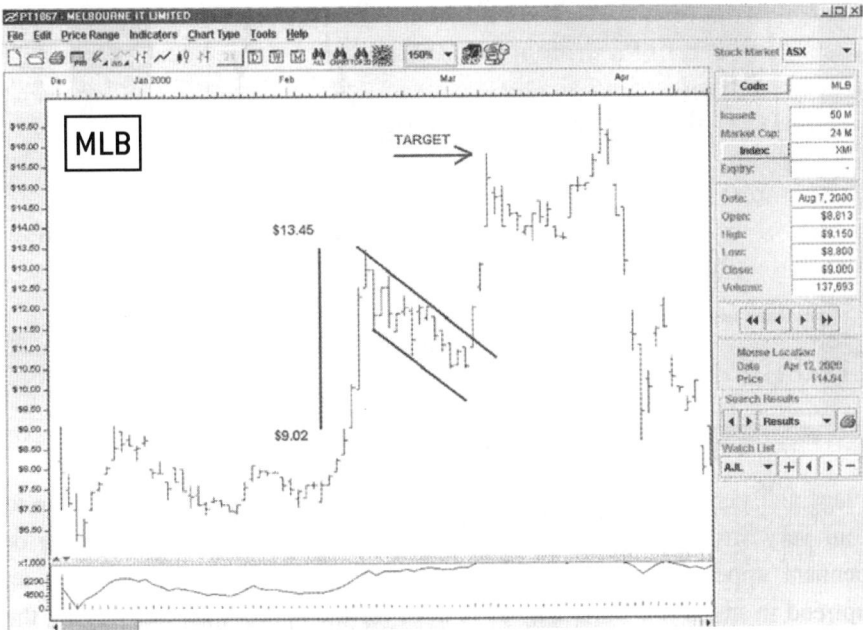

Measuring your profit target

While there are no official measuring targets, there is an old Wall Street saying, "Flags normally fly at half mast", inferring that the flag will appear halfway through a rally.

There are two schools of thought on measuring profit targets. My preference is to use the height of the flagpole as the measuring target, as shown below.

Add the height of the flagpole ($4.43) to the level from where prices break resistance (approximately $11.30) to derive your profit target ($15.73). The more conservative approach is to use the height of the actual flag as a profit target.

3 | Buy signal three

Saucers

Saucer formations are rather rare. There will generally be a spate of them towards the end of a prolonged bear market. A saucer derives its name from its rather obvious shape. It is a semi-circular price bottom. Saucers are a very reliable and profitable pattern to trade.

Saucers usually occur in low priced stocks, and form over an extended period of time, usually taking many months. Volume will tend to follow the shape of the saucer.

Trading a saucer

- Draw a resistance line at the top of the saucer. (In Allied Coal, shown above, the resistance is at 27 cents).
- Check the low point on the chart (10 cents).
- The depth of the saucer gives us the profit target.

In the case of Allied Coal (CNA), the depth is 17 cents. Once resistance at 27 cents is penetrated we can expect prices to rally at least a further 17 cents, giving us a profit target of 44 cents.

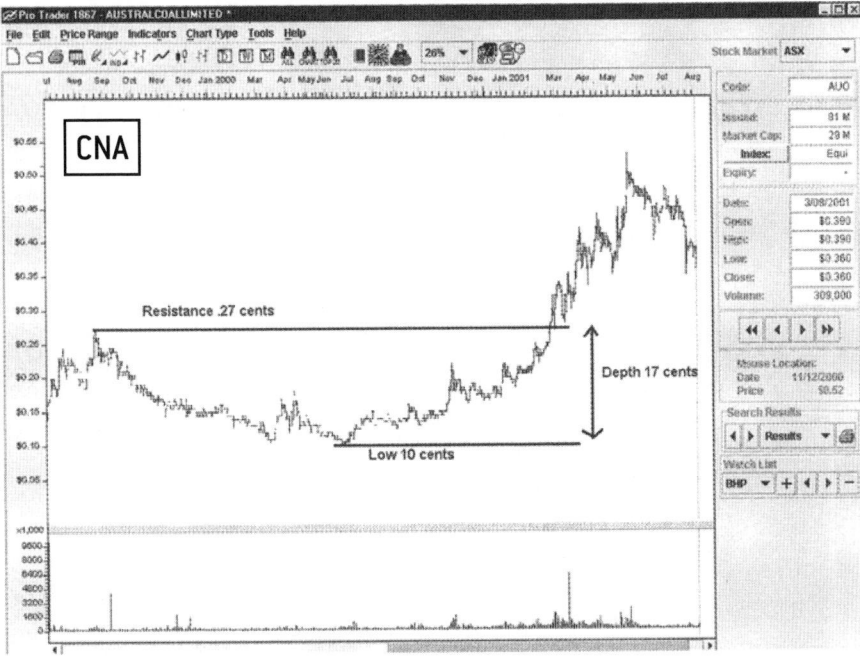

8

Confirming your buy signals

"Ground control to Major Tom ..." David Bowie

As previously mentioned, you want the overwhelming weight of evidence in your favour before buying shares in a company. It may not be sufficient to invest in a company on the strength of one buy signal alone, no matter how good that signal is. This chapter is about using other supporting indicators to help confirm the buy signals discussed in the previous chapter.

You've decided that a trip to Paris for six nights is just what the doctor ordered. You've checked around to find the best deals and then finally decided to book your holiday through your local travel agent. You've received all your flight documents and itinerary. You're generally feeling pretty pleased with yourself, already practising your French accent with the limited vocabulary you learned at school. Now, what is the last thing you do? Yes, of course, you ring the airline to confirm your booking and flight departure time!

That time arrives and you're buckling into economy class, daydreaming of Parisian pastries. You feel confident, as you taxi toward the runway, that the pilot is now undertaking last minute pre-flight checks. The decision has already been made to fly to Paris - it's just a matter of checking a few important flight indicators for the comfort and safety of passengers and off you go! So it is with the selection of shares! It takes time, effort and careful planning. You know what you want to purchase and the reasons for the buy order - now check a few confirming signals just to ensure that your plan is a good one! A plan that minimises the downside and maximises the upside for your portfolio.

1 Buy confirmation one
30 day high

The 30-day high is a simple concept. If a stock has recently traded at, or is currently trading at a 30-day high, it is a positive sign. If a stock trades at a new 30-day high, the company must be doing something right.

One of the difficulties a new trader has is grasping the concept of buying a stock that is trading at a new high. There is the feeling that the price has moved "too much" and you may have missed the boat.

Buying something that has just risen in price to new high, flies in the face of every instinct we have developed during our lifetime. The habits you pick up all through your life are habits that will hinder your success as a trader.

For instance, if you were out shopping yesterday and saw a jumper that you wanted priced at $250.00, went back to buy it today, but the price was $270.00, the chances are you would not buy it. This instinct works against us when trading shares.

30-day high — ascending triangle

Assuming we were looking to trade the ascending triangle shown in Patrick Corporation (PRK), we can add the 30-day-high rule as confirmation of a strong break through the resistance level.

This will increase the likelihood of a strong move upwards. When Patrick Corporation broke resistance, it was trading at the highest level for thirty-seven trading days.

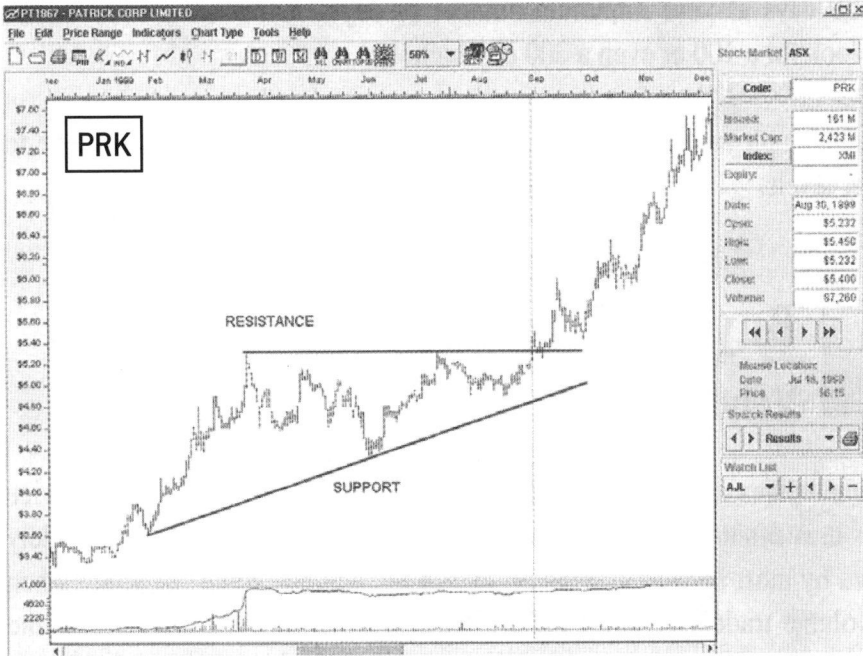

30-day high – resistance break

If you have drawn a resistance line on a chart and intend buying a break of that resistance, make sure that the stock trades and closes above the high of the last thirty days. Bear in mind: I am looking at thirty trading days.

Use 30 days as your minimum number of days. Other successful traders may look for a 100, or even a 200 day high.

In the example of Metcash (MTT), notice the increase in volume as the prices move to higher levels.

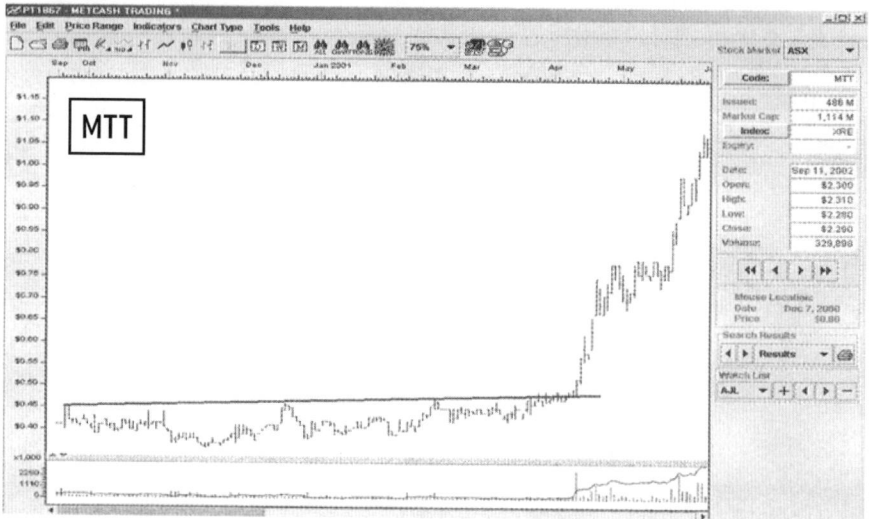

2 Buy confirmation two

Volume spikes

Volume spikes are often a prelude to a significant news release and price rise. It is often a sign that someone knows something that is not widely known by most investors. I would classify a "volume spike" as a day when the volume traded is at least 700% higher than the volume traded on the previous day. I like to see a large volume spike in a stock that I am about to purchase. The volume spike should be within the last three weeks data. A volume spike is most significant in lower priced or thinly traded stocks.

Isolated volume spikes

The stock, below, Hartleys Limited was thinly traded with an average daily volume, during February 1999, of less than 100 000 each day. Suddenly, on 2 March, nearly three million shares traded. This clearly raises some issues.

Why would someone suddenly wake up one morning and invest the best part of three million dollars into one stock? You can bet that most of the shares purchased that day were by one person. The very low volume traded

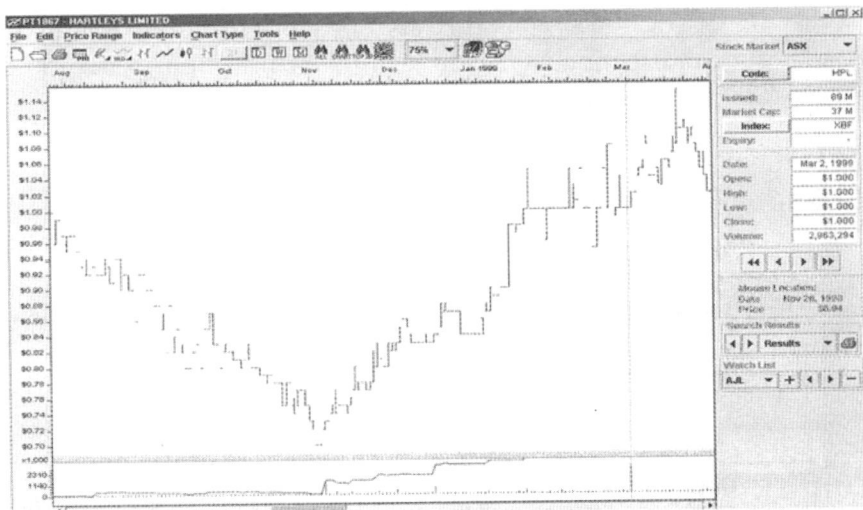

before and afterwards would indicate this. In the two days following the big volume day, only eleven thousand were traded.

What did the person know? It is also interesting that the open, high, low, and closing price was at $1.00. It is strange that on a very heavy volume day, the price did not move more than one cent during the whole day.

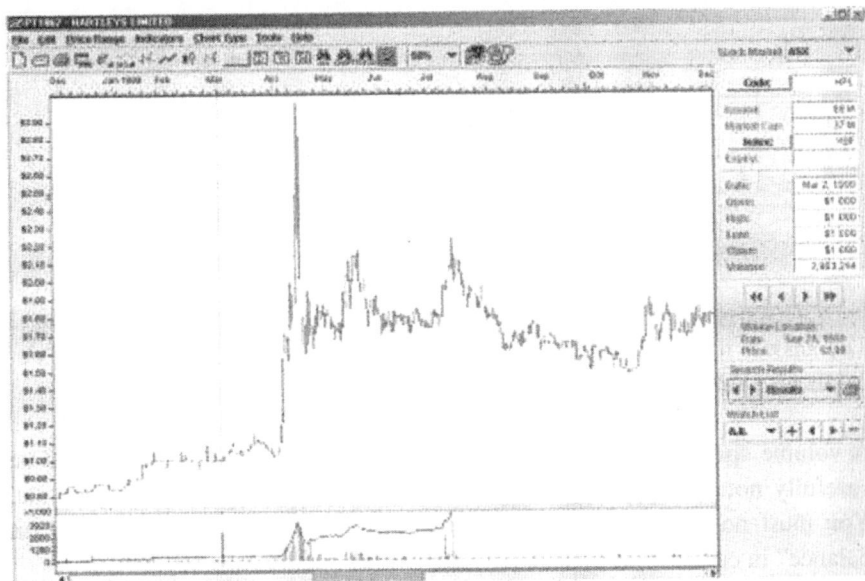

This type of volume spike can be used as a buy signal within its own right, as well as a confirmation signal. Sudden jumps in volume occur for a reason: "Someone knows something."

We can see the result: by April 16th 1999, the price had bolted to $3.00 per share. Not a bad result for eight weeks "work".

The following chart shows the subsequent price action. The jump from one dollar to three dollars was brought about by various stories promising a soon-to-be-completed Internet site, along with rumours of a takeover bid. The chart tells an interesting story.

Confirming a pattern

A large volume spike during the formation of a pattern, such as an ascending triangle or a consolidation phase, is a very good confirmation signal. It shows at least one buyer prepared to take a very large position in a stock that is trending sideways.

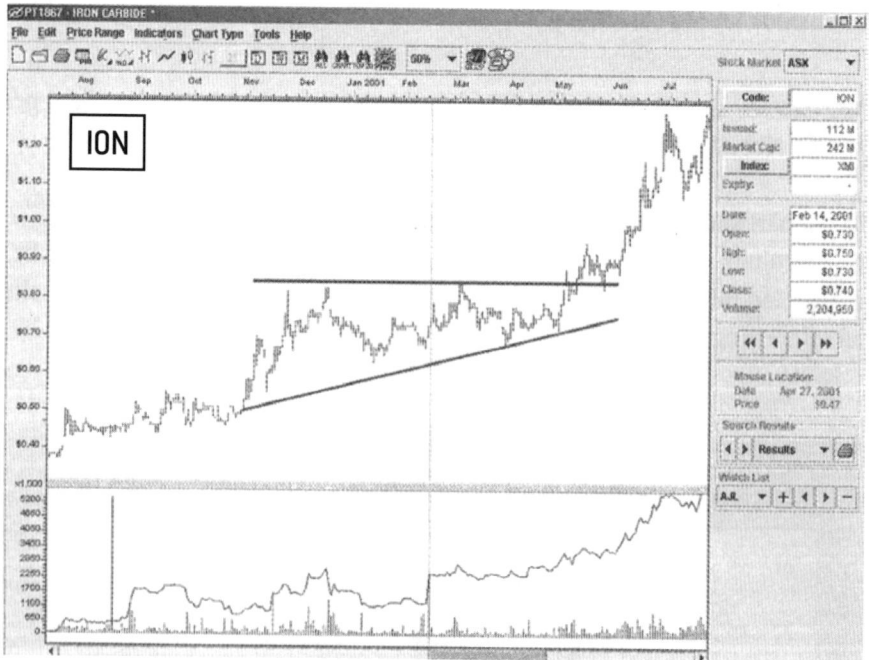

The chart of ION Carbide (ION) shows a very clear ascending triangle. It has taken some six months to form. In the middle of the formation is a large "volume spike". The only issue now is to determine whether or not the volume spike was a buyer or a seller. How important would this information be?

How do we tell whether the volume was buying pressure or selling pressure? The answer to this issue lies in a very simple computer indicator, called "on-balance-volume".

A volume spike is a very important initial indicator and one that should be carefully noted as you examine the rest of the chart for familiar patterns. You must now determine whether it is the buyers or sellers who are "on balance" in controling and determining the overall trend of the stock.

3 Buy confirmation three
On-balance-volume

OBV is a measure of volume rather than price. Prices are the consensus of value stock but volume is the consensus of emotion. If OBV is rising, it is an indication that buyers are interested in the stock. A falling OBV is an indication that traders are losing interest and beginning to sell the stock.

When we look at volume, we need to know whether it is people buying or selling shares. On-balance-volume is great for letting us know just that.

While volume is important, knowing whether the volume is buying pressure or selling pressure is crucial. OBV changes can precede

> *Prices are the consensus of share value, but volume is the consensus of emotions.*

price changes. Smart money can be seen flowing into a security by a rising OBV.

OBV is a running total of volume based on whether the buyers or sellers are in control. If a stock closes at a higher price than the previous day's close, the bulls (buyers) are considered to be in control.

135

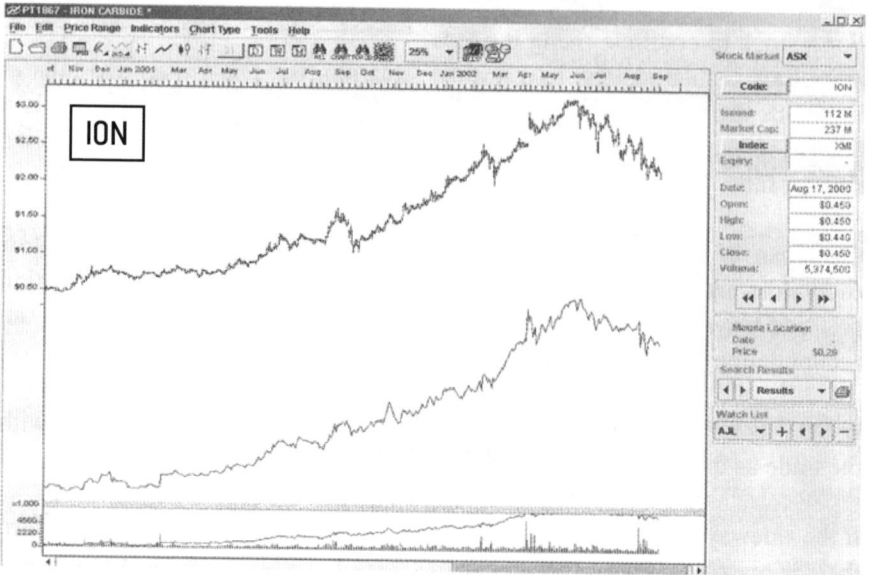

That day's volume is added to the previous volume total. On a day when a stock closes lower than the previous day's close, the bears (sellers) are in control and the volume for that day is subtracted from the previous total.

The OBV shows as a continuous line that rises and falls in concert with the buying and selling of the particular stock. Very simple and extremely effective!

The chart of Ion Carbide shows the on-balance-volume indicator plotted underneath the price plot.

In this instance, we can see that the on-balance-volume is moving in unison with the prices. This is a normal situation - as more and more buyers enter the market, the prices rise.

How to use OBV effectively

On balance volume does not generate buy and sell signals in the manner of other indicators. It is effective when used to *confirm*

> *OBV is a leading indicator, which means that OBV often rises or falls before the price rises or falls.*

price movement.

For a stock to continue rising, it needs more buyers than sellers. In a normal situation, the OBV rises and falls in line with the price, and this confirms the strength of the trend. OBV is a leading indicator, which means that OBV often rises or falls before the price rises or falls.

OBV can be of enormous value during a period of consolidation. Most oscillators and indicators are left lamenting during periods of consolidation or sideways movement. These sideways movements may be an accumulation or distribution phase.

If OBV is rising during sideways trading, the trader has reason to stay with the trade as the buyers remain in control.

If the sideways movement then turns into a recognisable continuation pattern, there is reason to buy further stock.

On-balance-volume as a leading indicator

Looking at the following chart of ION, we can see that for a six-month period the stock price was in a consolidation or sideways pattern.

This is a time when a trader can get frustrated, wondering whether or not the price will continue higher. A quick check of on-balance-volume can often answer this question. We can see at a

> *I would never look at buying a stock without using the on-balance-volume indicator to confirm that the buyers are in control.*

glance that the buyers are "in control" because the OBV was increasing, a certain sign that the smart money is slowly and gently absorbing all the stock offered by the weaker and frustrated traders.

This is a clear picture of OBV as a leading indicator.

As with all indicators, we are only looking at signposts! These signposts give us an indication of the general direction in which we should travel as we approach our desired destination; however, these signposts, unlike a road map, are imprecise, so you must gather as much corroborating evidence as you can before reaching a decision.

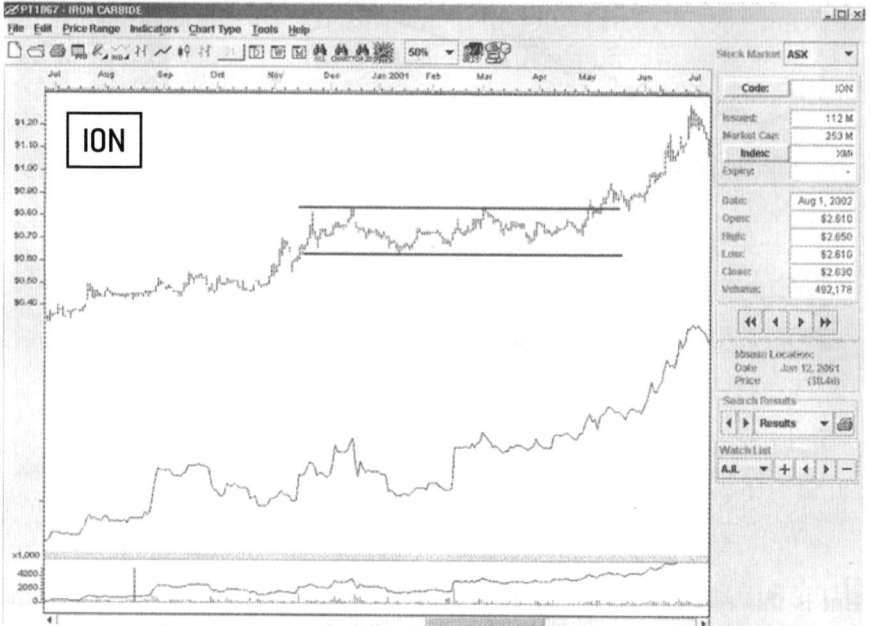

On-balance-volume divergence

The term *divergence* is used in technical analysis to describe a situation when prices are rising and an indicator is falling, or vice versa. Divergence between the OBV and the share price is an advance-warning signal that a change in trend is about to occur.

This was the case in Wesfarmers (WES) shares as early as February 2002. There was a clear divergence between the *rising* price and the *falling* on-balance-volume - a clear warning here that a change of direction (down) may be imminent.

But is this type of signal enough to warrant selling the shares? This is the sixty- four dollar question. For me it is! But for many people I spoke to at the time, the attitude was, "I bought these for the long-term and I am not selling."

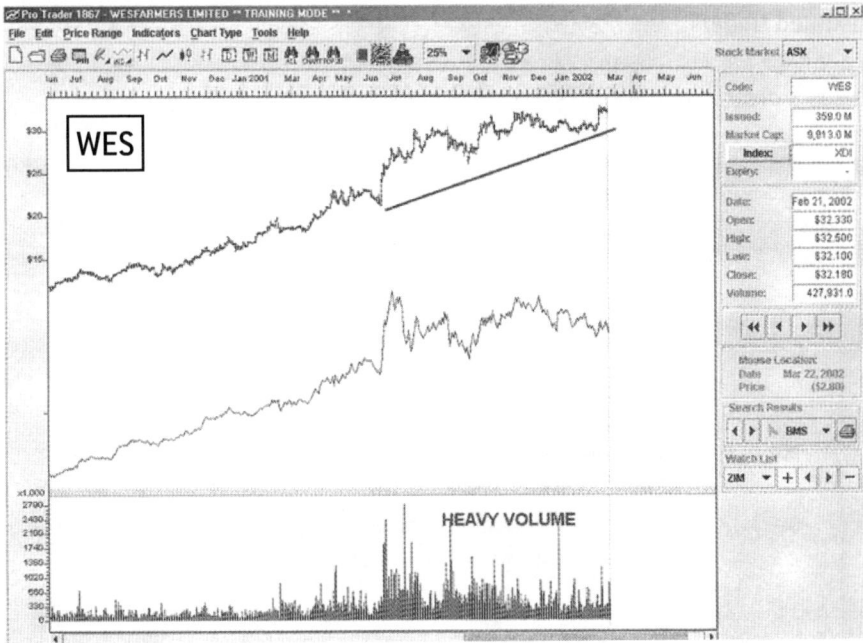

It will take some time for a new trader to develop the knowledge and belief that a computer can out-perform a human in this market. The reason is simple. The computer has no emotion.

Exploding the Myths

A downward escalator at CML

On the 22 Feb 1999, approximately 95 million shares were sold at around $8.50. Someone took over three quarters of a billion dollars out of the market that day. If it's good enough for him, it's good enough for me. I would be inclined to sell.

It is a matter of deciding which group is more in control at that point of time — buyers or sellers? Sure, someone else bought the shares but the OBV is telling us that the seller was the dominant player in the market.

Also, following a run from $6.00 to $9.00 in the previous six months, my money would be on the profit taker, not the buyer. This is common sense to me.

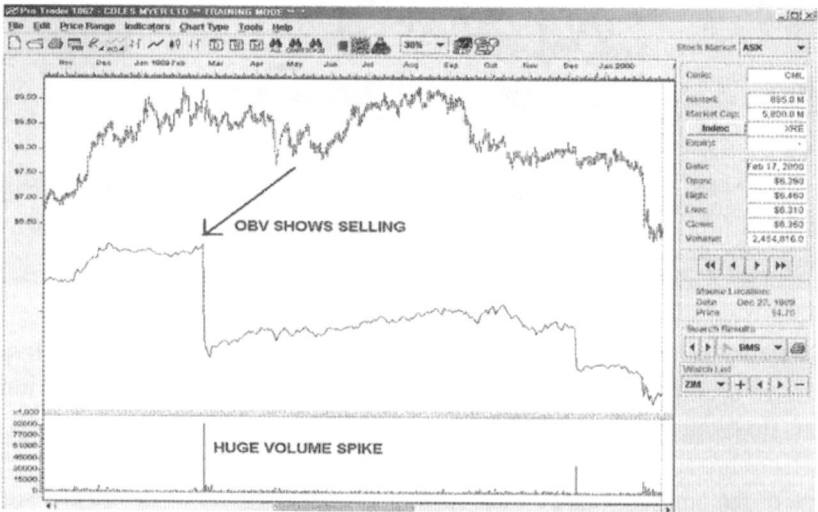

Nearly four years later, Coles-Myer has shown no sign of recovery. Again, a dividend is not enough to warrant holding onto a stock that is clearly falling in price. Even the discount card cannot justify holding shares in a situation like this.

Some further examples

The on-balance-volume on the Davnet (DVT) chart shows some interesting features. Firstly, there was massive buying of Davnet during the Telco boom, pushing prices from 50 cents to a high of exactly $6. The buyers were in control and in droves. Unfortunately, OBV is also telling us that there has not been any significant sell-off since the peak.

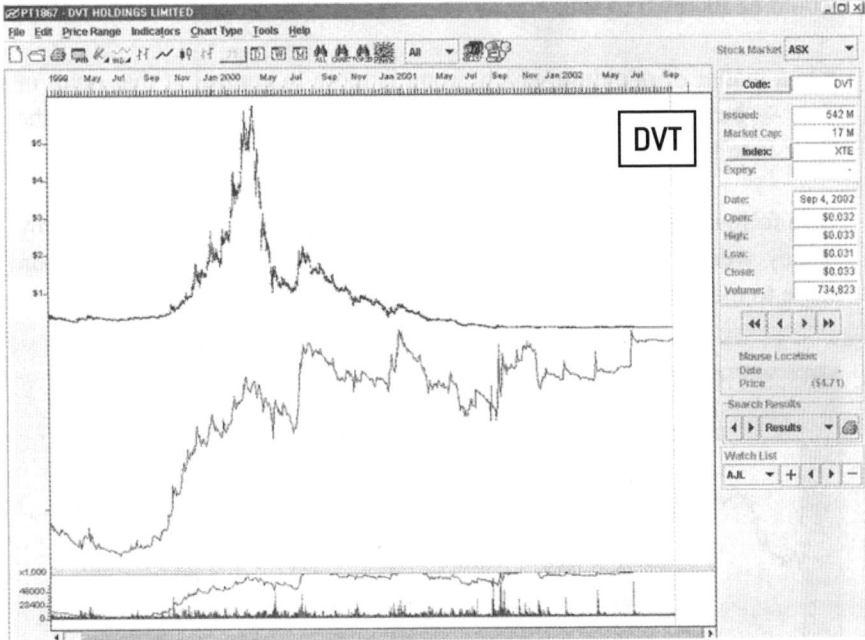

Obviously, people have put Davnet in the bottom drawer and are now living in hope of a recovery one day, having turned a short-term trade into a long-term investment. The stock languishes at prices less than ten cents.

One of the problems here is that each time Davnet shows some life and signs of a recovery, disillusioned owners will sell into each rally and keep a lid on any significant price rise.

Another example which highlights the use of OBV in your decision-making is Pasminco. The on-balance-volume indicator clearly confirms the downward trend in the price. When you get a chart like this, no recommendation should entice you into buying the stock. This is just downhill all the way!

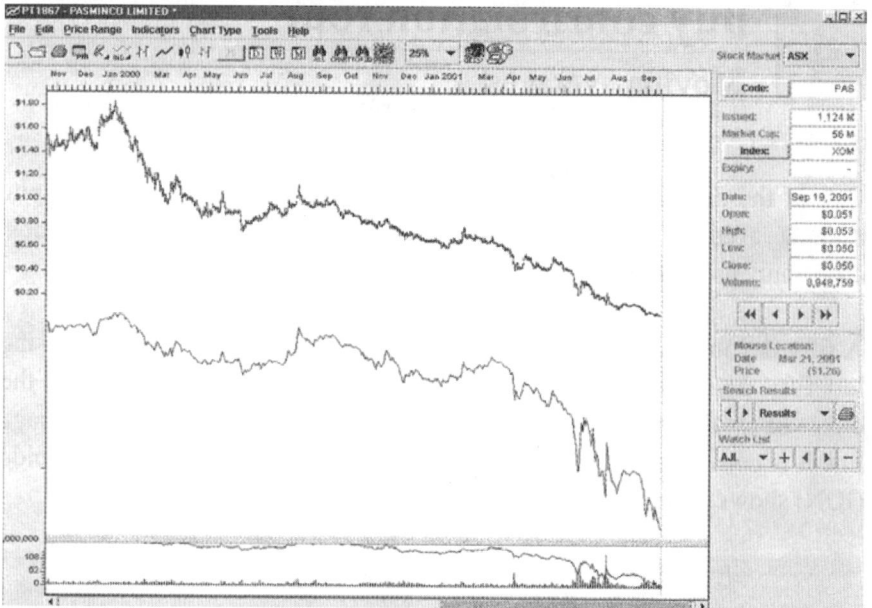

The accompanying chart of Ion Carbide shows an ascending triangle. The on-balance-volume indicator shows a clear rise during the formation of the last part of the triangle. This confirms the buyers are "in control" of this stock. I cannot stress enough the importance of volume interpretation in your decision-making.

I would NEVER analyse a chart without using the OBV indicator.

Many analysts will use other indicators as further confirmation and I support that view, but in my opinion, OBV is the most important confirmation factor.

4 Buy confirmation four

Moving averages

One of the oldest indicators used in trading is a moving average. Despite moving averages being a "lagging" indicator, they are still the most commonly used in determining whether a trend is rising or falling.

A fifty-day moving average is calculated by adding the closing prices of the last fifty days and dividing that total by fifty. A moving average has the effect of smoothing the data. As prices first cross above a moving average line, it is considered a buy signal. The accompanying chart of Ion Carbide (ION) shows a simple 50-day moving average line.

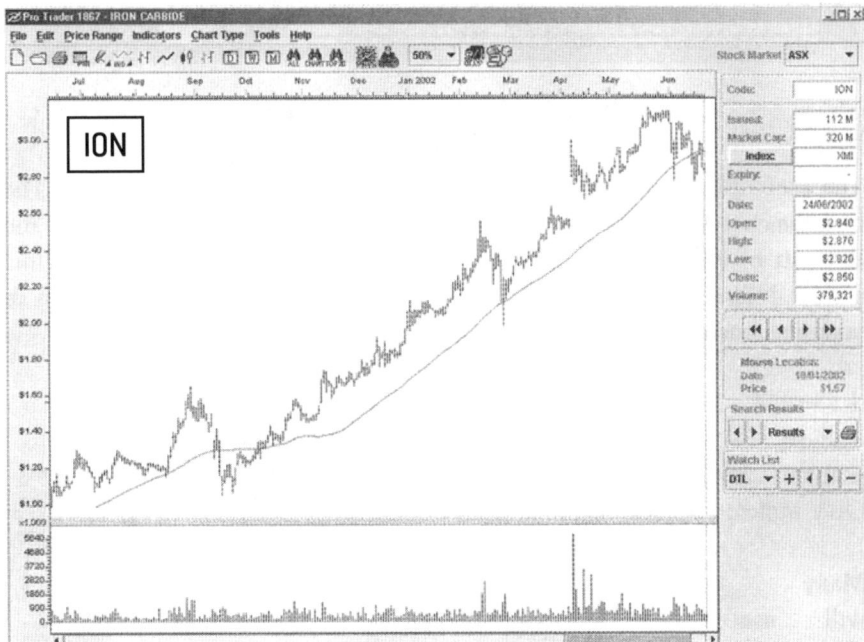

50 day moving average

Moving averages generally work best in trending markets. Using a moving average in markets that are in a sideways trend will often give you false signals; unfortunately, it will take a few false signals before you can recognise a sideways market.

Sideways markets are a major problem for most computer indicators. When prices are generally below a moving average, the trend is considered bearish. On the other hand, when prices are above a moving average, the trend is considered bullish.

The most common question I am asked is, "Which moving average do you use?" Unfortunately, there is no simple answer to this. There is no one moving average that works on all stocks or in all market conditions.

I only ever use a single moving average as a confirmation of a buy or a sell signal, never as a buy or sell signal in its own right.

Weighted Moving Average

A Weighted Moving Average (WMA) is similar to a Moving Average, except that the most recent data is weighted more heavily than older data.

Moving averages are another way for us to get a good feel of where the market is heading. A moving average is very similar to a trend-line, and in fact, is sometimes referred to as a "moving trend-line".

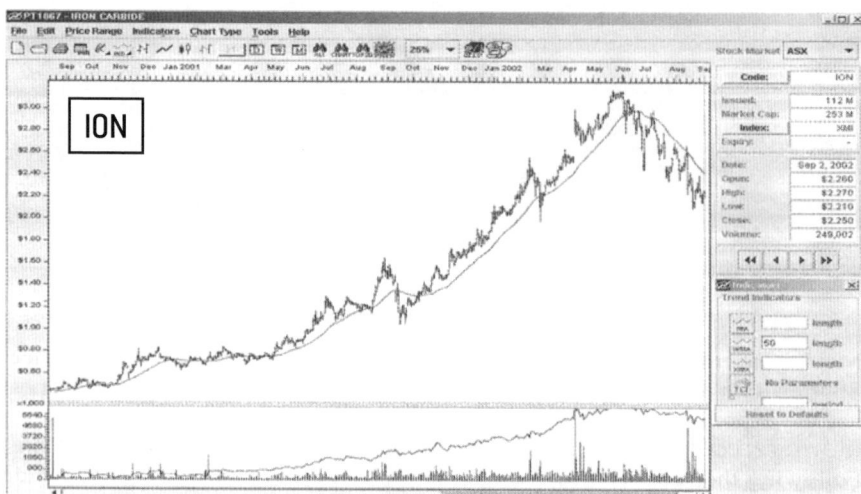

50 day Weighted Moving Average

Exponential Moving Average

An Exponential Moving Average (XMA) is similar to a moving average, except that the most recent data is weighted exponentially. A percentage of the previous day's MA is added to a percentage of the current day's closing price.

There is very little difference between these three moving averages. I have a preference for using an Exponential Moving Average but other traders have their own favourite.

Regardless of your choice, I would make the point again: do not use any single moving average as a stand-alone buy signal. I use them to confirm other buy signals.

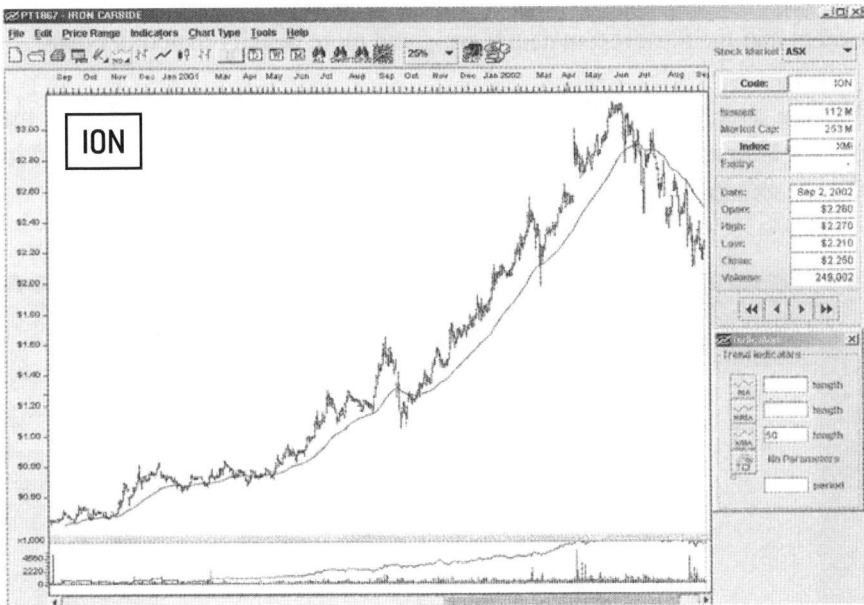

50 day Exponential Moving Average

Moving averages are an excellent guide to the trend of a stock's price. Shorter-term traders will generally use a 30-day moving average and most use the exponential MA.

Following the formation of the ascending triangle, the chart of Ion Carbide showed several confirmation factors:

- The trend was clearly rising.
- Prices were above a 30-day high when they broke the resistance line.
- On-balance-volume showed the buyers were in control.
- There was a volume spike during the formation of the triangle.
- On-balance-volume shows that the volume spike was a buyer.
- Prices were above a 30-day moving average as they broke above the resistance line.

This is a "must buy" on a break of the resistance line. The weight of evidence is in your favour.

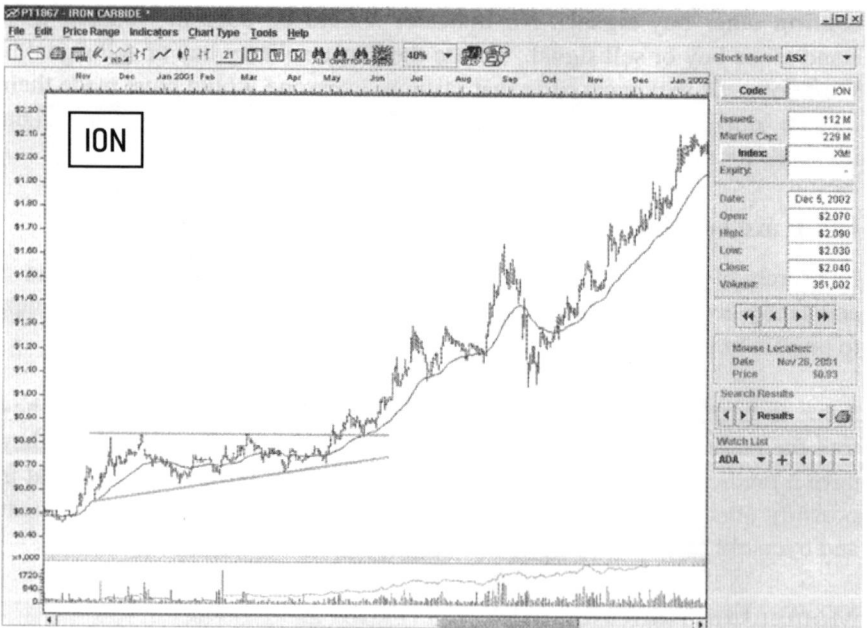

Strange but true!

All the information I need is on the chart. At the time of trading this stock, I had no idea of the business activity of the company, and I still have no idea what sector the stock belongs to. There was no attempt to purchase this particular stock in an effort to "balance my portfolio". It was simply a stock that gave me an above average opportunity to make a profitable trade.

If you continued to trade stocks like this, you would be very profitable indeed, provided you have a set of money management rules.

Computer indicators

The computer has also brought about a proliferation of "computer indicators". Much of today's software is built around these indicators, with some software containing over one hundred of them. Most professional traders would find it unnecessary to use any more than half a dozen indicators during the course of their daily analysis.

With more indicators evolving at a rapid rate, most of them are superfluous, many are plain useless. At best, some of the indicators can be used to confirm other buy signals. No indicator should be used in isolation as a stand-alone buy or sell signal. To use them as a solitary buy or sell signal is sheer folly. If they worked in that fashion, everyone would have made their fortune since the advent of these indicators. You need to use the right indicator for the right job at the right time.

What are computer indicators?

In search of the "perfect" trading tool, computer program traders have constantly been developing indicators to help analyse past data in an attempt to predict future movement.

Some indicators are categorised as "lagging" indicators, insomuch as they trail the price movement; others are considered "leading" indicators, as they have a predictive quality and warn us prior to price movement as to what is possibly about to happen. Yet others are designed to measure overbought and oversold conditions.

Momentum indicators

In general, these indicators attempt to measure price velocity and give us prior warning as to whether a price is weakening or strengthening. This can have the affect of allowing us to monitor when price reversals are about to occur.

The easiest way to think of momentum is to imagine throwing a ball up into the air and catching it again. Maximum velocity is reached as the ball leaves your hand. From that moment onwards, it is losing momentum and velocity. You can almost see this and predict when the ball is going to start falling again. We have tried to replicate this action in the share market with momentum indicators.

5 Buy confirmation five
Relative Strength Index

The Relative Strength Index (RSI) is a momentum indicator that measures an equity's price relative to itself. This indicator is said to be a trend-leading indicator, as it turns before the market. The indicator moves between three zones:

- Above 70% or 80%, representing the overbought zone
- 20%–80% or 30%–70%, representing the neutral area
- Below 20% or 30%, representing the oversold area.

Traditionally, the RSI has used 30/70% to indicate the oversold/overbought areas; however, traders are increasingly using 20/80%. Theoretically, the indicator tends towards the 50% level, so the stock will trend up when below 20%, and down when it is above the 80% line. Buy/sell signals are generated with movement around these lines.

The period used in the calculation of the RSI indicates the number of trading periods over which the calculation is based. The default of 14 is generally considered to be a good starting point. Use the RSI to confirm the strength or weakness in the stock as prices are giving you an entry signal.

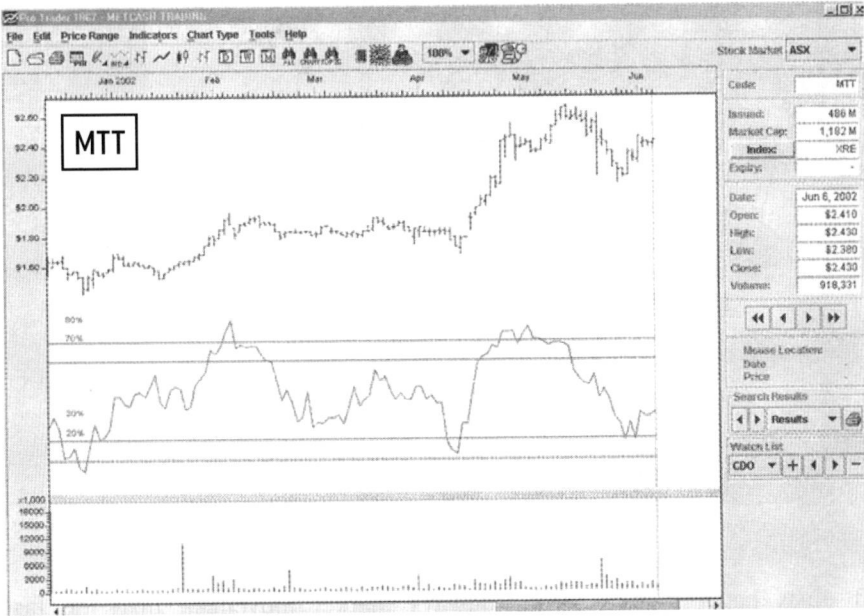

---

6   Buy confirmation six
The Stochastic Oscillator

The Stochastic Oscillator is displayed as two lines. The main line is called "%K." The second line is called "%D," and is a moving average of %K.

The Stochastic Indicator is a line oscillator that compares range and closing price. It is best used with a bar or candlestick chart. The fast stochastic line is considered too noisy without extra processing. The slow stochastic uses the same formula as the fast stochastic and then uses an exponential moving average to reduce the volatility of the oscillator.

It gives better signals in a sideways market movement than the fast stochastic, but responds more slowly than a fast stochastic in a volatile market. The slow stochastic is best used on slower moving stocks trading over longer periods. The momentum indicators I have mentioned are a very small sample of those that are available in some software packages. They are basically performing the same or at least a very similar function. Be very wary using these indicators in isolation as buy and sell signals.

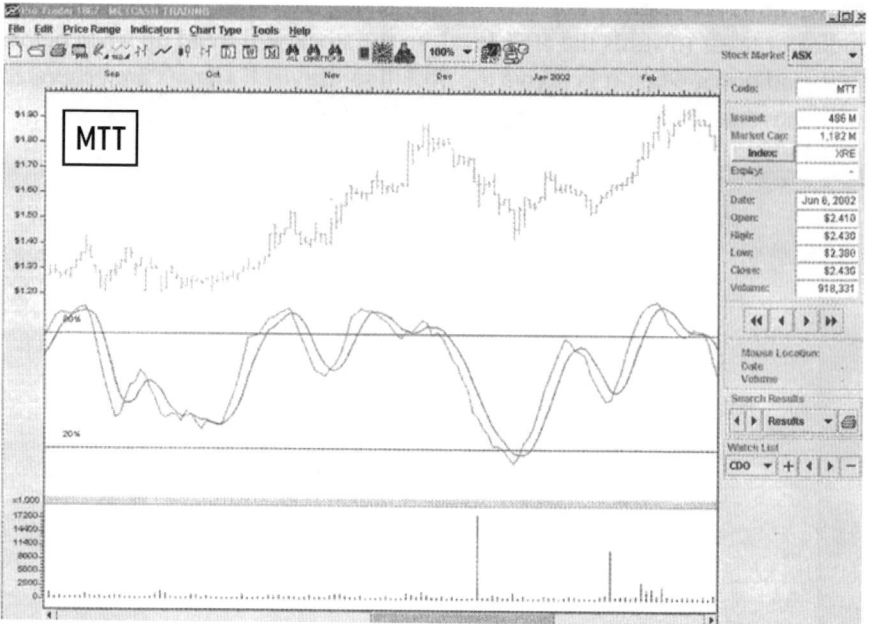

7 Buy confirmation seven

Moving Average Convergence Divergence

The Moving Average Convergence Divergence (MACD) oscillator is comprised of two lines with a zero reference line.

The first line tracks the difference between a 26 and 12 day Exponential Moving Average (MACD Line), while the second is a 9 day Moving Average of the first line (Trigger Line).

A MACD is essentially a momentum oscillator that measures the velocity of the share price. As with the moving averages, trading the MACD is simply done by buying and selling on the crossover of the two lines.

Caution needs to be taken when using any indicator on its own, and you would not simply buy just because two lines crossed. Confirmation from other signals adds more weight to any buy signal.

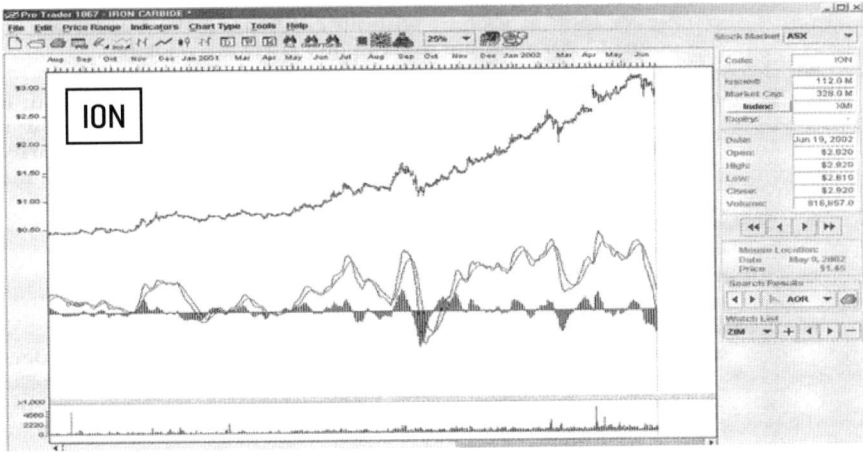

Exploding the Myths

Confirmation factors must be used to add weight to any buy signal. I have detailed seven confirmation signals:

- 30-day high.
    - Used to confirm strong new highs as prices break resistance.
- Volume – rising volume and volume spikes.
    - Rising volume and rising prices go hand in hand while individual high volume days alert us to the possibility of large moves as "someone in the know" makes his presence felt.
- On-balance-volume indicator.
    - Never look at a chart without confirming the buyers are in control. An absolute must in any software package.
- Moving average / dual moving average.
    - If you were to apply one overall rule in your trading plan, it should be "Never buy a stock if current prices are below a thirty day moving average". This will not necessarily guarantee your success, but it will keep you out of the majority of poor trades.
- Relative strength index
    - Used to confirm very short-term turning points.
- Stochastic
    - Another oscillator designed to pick turning points.
- Moving average convergence divergence
    - Use the M.A.C.D. as a confirmation factor. Some traders will use it as a stand-alone buy and sell signal. If that works for you, then "just do it". Unfortunately, I saw many clients come unstuck doing just that.

Using these confirmation factors in conjunction with any of the buy signals in the previous chapter will give you confidence in your purchase of stocks. The next job is to minimise any potential risk.

9

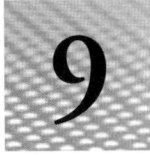

Damage control

"If I could turn back time!" Cher

Imagine you are at the Melbourne Cup, a trainer has given you a hot tip on his horse, it's a dead cert and you have plunged your spare five thousand dollars on the result. The horses line up, they jump from the barrier and head to the first turn. But your horse slipped at the barrier and is ten lengths behind the field. There is no chance of the horse winning.

Before the horses reach the first bend the bookie asks if you would like to cancel your bet in return for a fee of five hundred of your five thousand dollars. What would you do? I know I'd leap at the chance, take the four and a half thousand and run.

You have the opportunity to cancel your investment in the share market if things don't run according to plan. If the hot favourite you bought for three dollars a share does not go up, and indeed, begins to fall, get out! You can't turn back time, but you can change your mind before things get worse.

There are risks in almost everything we do on a day-to-day basis; crossing a road can be dangerous enough. There are risks owning houses, cars, boats and the like. Overcoming the day-to-day risks is a natural subconscious act. Responsible house and car owners take out insurance policies to minimise financial risks. It is almost an automatic reflex action.

The risks involved in trading are usually only discovered at the end of a boom when shares turn south. While no one wins every trade, it should surely be your ambition. There is no point being content with profits on seven or even eight out of ten trades. But it is those few losing trades that you need to protect yourself against.

A responsible person will take out an insurance policy as protection against damage. You take out home and contents insurance to protect against loss. Public liability, life and income replacement insurance are paid to cover various other risks. Whatever the policy, it is a form of damage control. Why not take this approach when share trading? Why is it that the industry makes very little attempt to teach traders about the risks involved in trading and the various methods of risk minimisation? Could it be that brokers won't mention risk because they might talk you out of trading and lose a commission? Are brokers aware of risks? Or do they really believe that diversification and time are the answer?

I think the latter is the problem. The only attempt the experts make in controlling risk is to diversify, or to sit back and wait for time to do the job. This obviously does not produce the higher returns we seek. The industry has yet to wake up and use the solutions that professional traders have been using for decades. The solution is a stop loss.

What is a stop-loss?

A stop-loss is an instruction given to your broker to sell your stock if prices fall to a level beyond the amount you are prepared to risk. A stop-loss is the educated trader's insurance policy.

> *A stop loss is an instruction given to your broker to sell your stock if prices fall to a level beyond the amount you are prepared to risk.*

A stop-loss is what lets you go to work each day, or play golf without worrying, secure in the knowledge that if your stocks fall to a level beyond the amount you are prepared to risk, your broker will sell the stock.

It sounds simple – and the concept *is* straightforward. In practice, the only difficulty is choosing the sell point. You should always calculate your risk and place your stop-loss order *prior* to purchasing a stock. This is because a stop-loss should be part of your total trading plan, worked out at the same time as you work out how much to invest in the stock, and how much profit you plan to take from the investment.

Never lower a stop - only raise it. As you raise your stop to a higher level you are locking in more profit.

A sound knowledge of how to apply a stop-loss is one of the very first steps towards a profitable trading career. The stop-loss has been in common use in the US stock market for at least fifty years and I have used stop-loss orders in the futures market for at least twenty years. Unfortunately, the Australian share market is lagging far behind and only recently began to accept the use of a stop-loss order.

However, it is still very difficult to find a broker in Australia who will accept a stop-loss order, or an financial educator who really knows all the intricacies involved in the correct use of stop-loss orders. Keep looking! They do exist, and a broker who will accept this type of order and transact it correctly, is worth his or her weight in gold.

The trick is to minimise trading risks. Most newcomers enter the market on a tip they have picked up from a newspaper, a friend or, surprisingly, a stranger! They do so with little consideration for the risk they are taking. In this chapter, we will look at specific technical steps available to you, with an in-depth examination of "stops" and "support", but first, we will take a closer look at the nature of risk.

Defining the risks

Trading shares exposes you to two sources of risk: market risk and individual stock risk.

Individual stock risk

Let's look firstly at individual stock risk. Mayne Nickless (MAY) is a good example of individual stock risk. Most people are familiar with this company. The shareholders have had an interesting roller-coaster ride over the years. From a peak price of nearly $10 per share in August 1998, the share price tumbled and traded under $3 per share, less than two years later.

Prices then recovered from the June 2000 low of $2.87 to a peak of over $7.50 by October 2001, more than doubling in price in twelve months. During this time, Maynes enjoyed a successful high public profile, with favorable press reports and many broker recommendations. Unfortunately, like all other good upward moves, it came to an end.

The end was not a sudden plunge as people often imagine happens with shares, but a gentle decline until two unfavorable reports hit the market. The next chart of MAY shows two particular sharp jolts down as unexpected news was released. MAY remains a "good" stock, but there is little point watching it halve in value. You need to protect your capital so that you live to invest another day.

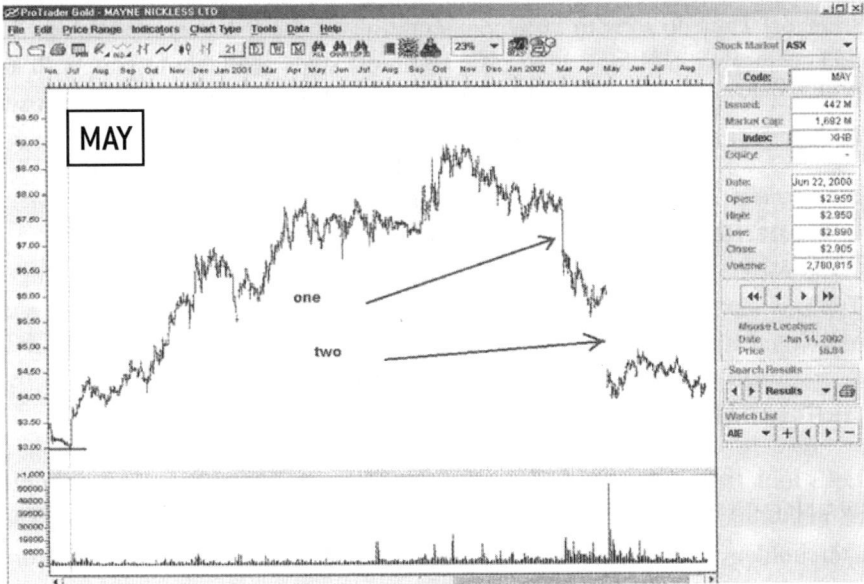

Regardless of the stock, a stop loss is more necessary in today's market than in the past. News travels at the speed of light these days, and the market reacts with the same speed. The only safe way to trade is with a stop loss.

When purchasing shares, pick a level of risk that is appropriate and place an order to sell the stock at that level. In other words, work out how much you are prepared to risk in order to see if your decision to buy is correct and the price does indeed rise. The answer to this question determines the level at which you place the sell order.

Telstra - a blue chip?

Telstra is, or perhaps was, rated as a blue chip company. The general public has come to realise that ownership of long-term blue-chip shares is not a guarantee of profitability. The Telstra float attracted many newcomers to the stock market. It first traded above $9.00 per share on 1 February 1999. The price nearly three years later was around $5.50.

Placing a stop loss order and selling Telstra would have saved investors a lot of grief over the last three years. Don't get me wrong: Telstra *is* a good stock that has every chance of trading higher than $9.00 one day. But why wait years and years and tie up your capital unnecessarily?

Owning a blue chip share does not reduce risk. Newcomers have the perception that purchasing a blue chip share almost assures them of risk free trading. Blue chip shares are subject to the same large price fluctuations as any other stock.

My view is that when I buy a stock, I lend the company some money in the expectation of a reasonable return in a reasonable time. If the company does not perform, then I withdraw my money.

Market risk

The second risk is market risk. I have seen many events during the past thirty years that have "rocked the boat" for a moment or two, but by and large, the market is very resilient following a crisis. Almost without fail, when disaster strikes, opportunities appear and the market rallies from these "one-off" events.

The events and reactions, shown below, are ample proof that what is considered market risk, is, in fact, market opportunity. Unfortunately,

Exploding the Myths

World markets get a thump - then recover!

Event	Initial reaction	% change one month
Pearl Harbour Dec. 1942	- 6.5%	+ 3.8%
Korean War June 1950	- 12.0%	+ 9.1%
Cuban missile crisis Oct. 1962	- 9.4%	+ 15.1%
Kennedy assassination Nov 1963	- 3.0%	+ 7.0%
October 1987 market crash	- 34.0%	+ 12.0%
Gulf War January 1991	- 4.3%	+ 17.0%
WTC attack September 2001	- 12.0%	+ 11.0%

traders need to go through a couple of these events before they realise they are opportunities.

Market risk is with us all the time; however, as you can see from the table opposite, it can also be a buying opportunity.

How does a stop-loss work?

Assume you are about to purchase a stock if it breaks through resistance at $1.00 per share. What is a reasonable risk to take in an effort to see whether your decision to purchase is correct? In other words, how much are you prepared to lose, or how much are you prepared to see the stock price drop before you quit? Ten, fifteen, or perhaps, twenty cents? This is your decision and your decision alone. No one can help you, but let's assume you have chosen to place a stop loss at 94 cents. This is an instruction to your broker to sell stock at MARKET immediately the market trades at 94 cents.

So, 94 cents is the trigger price that sets off the broker's selling action. By the time the broker goes through the process, the price will probably have fallen lower than the stop-loss price. Your order may be executed at 93 cents, or even lower if there are others selling stock at the same time.

In most instances, a stop is transacted smoothly and effectively. There are rare disaster days, when the market plunges through your stop. For example, a large overnight fall in the Dow Jones may cause your stock to open at 75 cents, having closed the night before above 94 cents. In this case, your stop-loss order will be triggered and your stock sold at around 75 cents. On those rare occasions, I believe you are better off canceling your stops. Go and play golf for the day. Remember, the market generally recovers well from those disaster days.

Did you say crop loss or stop-loss, Brian?

Brian and I were playing cricket one day when we were younger and in a considerably better physical condition. As farmers' sons, summertime was cricket interspersed with the wheat harvest. It was a particularly hot, nasty December day with a strong northerly blowing. During the afternoon, someone spotted an enormous cloud of smoke well to the north. A large bushfire was burning out of control. During drinks I pointed this out to Brian. He looked north, turned a shade of white and said,

"That's got to be close to my farm. Things were a bit tight this year and I didn't take out crop insurance. I wonder if I'm too late?"

Too late! Hundreds of thousands of dollars had just gone up in smoke. Share trading can be like that - if you don't protect your assets, you can watch a lot of money disappear in the blink of an eye. The only way to keep your capital intact is to have sound methods for controlling risks - methods like the stop loss.

Trailing stops

A trailing stop-loss is a method of raising your stop-loss as the price of the stock rises. This simple process requires a review of your stop-loss on a daily basis. Keep raising the stop as the market rises. At some stage the market will turn down, trigger your stop-loss and the stock will be sold. This method overcomes the problem of when to take profits. Let the market decide for you! Most newcomers try to sell stock at the top of the market. But the more you think about this and the more you trade, the more you realise the futility of trying to pick the top.

The more you trade, the more you will realise that the difficult part of trading is selling, not buying. A trailing stop-loss, along with a plan that defines where to place the trailing stop, is the best way to safely stay in a stock that is trending upwards for a long time. The trailing stop-loss is similar, in some ways, to insurance. You should increase the value of a house and contents insurance policy as the value of your property increases!

Percentage value stops

How do you then choose the price point at which to place the stop-loss? Some so-called experts recommend a percentage stop-loss. Making a presentation at a seminar, they will say: "I always use a 7% stop-loss and take a 20% profit." This is a good time to walk out. The percentage approach just doesn't make sense.

Suppose you had purchased a speculative stock trading at 8 cents. A 7% stop-loss would be set at 7.44 cents! This is far too close. A small market fluctuation will stop you out. Can you see how ridiculous this is? A stop this close to entry may well be filled seconds later. The 7% stop-loss may be the difference between the bid (what the buyers are prepared to pay) and the offer (that the sellers would like to receive)

In contrast, consider using a 7% stop on a $50 stock is too much to risk. If you need to risk 7% of the value of a fifty-dollar stock your entry level is incorrect. Remember, you don't have to

> *The key to successful stop loss placement is to have the stop at a level where you do not expect the market to trade.*

own this stock. If it doesn't fit your plan, find a stock that does. There are well over 1500 to choose from. The key to successful stop-loss placement is to have the stop at a level where you do not expect the market to trade.

In other words, if the stock drops beyond a certain level, it is an alarm bell that something is going wrong with the stock and it's time to get out. You cannot place a stop-loss at a level simply because it is convenient!

Dollar value stops

Talking about placing stops at a convenient level is another suggestion made by "expert" presenters. You will hear them suggest that you should not risk more than, say, $500 on any stock. These people are also the ones who tell you that if you take a $1500 profit on your winning trades and use a $500 stop, you have the key to great wealth. If it were that easy, we would have been doing it for the last 150 years.

A dollar stop carries the same flawed logic as a percentage stop. Unfortunately, even in an upward trend, a stock price may fluctuate far too much for a $500 stop to survive those fluctuations. For instance, you buy 100 000 shares at 10 cents each in a small spec company. Your outlay is $10 000. A $500 stop-loss would knock you out of the market at 9.5 cents per share. This could well be within a normal daily fluctuation.

Moving average stops

A sensible way to set stops is to use methods that take into account longer term trends and iron out the effect of daily fluctuations. A moving average is a good practical method to manage risk, as well as a sensible way to place stop-loss orders. If the price today is above the average price of, say, the last thirty days, the trend is up. If the price is below the average price of the last thirty days, the trend is down. Place a stop-loss order at a price level below the level of the 30-day moving average.

This method does have a shortcoming. There are times when prices fall suddenly and the 30-day average fails to give a sell signal early enough. A lot of hard-earned profit can be lost. Despite this shortcoming, it is a useful tool and far better than no stop-loss at all. Newcomers will do well if they apply one simple rule: place a stop-loss below a 30-day moving average. Moving averages were part of a traders tool-kit long before computers came on the scene. These days, the calculation is done for you by any software analysis package, making it a quick and simple operation to find where to place this type of stop-loss.

Stops under support

The safest place to have a stop-loss is under a strong price support level. The trick is to buy stocks just on or just above that support. Assuming that you will place a stop-loss underneath a strong support level, the closer you buy to this support, the lower your risk becomes.

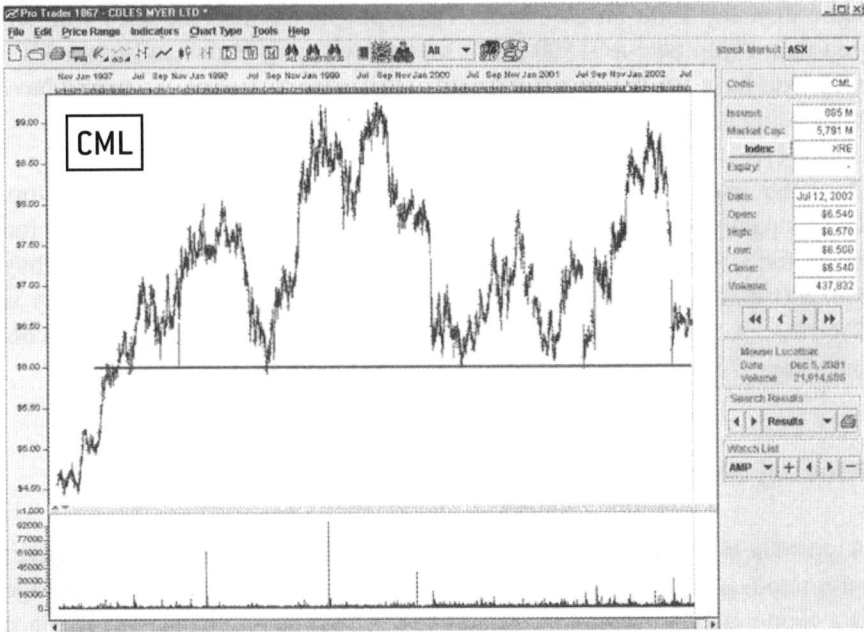

Coles Myer (CML) price support is at $6.00, in the above chart. The failure of prices to maintain support is a warning of a continuation of a down-trend. In other words, when prices fall below the support level, through the low price barrier, there is usually a reason for it – a reason that will cause prices to continue falling.

This is a signal to sell. This is where the stop-loss comes in. Place it just below the support level.

Money management

Again, newcomers have no concept of money management in the share market. They rush out and plunge their nest egg into one stock. This is the supreme gamble. Even an irrational gambler will not plunge his whole stake on one horse in the first race of the day, but a new share trader will. If you are paid a fortnightly wage, you will probably need to plan and run a budget to get through to the next pay period. Trading requires the same type of planning and a set of money management rules.

So what would you consider to be a sensible portfolio of stocks in terms of the amount of capital devoted to each holding? As a rule of thumb, I would have the following suggestions -

- A $10 000 account should hold a maximum 4 stocks.
- A $20 000 – $50 000 account should hold a maximum 5 stocks.
- A$100 000 account should hold a maximum 10 stocks.

Remember what I have already said about over-diversifying. Professional traders living from the market with limited capital specialise in order to make high returns; they do not rely on diversification.

The 2% rule

The "2% rule" is an old futures market method of risk management that I first saw in the mid nineteen eighties. It was designed for trading a $100 000 commodity account. Authors and educators have picked up the concept and advocate its use in stock trading. Exhaustive testing has shown that a trader should risk no more than 2% of total equity on any trade.

Therefore, the risk on the first trade was limited to $2 000. If the first trade lost, the trader would have $98 000 left, so the risk on the second trade would be set at $1 860 (2% of $98 000). There is no reason that the same principle should not apply to smaller accounts in the share market.

Do not confuse this with a 2% stop-loss. A $10 000 account should risk no more than $200 on any single trade; a $20 000 account, $400. For example, if you purchase 5000 shares costing $2 each (a total investment of $10 000), a risk of $200 is only 4 cents. If you stay in the stock beyond that level, you have risked more than 2% of your capital.

If, however, you sell at $1.96, you limit your loss to $200. This amount would then be subtracted from your total investment allowance, giving you a new total of $9 800 to invest in your next stock choice, with a risk of $196 (2% of $9 800).

The 2% rule will achieve the following:

- If your account balance falls during your early trades, then the amount risked on each successive trade also declines proportionally.

- Rigid adherence to the 2% rule will keep you out of riskier trades.

- A string of losses will not wipe out your account.

- The use of the 2% rule will ensure that you get rid of non-performing stocks. You need to abandon losing trades, and stay with winning trades.

- The 2% rule will stop you overtrading, as you will need to search long and hard for a suitable stock to trade.

Exploding the Myths

I devoted a whole chapter to discussing risk and ways to minimise it, because most newcomers to trading give no thought at all to the risks – until it is too late. With a little thought, planning and care, it is possible to begin share trading without blowing your hard-earned capital. And let's face it, for most of us, accumulating that nest egg in the first place was hard work. Why give it away so quickly and easily?

10

Profit taking

Taking profits is, without doubt, the least planned area of trading. When you first begin to trade, who thinks of getting out of the market? No one! There is only the excitement of purchasing shares and the anticipation of making some easy money. But, when do you take profits and where? Without planning there is every likelihood that you will buy a share and watch it rise for a while, then watch it fall back to the purchase price, or perhaps, lower. Perhaps this explains why most people fail to end up with a profit.

You need look no further than Telstra and AMP for examples of people buying a stock and watching it go up and down. Fortunately, there is the odd stock like the Commonwealth Bank that has continued a staggering rise since the day it floated. This is the exception, not the rule. Patterns once again give you a pre-defined price level for taking profits.

The decision to sell a stock becomes a major dilemma for most newcomers. Everyone wants to pick the top. If you stop and think for a moment, you will realise this is impossible. You only know it's a top well after the event. There are various measures you can take to ensure that you maximise your profits. Profit taking rules must be incorporated in your trading plan, perhaps, under a heading of "Exit Strategies". Apply these pre-determined rules to each individual trade, determining the method of exit prior to entering the trade. I have pointed out the importance of preserving capital. It is just as important to preserve profits. It is heartbreaking to see a profitable trade turn into either a loss or into a long-term hold because you are waiting for a recovery in prices. The process of entering stocks is broken into two areas; first the buy signal, then the confirmation factors. I use the same process when exiting the market as I use upon entry - use exit signals and confirmation signals, when practical.

Split your parcel on exit

One point that most people fail to understand is that you can sell your parcel of shares in two or three lots. I make a general habit of buying shares in multiples of 3, three hundred, three thousand, thirty thousand or even three hundred thousand. Let's assume that I have bought thirty thousand shares in a company, I will often sell three parcels of ten thousand shares in stages. Yes, it will cost more brokerage, but that is a small price to pay for the chance to stick with a long-term trend, should a trade unfold that way.

Pattern recognition exits

Taking profits at pattern recognition targets can be a bit annoying for new traders. They trade by the rules and take a profit, only to watch as the stock trends higher and higher. There is a feeling of disappointment when this occurs. The thing to bear in mind is that you can always get back into the stock if you have the relevant buy signals according to your rules.

Alternatively, split your parcel in two when it comes to taking profits. Half your holding can be sold at the measured profit target and the balance when a trailing stop-loss is triggered.

Trailing stop-loss

As a general rule my best advice to any trader is to use a trailing stop-loss. This alleviates the whole issue of when to take profits. With a trailing stop-loss, the principle is that at some stage prices will turn down and the stop-loss will be triggered. I am often asked where I place my stop-loss? At a level where, firstly, you do not expect the price to fall to, but if it does, you certainly want to be out of the stock.

1   Exit signal one
Key reversal top

A key reversal top gives a very clear and strong exit point. Again, the software I have developed scans all the stocks listed on various exchanges and finds key reversals in a matter of moments. Unfortunately, they are a rare signal. Given my experience, I would sell all stock on a key reversal signal without any hesitation. Just as a key reversal bottom is a great entry point, the key reversal top is a great exit.

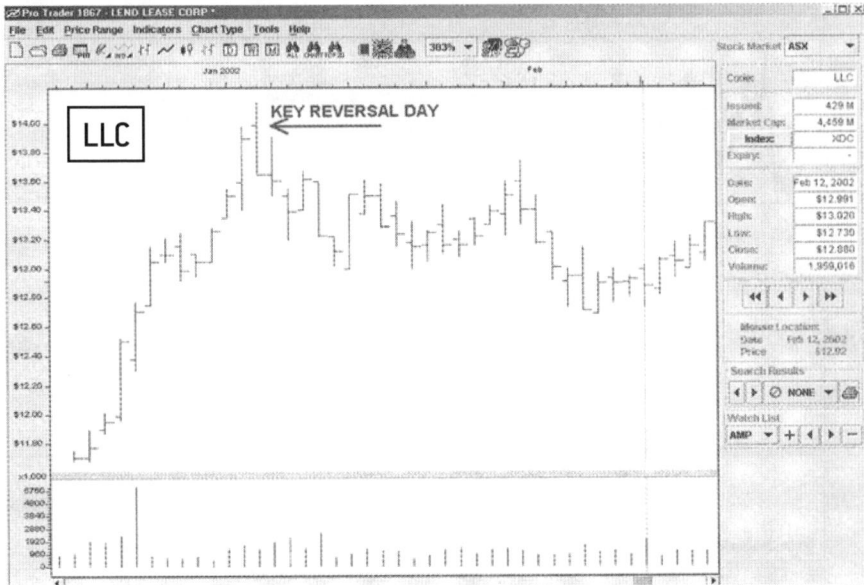

A key reversal top is really a "one day pattern", occurring after a strong move up. The overall run up may last many days and, perhaps, several weeks. It tends to be an "exhaustion" move, as it occurs after a huge run up in price and volume. On the key reversal day the market opens higher than the previous day. Prices may or may not trade higher than the open but, by the end of the trading session, prices close lower than the previous day's close. A key reversal can be used on weekly and monthly charts, as well as a daily chart. If I have another profit target placed or am using a trailing stop, I cancel these orders and exit the market according to the key reversal. The method of using a key reversal to exit is to place a stop loss at a point just below the low price of the day of the key reversal. There are no confirmation factors to use when using a key reversal exit.

2 | Exit signal two
Breaking support

Just as breaking resistance is a good entry method, breaking below support is a good exit strategy. We can see that a stop placed below support on a Telstra (TLS) chart would have been a wise strategy.

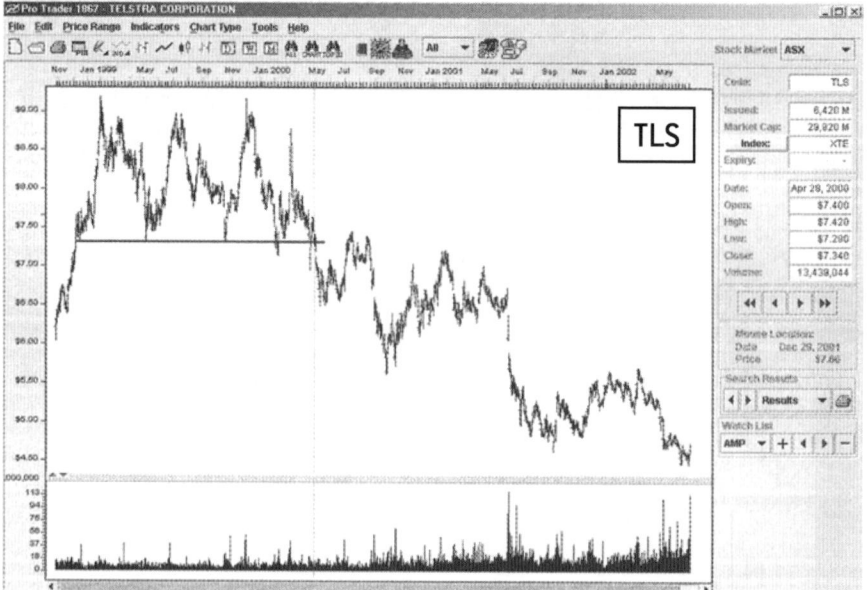

Confirmation signals should be used to confirm weakness as prices break support. Confirmation comes from various indicators:

- Use a dual moving average. On a higher priced stock, I usually use a 45 and 90-day dual moving average.

- Ensure on-balance-volume is declining, indicating the sellers are in control.

- Computer indicators, such as the Relative Strength Index (RSI) and the Stochastic, should be indicating further weakness.

- Unlike a buy signal where you want the overwhelming weight of evidence in your favour, I will act on a sell signal, with perhaps just one confirmation factor.

Let's look at the on-balance volume and dual moving average when Telstra broke through support.

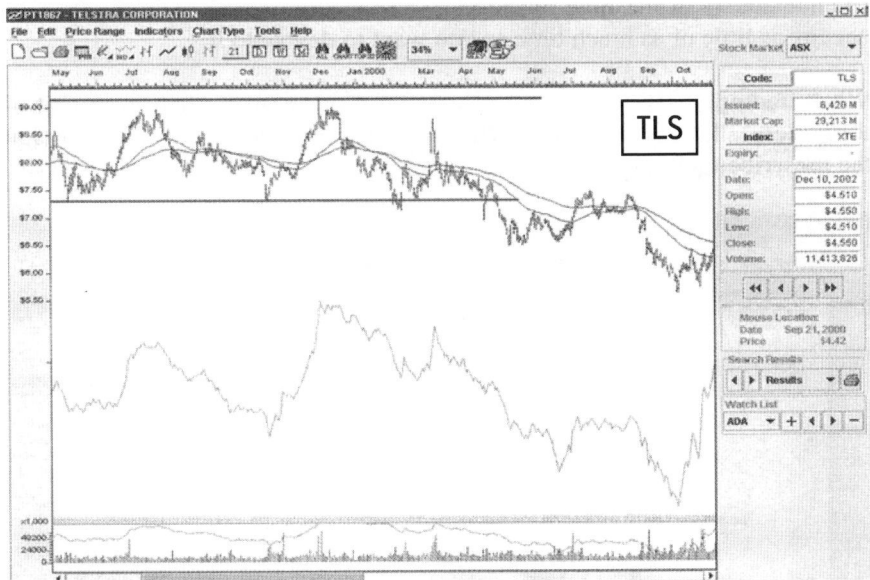

The OBV clearly shows a downward trend with the sellers "in control" of this stock. There is enough "evidence" on the chart to warrant selling the stock.

If you find a chart that shows a long-term support line, then check the length and strength of the line. The more a share touches a support and then bounces upward, the stronger the support. Similarly, the longer the period of time the support line exists, the stronger the support. I would have no hesitation selling a share if it traded below the support line, or an extension of the support line, provided the "weight-of-evidence" or other confirmation factors were in place. Always remember, you can get back into the stock whenever you choose. Despite any profit targets or other method of selling that you have in mind, a stop-loss below the long-term support is vital.

3 Exit signal three
Pattern recognition targets

This has to be the easiest way to trade. All buys, stops and targets precisely measured prior to entry. All risks are assessed and all orders placed simultaneously at the time of entry. This is why trading for a living need occupy as little or as much time as you want to devote to it.

When trading patterns, all profit targets are based on the depth or height of the pattern. There is no need to confirm this exit signal, just take profits at the prescribed target level.

The ascending triangle pattern on Catuity Inc. (CAT) was a very clear precise pattern and the profit target was met with a minimum of fuss. Trading patterns has the very real benefit of allowing you to trade stress free. Place the orders, go back to work or go on holiday and wait for the broker to ring you, generally with a profit result, but occasionally with a loss. With well developed skills, pattern trading should bring at least seven profits from each ten trades entered.

4   Exit signal four

Multiple moving average crossover

The chart says it all. Moving average crossovers are designed to give buy and sell signals. I doubt that there is any software in the world that does not generate buy and sell signals in this fashion.

Most software packages allow the user to select the type and the length of the moving average. At the "click of a button", the software program will generate moving average crossovers, giving you reliable buy and sell signals. All that is required is the discipline to stick with the system.

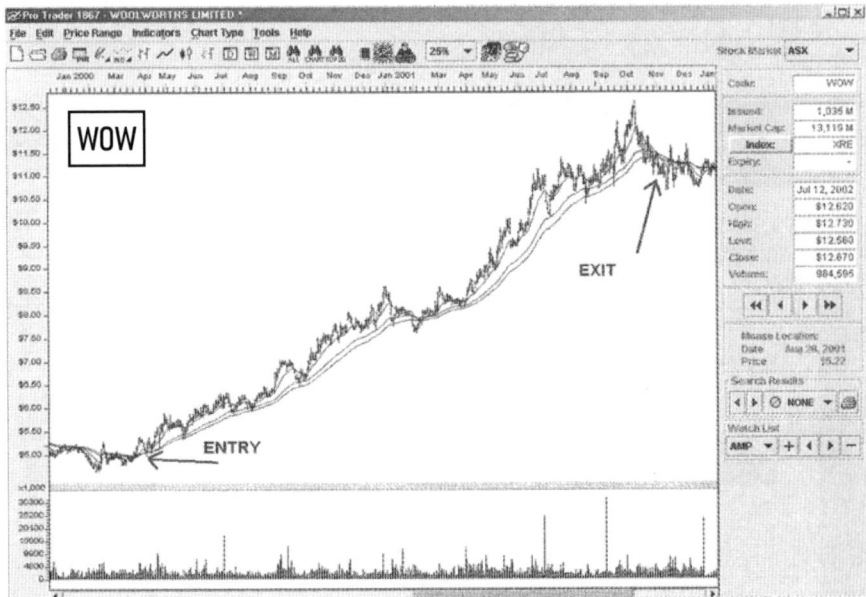

Most software will allow you to scan the total data-base and find any stock that has crossed your particular set of moving averages. As I have stated, my preference is to use a 21, a 34 and a 55-day multiple moving average for entry and exit.

I would also generally stay within a price range between 75 cents and $3.50.

5 Exit signal five
Past resistance levels

A price level that has provided support in the past will often provide resistance in the future. The chart, below, shows this feature. We have a potential "saucer bottom" in this chart of Data#3 Limited (DTL). The current data at the top of the saucer is having a little difficulty in breaking through the resistance level at $1.40. The resistance level at $1.40 was a past support level (see below).

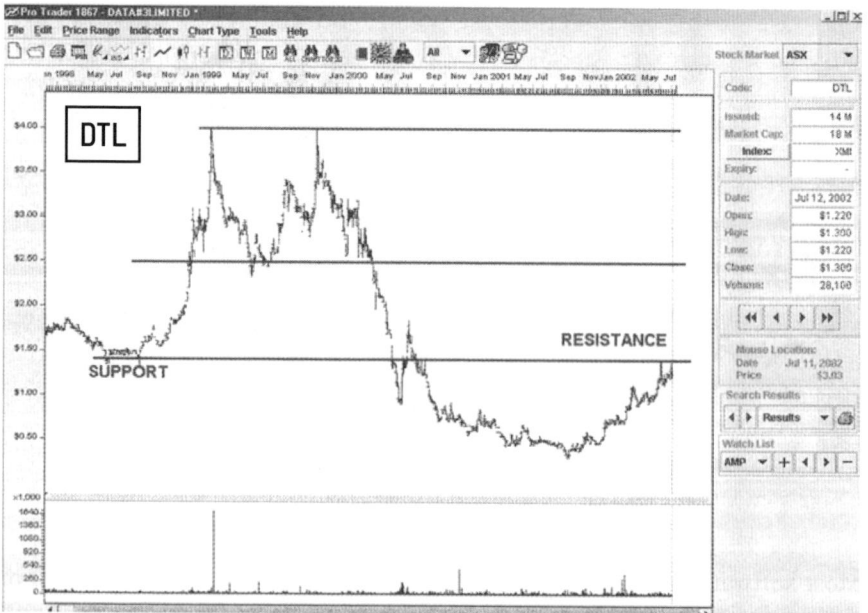

If DTL breaks upwards again, we can expect it to trade up to the intermediate resistance level that I have drawn on the chart. Finally, the big test will come as prices touch the historic highs. Prior resistance levels can be a sound area to take profits. You can always re-enter the stock if the resistance level is penetrated.

Invariably, prices will spend a considerable length of time consolidating at resistance levels. If price penetrate these levels quickly, then the stock is extremely strong. As a general rule, I will take profits on at least half my holding at a resistance level. As I do this I place an order to re-buy the stock if it trades above the resistance. Whenever you purchase a stock, check to see how far away the nearest resistance level is, thus ensuring that any profit target covers brokerage and leaves you with a satisfactory profit.

Exploding the Myths

As with all other aspects of trading, consistency is important when taking profits. Only through consistency can you measure results and improve performance.

Regardless of any other influence, I will always take profits and exit the market on a key reversal top. A key reversal top is my highest priority exit signal. Unfortunately, they are rare.

If I enter the market using a multiple moving average crossover as my entry signal, I will also use it as my exit signal, unless a key reversal comes along first.

If I use a pattern as my entry signal, I will always take profits at the pattern target on half my holding, and let the balance run with a trailing stop-loss.

"Where do you think the overall market is at present?
Does it matter?
The truth is that there are stocks going up and
stocks going down all the time!
Just make sure you are continually in those stocks
that are trending up.
The trend is your friend."

11

Developing your trading plan

The only place success comes before work
is in the dictionary — Proverb

If you are approaching trading for the first time, you are in a strong position to get it right – avoiding the pitfalls and heartbreak that beset the majority of newcomers to the market. You can assess yourself, your finances and risk profile; clarify your goals; then write a trading plan to suit your own goals and personality. If you take the time to do this, you will dramatically increase your chances of trading for profit, and minimise your losses.

This chapter, hopefully, will go a long way towards answering many of the questions that people usually learn by trial and error. There are tips on how to get started, as well as practical suggestions on the equipment you need, developing a plan and placing your first trade.

Why bother with a plan?

Remember the AMP float? It was a big day. Another million or so ordinary

Aussies were about to be introduced to the Australian share market. Along with everyone else in Australia who had a vague interest in the share market, I had been eagerly awaiting this float. Around the traps, everyone was guessing the opening price. Early predictions suggested a value of $8.00 to $10.00 per share, but they rose as float day neared. *Shares* magazine, just before the listing day, emblazoned, "BUY $16.00, SELL $20.00" across the cover. The following story demonstrates how a lack of forward planning and an inability to act on that planning can be costly!

───── **Exploding the Myths** ─────

Procrastinate and burn, baby ...

I was driving Brian to my stockbrokers' offices – where they had a private client trading room – to watch the first trading session. Brian had been issued 500 shares in the float. It was another part of history in the making. There had been intense hype and media coverage given to the float of this Australian icon, and today was payday for policyholders.

"They'll come on at $22.00." This was my final guess. "You've got to be joking! I'd sell them at that level right now if I had the chance," Brian said. We arrived in town, made our way to the trading room and were just in time to see the pre-open bids and offers flash up on the screen. The pre-open showed bids at around $35.00. This was way beyond even the most outrageous guesses.

"Must be a mistake. It's meant to be $25.00," I told Brian. Then I saw trades actually go through at $35.00 and buyers were coming from everywhere. Obviously, some people had given orders to "buy at market". This simply means buy the shares at whatever price is offered, a pretty dangerous instruction in a situation like this.

I started yelling at Brian, "Sell, sell, sell." Brian's 500 shares were suddenly worth $17 500. "Why?" he yelled back.
"Just sell them! This is crazy. The market's over-reacted." In fact, I could hardly believe my eyes. "How many should I sell?" he asked.
"The lot, just dump 'em, now!" "But these shares are a long-term investment!" he argued.

The shares were now trading at $40.00. After another three minutes of discussion, I dragged Brian to the reception desk and asked for my broker. After another delay, the broker appeared. By the time Brian had procrastinated a little longer the shares had been to a high of $45.00 but were now trading at $28.00. AMP had fallen $17.00 per share in about 10 minutes! He finally sold late in the day at $23.00.

Brian was pretty happy with the day's work because he had received these shares "free". I had a very different perspective. Brian missed out on the best part of $6 000 because he had no plan and he couldn't make a decision when it was needed. A stop-loss should have been placed the moment the shares first traded.

What would you prefer to do, work for a day to receive $17 200, or do the same day's work and receive $11 500? The choice is yours. If you choose to trade shares, you may well face this dilemma at some stage – as Brian did.

If only Brian had stuck with his first thought of selling anything over $22.00 and made this his plan, he would have placed the order before the market opened. A simple phone call to his broker with the instruction to sell 500 AMP shares at $22.00 or higher would have given him the opening price of $35.00 and an easy profit of $17 200.

1 Trading plan one
Self assessment

Is age a factor? Go to a financial advisor as a 25 year old and take a 50 year old with you. You will get different advice. The 50 year old will be told that he can no longer afford to take any risks as he has little time to recover from any losses. The 25 year old is told that he can take some risks as he has time on his side. I find this is such an incredibly negative view. It implies that you are automatically going to lose. It is an amusing but tragic mindset. Surely anyone, regardless of age, should be striving for maximum returns with minimum risk. It is possible to have your cake and eat it, too.

Traditional thinking is that once you can see retirement creeping around the corner, you cannot afford to take risks. My attitude is different: if retirement is approaching and you have not accumulated enough to retire comfortably, you may as well take a risk in an effort to avoid the pension. You don't have time on your side.

While every situation is different, whatever your age, surely the answer is to find a trading method that *eliminates the majority of risk*. Age should not be a factor. Maturity is the issue. A mature person, regardless of age, may well take more time to assess risk and be less prone to impulsive decisions. The market offers a stimulating challenge that can be appreciated by anyone at any age, and can keep producing a challenge long after retirement.

You cannot eliminate all risk, and any good trader will tell you that you will inevitably lose a few trades. Losing trades are part of the business. However, your goal must always be set at winning 10 out of 10 trades.

Consider your risk profile

Most people tell me that they are not risk takers. However, some of these people go to the races and the local casino. Others drive fast cars too fast or go bungee jumping. And some will suddenly decide to sink a few thousand dollars into shares that catch their eye! The point here is that nearly everybody is prepared to take some sort of risk – whether big or small.

You have to be realistic in determining how much risk you are prepared to take, because it's your future and your hard-earned assets that you are staking. Your personal risk profile will be reflected in your trading plan. Whether you enjoy risk or are risk adverse, your plan will need risk management rules in order to survive.

You need to consider the following -

- How much will you invest in each stock?
- What are your entry rules?
- What are your exit rules?
- How will you control risk?
- What is the maximum number of stocks you will own at any one time?

Location

Choose your trading environment with a great deal of thought. You cannot afford any distractions. Whether you are going to be at the computer all day as a day trader, or whether you simply need to put aside an hour or two each day for your analysis, you need to be comfortable, well equipped and uninterrupted. While it makes sense to trade from home, there are many distractions. Children, pets, spouses and the television can be left outside!

Define your personal philosophies

I have a set of rules stuck on the wall in front of my computer. I call them my "Ten Commandments". One of those rules states, "I will never knowingly own shares in an airline company." Obviously, I have missed out on a few good trades here and there, but so what! My philosophy is simple - I would not want to be holding shares in a company if one of their planes crashed.

To me the market has enough risks, there is no point taking on more risk if you can avoid it. You need to be comfortable with the manner in which you invest.

Do you have any philosophical aversion to any particular market sector or enterprise? Perhaps you are opposed to uranium mining, or insurance stocks. You may decide to concentrate your investments into green companies, or healthcare and biotechnology. Make rules based on your ethics, write them down and stick to them.

What sized account?

What proportion of your assets will you invest in shares? My broking experiences showed that people with a large net worth investing a small portion into shares are just mucking around and they have a very cavalier attitude. They will tell you differently, but I have seen the results. Clients managing their own super funds are very serious and generally do well. Someone with a very small starting capital and a low income will also work very hard.

There is no "right" or "wrong" amount to start trading with. Just make sure that you are trading with money that you can afford to be without. If you trade while under the pressure of needing to earn your next mortgage payment from the market, I can almost guarantee your failure.

What form of analysis?

If your intention is to add to your net wealth, a trading plan is a critical step in the right direction. Part of this plan involves deciding what form of analysis you will use to aid your investment decision. If you have traded in the past, what has been your method of making a trading decision? Has it been a hot tip from a friend, or perhaps a newsletter or a tip sheet? I daresay this has not been successful for you. A more methodical approach is required. A combination of chart analysis and a few solid fundamentals would be far more applicable.

Stock price levels

You need to consider the price level of shares that you intend purchasing. Stocks under 50 cents should be considered as very speculative at best. This is not to say that they should not be considered for purchase, but if you do trade at this level you need to be extremely cautious. Generally, higher priced stocks may produce a dividend, but it is more difficult to make large capital gains. Personally, I tend to concentrate on stocks priced between 75 cents and $3, occasionally going down to 50 cents.

I do things a little differently during a boom. I will open a second account just for trading spec stocks, that is, stocks lower than 50 cents.

2 | Trading plan two
The tools of the trade

If you are serious about trading, a computer is essential. Charting by hand these days is ridiculous. Any new computer that you buy these days will be capable of running the software required for analysis and managing your trades.

How good are your computer skills? Can you do any more than tap away on a keyboard? Do computers scare you? If necessary enrol in a TAFE course, you may be surprised how easy it can be to become proficient with computers.

The Internet

You will need an Internet connection for analysis or for retrieval of daily stock prices. The moment you intend using the Internet you should ensure you have the latest virus protection software and keep it up to date. Each day you need to update your software with the latest share prices. This is a very simple procedure these days, with the Internet providing a fast, efficient medium for data transfer.

Technical support

Technical support is essential. No matter what you buy, at some stage you will need technical support. Are you going to call a message service or listen to a tape-recorded message and wait for an operator for ages? Will you get a response today, tomorrow or next week? You cannot afford any downtime in this industry. Before you buy anything, ring their support people and see what reception you get.

Trading software

It is impossible to do justice to your trading activity without appropriate software. One thing I have learnt is that the cost of share trading software does not correlate with value. Don't get conned into spending thousands of dollars on it – you cannot buy profits. Fortunes were made long before the advent of computers, software and computer indicators.

Time and time again I meet people who have been to the latest "wealth creation seminar." They walk out with their eyes glazed, having just learned that a Bollinger band or a Chaiken line is the magic key to making a fortune. Just click a button on the latest piece of software, buy the stock, sit back, relax and watch the money pour in. Sorry, trading just isn't like that.

Thousands of people go out every day and buy software without any idea of what software can do or will do. Most end up with a piece of software that was sold to them because it would help them make a fortune. Software

183

does not do that. Neither a fool nor a wise person will make a fortune because of a piece of software. But a good trader will be able to make money with virtually any piece of software - because of his plan, his money management and his discipline.

Before you buy software, you should find out the following:

1.   Is the software easy to use? (Try it - don't take the word of the salesman)
2.   Is it well supported?
3.   How long has the company been in existence?
4.   Is the software upgraded regularly?
5.   Are the upgrades free?

Analysis can be broken into various areas. I believe these are the most relevant.

1.   Fundamental analysis – studying the financial health of a company. There is software specifically designed to scan the market and look for trading opportunities, according to various formulae.

2.   Computer analysis – I define computer analysis as analysis comprising the use of computer indicators. Some software has over 150 of these indicators, and the number grows every day.

3.   Technical analysis – technical analysis is the type of analysis described in the book, "Technical Analysis of Stock Trends", written by Edwardes and McGee in 1948, prior to the advent of computers. Technical analysis is what I call "pattern recognition".

Then there are the two main branches of analysis that seems to suit the sophisticated trader who is looking for something different.

4.   Gann Analysis – I couldn't attempt to describe Gann analysis other than it appeals to a small select group of traders who seem quite fanatical about Gann's method.

5.   Elliott Wave Analysis – Again, a pretty complicated area of analysis that also suits a small number of fans.

Assuming you have never traded before or are struggling to make a profit, you need to have some basic idea of what suits you. This is a bit of a catch 22 – if you don't know what you are looking for, how will you know when you have found it. You need to go and talk to people and ask what works. Bear in mind that you need some evidence that they are making a profit. I know many people who have bought software, do not make a profit, but will tell everyone the software is fantastic. Obviously being a technical analyst, I will always advocate software that scans the market and finds recognisable patterns.

This brings up the next issue. Regardless of what software you purchase – you need to get an education showing how to best use that particular program.

3   Trading plan three
Daily record keeping

In the early stages of your trading career, you may spend hours and hours each day developing your skills and knowledge. Once you have established the necessary knowledge to develop a plan and proceed, trading will probably occupy between 30 and 60 minutes each day.

All your analysis should be conducted outside market trading hours. This is when you can make an unemotional decision. Place all your orders pre-market. Watching a "live data" screen will not help you in any way. Why do you think brokers sit in front of live data all day placing your orders, rather than sitting at home trading their own account?

Maintain a trading diary

Keeping a trading diary is essential if you want to continuously improve your plan. The best tool you can develop for improving your trading plan is an accurate record of every step and decision you make in your investing activities. Entries should include the following -

1. What bought this stock to my attention?

Answers may include: hot tip from a friend, brokers research, newspaper article, my research or a multitude of other reasons. If, after a number of trades, you find that the majority of losing trades are coming from newspaper articles, you will soon stop buying the paper and using it as an investment tool. It is only by keeping a diary that you can perform any serious analysis.

Despite your best efforts, you will be convinced at some stage to follow a tip. Whether it comes from a broker, your best friend, a newsletter or plain gossip, you need to record it and the outcome. You will then be able to determine which sources provide the most accurate and useful advice – and which to ignore in future!

2. Record your entry levels and the reason for entering

Your reasons for entry may include: hot tip, broker recommendation, fundamental analysis, technical analysis or, perhaps, newsletter recommendation.

Also included could be one of the seven buy signals I have detailed, along with some confirmation factors. Regardless of how you enter, it is the record keeping that is essential. During periodic revision you may find that you constantly "enter too early" or "enter too late", or the trade that is a "hot tip" is usually a losing trade. Either way, it is the diary that will allow you to lift your game and improve your trading.

3. Record your method of entering a stock

Was your entry the break of a resistance level, were you trading an ascending triangle or perhaps a saucer pattern? Again, revision will lead you to improvement. If all the buy signals are confirmed and you believe a good opportunity exits, then enter the market without hesitation. Don't attempt to buy one or two cents cheaper. I have seen too many people miss good trades by being too intent on trying to squeeze every drop of blood from a stock.

Plan your entry and orders in the quiet of the evening, not on an intra-day impulse. Place your orders outside market hours. Find a stock with a pattern that is ready to be traded and place your orders, at least a buy and a stop-loss. Never become complacent about a large paper profit.

4. Record your method and reason for exiting

Why did you exit this stock? Was your stop-loss executed? If a series of stops are executed, you may work out that they are placed too close. Was your exit by a "trailing stop-loss" or "key reversal top"? How successful was this?

Do not continuously take small profits. You must let profitable trades run as far as possible. As much as possible, use the trailing stop as your main exit strategy for major positions.

5. Record your results

Keep a record of the result of each trade, if possible highlighting what you did right. Above all, write down your feelings as you enter and exit each stock. I have found that the more apprehensive I am upon entry on most occasions the better the result has been. The diary will help you work out your strengths and weaknesses.

Ultimately, you will find much of what you do will be on autopilot. Champion golfer Tiger Woods would make very few decisions when teeing off in a major tournament. His grip, stance, back-swing and follow-through are on autopilot. There are only a few minor considerations to make; the length of the hole, the wind and, perhaps, an obstacle (bunker) to negotiate. Probably, 90% of making a successful tee shot is automatic; there are only a few fine details to work through, given the conditions on the day.

So it is with trading. A plan is a bit like systemising office procedures, or becoming a good golfer. Develop a blueprint and stick to it. Keep it simple and straightforward!

Everyone will develop their own trading plan and no two people will trade with the same rules. Risk profiles are different, starting capital is different and goals are different. The best I can do is pass on some of the basic elements that I believe help to make an effective, workable plan, and to outline some of the rules that I observe.

4 | Trading plan four
Establish your goals

Before we go onto goal setting, you need to seriously question your motives for wanting to trade. As a word of warning, industry statistics suggest that 80% of traders lose. If 100 people begin trading today, only 20 will go on and trade profitably for the rest of their lives.

This 80/20 rule is a well- known phenomenon. In business analysis, 80% of a business's profit comes from 20% of its customers; or 80% of sales come from 20% of products. This rule is applicable to the share market. If you want to be a successful trader, you need to understand *why* 80% lose.

Then you have the choice: join the mob, make the same mistakes that newcomers have been making for decades – and lose; or eliminate the mistakes and join the 20% in the winners' circle. One thing that is clearly obvious; of the 80% who lose, 100% of them do not have a profitable plan.

Establishing goals

This should be your starting point. Goals determine *why* you are trading. When faced with a decision, goals help you choose the path that best suits you.

> *Setting a goal is not the main thing. It is deciding how you will go about achieving it and staying with that plan.*
>
> Tom Landry

A goal can be very specific, like achieving a nest egg of a specified sum, or to earn a satisfactory income through trading or a solid retirement income. It doesn't have to be complex – in fact, the best goals are simple and easily defined.

A goal can also be more general, like: "I want enough money to be able to make choices in my life." However, my experience is that the older we get, the more necessary it becomes to define the goals a little more closely. Goals need to be revised from time to time. As our circumstances change, and perhaps our priorities, we may find that goals we set some time ago no longer accurately reflect our current aspirations.

Profit objectives

What sort of returns can you achieve each year from your trading activity? Be realistic. Over any given decade, a good portfolio of long-term stocks will return around 10%.

> *In investing, the return you want should depend on whether you want to eat well or sleep well.*
>
> J Kenfield Morley

Given that this type of return is made without thought, planning or stop-losses, you should expect to do better if you are more actively involved in trading. You might aim for a portfolio average of 10% plus the inflation rate, plus bank interest, plus 15% for time and effort. Currently, this equates to around 30%.

5 Trading plan five
Practice makes perfect

Practise trading? Why not? Commonly called paper trading whereby you "pretend" to buy and sell stocks and follow their progress on paper before risking capital. If you are going to paper trade for a while you need to be honest with yourself.

I almost hesitate to recommend paper trading because I have never seen a "paper trader" lose. They always seemed to work with a sheet of graph paper, a pencil and an eraser.

I have watched hundreds of people paper trade and saw them time and time again using the eraser. They were invariably rubbing out mistakes.

Sorry folks, that doesn't work in real life. Don't overdo the paper trading as this can lead to overconfidence. Paper trading does not give you any feeling of the emotional side of the market.

Almost without exception, the people I saw paper trading failed once they entered the real world of trading. Not one of them drew up a written trading plan with money management rules. If you are going to paper trade, do it properly and use the experience to develop a plan, always remembering that it is going to be real money that you trade, not monopoly money.

What will planning achieve?

It is not sufficient to just wander out and buy a share in the hope of a price rise and a profit. You need an understanding of why you need a plan. The main obstacle to successful trading is the trader's emotions. Listening to hot tips, blindly following brokers, tipsters' letters and allowing greed to affect a trading decision is the downfall of most new entrants to the market.

Apart from the obvious profits a trading plan:
- will bring *discipline* to your trading
- will help you *manage risk*. Having a system makes you define the risk on each trade. If you don't define the risk then how can you control it?
- will bring you *consistency*
- should *limit your losses* and *let your profits* run the full course of the trend
- should allow you to *participate in major moves* and trends.

Can you imagine going to an auction to buy your first house without having a plan? Would the Australian Test Cricket team or the Wallabies enter a match without a plan? Did you plan your last holiday? People take more time planning a holiday than they do in planning a share trade.

Crazy but true! Cars get serviced and refuelled, bags are packed and a departure date is set. Maps are scoured, accommodation is booked, the newspaper is cancelled and away you go. Not so with trading. For most newcomers there is a tip from an acquaintance, and the following day the last of their precious savings has been spent – and potentially lost.

—— Exploding the Myths ——

Look for the silver lining ...

In Adelaide in 1983 I had purchased a silver contract in the expectation of rising prices. I was sitting in a trading room with eight or nine other traders and would admit that we were a desperate bunch of mad-dog gamblers.

At the time, we thought we were pretty astute investors. Silver was trading at around $13 per ounce (U.S.) and regularly moved in a 25 cent range each night.

Each one-cent move was an increase or decrease of $50 U.S. per contract and the contract fluctuated up or down one cent each second or two.

I was the "newbie" to futures trading. One of the guys in the room gave me a valuable lesson. He pulled a roll of $50 notes from his pocket and placed them in front of me. Each time silver fell one cent, he removed $50 from the stash— if silver rose 1 cent, a $50 note was replaced.

In about five minutes flat, silver had declined by 10 cents an ounce, Derek had removed 10 fifties from the stash and I had broken into a cold sweat. Derek asked how much pain I could tolerate. Without any further ado, I raced on wobbly knees to the order desk, closed my position and took a $500 loss in a matter of about five minutes.

I know that Derek saved me from disaster. If it weren't for the reality of watching those $50 notes disappear, I would probably have lost thousands. Don't be lulled into thinking that the money in your account is not real. I duly retreated from the market, went and practised and finally came back with a plan.

Always bear in mind that your own resolution to success is
more important than any other one thing.

Abraham Lincoln

It's worth putting time and effort into setting up your plan. It will help you to avoid the costly mistakes that all beginners make. It will help you to ignore those hot tips from workmates, friends, brokers and magazines. It will help you to make sensible purchases, to sell at the right time, to protect your assets, reduce your risks and minimise losses.

Take a step back before you trade. The market has been there for a long time and will outlast you and me. Study for a while and learn about the market before committing hard-earned funds.

The trader's lament

Shown, opposite, is a chart of NZO – New Zealand Oil and Gas. I use it as an example of one of the markets' frustrations. Here is a stock that has risen from around 35 cents in February 2004, to over $1.10 in February 2005 but has given no "perfect" buy signals. The most recent sixty days data shows an average of only 40 000 traded each day, no wonderful ascending triangles, no flags, no pennants and no saucers. Even the first clear-cut higher highs and higher lows were not obvious until the price has risen to close to the 70 cent level. Pattern recognition is not perfect, nor is any other form of analysis.

So how do we avoid "missing out" on a good price rise such as this one. Unfortunately, you need to accept that this is going to happen – it is basically impossible to find a legitimate "buy signal" that will get you into every rising stock at the most appropriate time and price.

*"Remember ... you must put time and effort
into setting up your trading plan.
The plan will give you direction and focus
and assist you to avoid costly trading errors.
A trading plan will help you to make sensible purchases,
to sell at the right time,
to protect your assets,
reduce your risks and minimize losses."*

12

Psychology and the market

There are many psychological issues to contend with and overcome in order to be a profitable trader. While you don't have to be a psychologist to succeed, it certainly helps to understand various aspects of the psychology of the market and market participants. I have no training in psychology, nor am I suggesting that I have any expertise in this area. I have, however, been fortunate enough to spend ten years in the broking industry watching the habits of both winning and losing clients. Much of what I write is common sense.

Every bull market has a different theme but the participants in each boom act in exactly the same manner. Having participated in four booms so far it has now become amusing. It is amusing because regardless of what I do or say, I cannot stop the greed that dominates the emotions of traders during a boom. It is like telling the two year old that the fire is hot. Until they actually feel the heat and burn themselves, nothing I can say will stop them from the wild gambling that they call astute investing.

The journey from the 1969 nickel boom to the 1999 Telco boom has proven that new generations do not learn from the mistakes of past generations. In every bull market, new traders get caught up in the exciting buying spree - believing the absolute rubbish that circulates and finally getting caught in the downturn at the end of the boom.

Bull markets are fantastic fun, full of excitement, hype, absolute bull dust, wild stories and gossip. To get a feel for the next bull market, let's take a quick look at past bull markets and pick the recurring theme.

> *Financial genius is a rising stock market.*
>
> John Kenneth Galbraith

Past bull markets

1969 - nickel boom

Poseidon was the word on everyone's lips and the main topic of conversation at every dinner table. The investing public was in a total frenzy as this small Adelaide-based exploration company (named after a Melbourne Cup winner) discovered nickel in outback Western Australia. Shares in the stock rose from around $1.00 in September of 1969, to a peak of over $270 per share by the New Year of 1970.

Everyone owned shares in one nickel company or another and were eager participants in every float that promoters threw at the public. These new companies raised close to one billion dollars from a sometimes gullible public.

Excited speculation and rumours of imminent nickel strikes pushed everyone to invest. Easy money beckoned and some fortunes were made. The odd fortune was kept and put to very good use after the boom. However, thousands gambled and lost as the boom petered out. It's a sad fact that during bull markets investors believe that prices will rise forever, even as the bubble bursts and prices fall and fall and fall.

Once the bubble bursts and prices slide into oblivion, new investors are told to "wait for the recovery". All too often, the recovery is far too late for many companies and shareholders.

As a warning to all investors today, who may be facing their first bull market: How many companies that floated during the 1969 boom do you think are still publicly listed today? I would doubt that one in fifty would still be in existence.

1980 - gold boom

Same theme, different metal! In 1980, the price of gold rose from $350 per ounce to around $860 per ounce in response to 20% inflation, 18% interest rates and the Russian invasion of Afghanistan. Float fever struck again and the tips and rumours were back with a vengeance. Once again, investors were caught in the bull market psychology – a belief that prices could rise and rise forever and huge profits could be made.

Gold fever ran rampant, perhaps more in Western Australia than the other states. People deserted the city in droves each weekend, clutching a gold detector and heading to the latest hot spot. Others lined up outside the Perth mint with any object made of silver. Silver prices had risen to US$48 per ounce and many family heirlooms were melted down to realise the intrinsic value.

Fortunes were raised again, from the greedy and gullible public to the greedy entrepreneurs, as new gold mining companies popped up like mushrooms in the autumn. Again, I would doubt that one in 50 companies that floated during 1980 exists today.

1987 - boom

The 1987 boom was not based on specific commodities. However, the entrepreneurs were at it again, raising small fortunes from the public, promoting speculation and public expectations as the "greed is good" syndrome hit the world with more impact than ever before.

More media hype, more outrageous capital raising and more promises of easy money. The reality check in the form of the 1987 crash was the biggest of all time. The Australian market, measured by the All Ordinaries Index became *very* ordinary, and lost 25% in one hour of trading. From the September peak of 2 312, it took just two and a half months to lose over 50% of its value.

2000 - Telco boom

Same theme, different industry. Suddenly, everyone thought they would make a fortune selling goods and services on the Internet. Float fever and fortune seekers ran amok. Gold mining companies re-invented themselves as dot.com companies, and again the entrepreneurs, raised billions of dollars from the public. The "new economy had arrived". Savvy media performers pushed the boom along by releasing optimistic statements of fantastic profit forecasts.

The media, sometimes unwittingly, helped the public along with almost inflammatory headlines: "Boom to continue" and, "The Year of the Rich", inciting more and more uneducated newcomers into the market. Generous television coverage gave us vision of teenagers worth millions of dollars. It was a race to see who could pay a million dollars to build a "web-site". Web sites can now be built for a tiny fraction of that cost. On-line chat forums played a part in promoting even higher prices and manipulating stocks. The new breed of "day-traders" arrived.

Once again, investors imagined that prices could escalate forever - that there was no end to the profits. Greed overcame sanity and it all finished with the same results - investors lost their stakes, companies filed for bankruptcy. Only this time the numbers were different: losses amounted to *billions* of dollars in company failures and write-offs. Once again, paper castles came tumbling down on 17 April 2000.

Classic features of a bull market

Bull markets may have different themes, but the participants in each boom generally act in a predictable manner. You'll find most of the following six features in nearly every market that exhibits the "bull frenzy".

1. The "hot tip" syndrome

The hot tip syndrome occurs when the publican, the cabbie and everyone around the barbecue becomes a share market guru. This really must be avoided. When you find yourself at a gathering and the main topic of conversation is the share market boom, it is time to reduce exposure to the market.

2. The media frenzy

The media frenzy occurs when the print media takes the booming stock market from the "business section" to the front page and the television stations expand the daily report from 15 seconds to 90 seconds during the news broadcast. (Since the "Telco" boom, we now get a market comment on the Saturday night news on commercial TV)

The following headlines appeared in the *Financial Review* during December of 1999, four months before the "Telco Crash."

Dec 15	"NET FEVER" – Stags clean up
Dec 16	"BOOM TIME" – Rates under pressure
Dec 20	"SURVEY" – Boom will go on
Dec 30	"YEAR OF THE RICH"
Dec 31	"SHARES ROAR" – Jumbo guide to the hot sectors

The print media devotes headlines and lead stories to the latest booming stock or market sector. I have found the printed media to be a great source for measuring public sentiment and helping me avoid the savage market downturns. During the last three months of a boom, you can expect headline after headline to be related to the boom.

So how can you use this information to your advantage? There are several choices; you can sell all stocks and stay sidelined until the depths of a bear market are evident. If you choose this path you would be observing the old market adage of "buy in the gloom and sell in the boom". This choice is generally overlooked by investors and not very practical.

My choice is to do what I always do, and that is to place my stop-loss orders and let the market tell me when to sell my stocks. People get the impression that one day you wake up and the market has crashed. This is not strictly correct. There are usually warning bells ringing everywhere for those who look. Let's look at the 1987 crash. This occurred on Monday October 19th in the US and flowed on to the Australian market on Tuesday 20th October.

The fact that most people fail to understand is that the market peak was during the third week of September, one month earlier. The All Ordinaries Index was down more than 10% prior to the October crash. The majority of stocks were well down from their high prices and there is a very strong likelihood that you would have been stopped out of most stocks well before the crash.

3.   Float fever

Float fever strikes new investors as companies raise billions of dollars from the public. Money that would never be raised if the public weren't so greedy and the prospectus so full of hype, hot air and, at times, total bull. All supported by an "Independent auditor", an accountant and given ASIC approval. The newspaper headline from December 15, "Net Fever - Stags clean up", mentioned above, is a sure sign that the public fundraising is reaching a climax and it's about time to reduce exposure to the market.

Exploding the Myths

Brian's dollars float away ...

Brian was on holiday in Perth at one stage and we got together for a game of golf. Following a good season, he had few "spare" dollars burning a hole in his pocket. On about the fifth hole he told me about the two engineers who were staying in the same motel. Over a good glass of red these two chaps told Brian the name of the well-known company they worked for, and mentioned that the company was about to float.

These two chaps were "high up" in the corporate structure and knew of several contracts that were in the pipeline, but not mentioned in the prospectus. The initial public offering was at a cost of $1.00. Now, Brian tends to stay away from these "expensive" stocks, preferring to gamble a bit on the penny dreadfuls, but this inside information was too good to pass up. Brian was assured that the stock would open at "somewhere above $1.20, and possibly up to $1.50".

We duly finished the round of golf and rather than playing the "19 hole", Brian had to shoot off, as he had some pressing business to attend to. He told me much later that he put every spare dollar into the I.P.O. Having guessed as much, I waited eagerly for the float and watched as the stock "came on" at $1.03, had a high for the day of $1.05 and finished day one at .99 cents. So much for the opportunity for a quick 20 to 50% profit. Brian watched the price sink slowly to 55 cents over the next six months. It was over three years later that the stock recovered and Brian sold at $1.10.

The good!

Melbourne IT (MLB) was offered to the public at $2.00 per share. They were extremely hard to get hold of prior to the float. On 14 December 1999, they were first quoted on the exchange, the first trade was at $8.20. This was a fantastic return for all involved. By 29 March 2000, the shares peaked at exactly $17.00. This is what I would call a great story and a great result, but only if you realised profits. What more could you possibly expect?

If you did not plan to take profits at some stage, choosing to hold on for the long term, your shares in Melbourne IT currently languish around 50 cents per share. That's right, from $17 to 50 cents.

> *The lesson? When the market is at fever pitch and you cannot get any stock in the latest hot float, a price top is not far away.*

The lesson? When the market is at fever pitch and you cannot get any stock in the latest hot float, a price top is not far away.

The bad!

Another float during the Telco boom, Seafood-on-line, provides a cautionary tale to all investors in danger of getting caught in the float hype. This glossy brochure offered the public the normal great opportunities. With very little fanfare, the company attracted $16 million of new capital through the initial public offering. Shares were offered at 20 cents, and the float was fully subscribed.

On the first day of trading, the shares managed a high of only 21 cents and have never risen above that level. Given the timing of this float - right in the middle of the Telco boom - it was a very poor opening; not a good omen for a profitable future.

After twelve and a half months the company was bankrupt. The profit forecast of $16.5 million shown in the prospectus was overstated by about $16.5 million. Always remember that the purpose of a prospectus is to raise money from the public. Many should be taken with a grain of salt.

The ugly!

The less said about Telstra the better. The general public have learned some harsh lessons from their long-term investment into this company. Some of those lessons are:

- Nothing goes up forever.
- Never let a winning trade turn into a losing trade.
- Timing the market is more important than time in the market.

> *Boom-time allows a company director to sell a shareholding in his company for much more than it would be worth in normal times.*

4. Your broker

Your broker is hard to get hold of during boom-time - he's too busy. This is a fact. No disrespect to the broker. The general public has no concept of the pace, the stress and just how busy it gets during the heady days of a boom.

Believe me, there's no time for anything. As soon as you start to feel frustrated at the lack of availability of your broker, and anger sets in as you feel you have

> *A broker's best client is not the richest client; it is the one who trades the most and generates the most commission.*

missed a trade, step back a little; a significant market high is approaching. If your broker is not there for you, then you're not trading enough for him.

5. Broking firms

Broking firms are advertising for new brokers and accounting staff. Industry advertisements during boom offer very high incomes. The more job advertisements there are, the closer we are to the top of the boom cycle.

During boom times, broking firms are extremely busy and need to employ more staff to handle both the trading, as well as the back office paperwork. Often during boom-time, brokers are offered salaries so the broking firm retains the high proportion of broking income. During the normal quiet times when fewer trades are transacted, a firm will often offer commission as the preferred form of remuneration.

In the past, a sure time of a top has been your account. There are often missing trades, incorrect trades, your account doesn't balance and the "back office" cannot accurately tell you how much spare cash you have in your account.

6. Politicians

Pollies are generally in on the act. How could you have a boom without the pollies taking the credit. Bless their little hearts! Just as they like to make mileage from sporting events, they also attempt to take credit for the boom, as if it is the result of some tremendous economic decision making process. We have seen more politicians in recent years with the floating of various public utilities. Pollies are often seen leaping in front of cameras as shares rise, but the tend to hibernate during a bear market.

The end of the boom

At the end of each bull market, newcomers lose heavily, dozens of "new companies" enter bankruptcy, and government regulatory bodies rewrite the rule-book in a belated attempt to ensure the protection of all concerned. Newcomers are unprepared for the down-turn, don't read the signs, and continue holding shares as they fade into oblivion. The memory soon fades. A new industry emerges and a fresh batch of traders makes the same mistakes all over again as the next boom rolls along.

Bear markets

Bear markets bring out the most pessimistic. During the Australian stock market downturn of 2001, thousands of brokers were laid off, back office staff were retrenched, relatively little stock was traded, and most commentators were very bearish – that is, they talked gloomily about stock prospects, supporting the general view that prices were falling.

You will find the following symptoms are characteristic of a bear market—

1. The media

The media is gloomy in its market reports and cuts back to a 20 second snapshot during the seven o'clock news.

2. The barbecue conversation

The barbecue conversation is devoid of any mention of the share market (other than a casual comment that the whole thing is rigged and it's too risky to trade shares).

3. Fund returns

Fund returns take a hammering and returns are worse than usual, with negative returns being commonplace. So much for diversification, it does not eliminate risk.

4. The brokers' office

The brokers' office is quiet, you wander in to see your broker and he's playing solitaire on the PC and the phone doesn't ring during your half hour visit. If you don't go to see your broker he will ring you. He now needs your business.

5. New floats

New floats are scarce and unsuccessful by comparison. Generally, they are of better quality, as only those firms that really warrant listing will attempt to raise funds in such an environment. Not only are new company floats scarce, but existing companies are struggling and, in some cases, liquidators are called in.

Making money in a bear market

Yes, it *is* possible to make money in a bear market. There are *always* stocks that perform strongly, even in the gloomy atmosphere of a bear market. I feel it is easier to choose a stock because not many are actually rising, but any stock that is rising in a bear market has a lot going for it. Between the April 2000 Telco crash and November 2001, commentators generally believed Australia was in a bear market.

Yet look at these stocks. From June 2000 to November 2001, Cochlear rose from $22.00 to $50.00, Bristile rose from $1.06 to $2.60, Lang Corporation rose from $7.50 to $10.80, Southcorp rose from $4.70 to $7.30, Healthscope rose from thirty cents to $2.40, Mayne Nickless rose from $3.04 to $7.14, Toll Holdings rose from $9.19 to $29.60 and St George Bank rose from $10.90 to $17.30 ... and the list goes on. If that was a bear market, then I say let's have a bear market all the time!

Getting married

Everyone "gets married to a stock" at some stage. I bumped into a young couple early in July 1999. They had borrowed $1 000 and bought 10 000 shares in Sydney Gas at 10 cents per share. The stock was trading just over the $1.00 level when we met. I suggested they take some profits, maybe sell 1 000 shares and repay their parents; or possibly sell 5 000 shares then wait and see with the rest. They were opposed to this, as their broker told them the stock was going to $9.00. Where this figure came from is beyond my imagination.

The stock has since been to $1.40, but three years later is at 45 cents. The young couple has done well, but they still own the stock and are still waiting for the $9.00 price tag. It is a toss-up as to whether the $9.00 comes along before the original entry level of ten cents.

If anyone, broker or layperson (or both), tell you that a ten-cent stock is going to go to $1.00, let alone $9.00, you need to ask a few questions. How does anyone know with absolute certainty that a stock is going to rise to a particular price? If this were possible, we would all be millionaires many times over.

Winners ... and losers

Winners have many of the attributes of a winner in any other field. Their cup is half-full, rather than half-empty.

1. A successful trader knows that trading is relatively simple and often quite boring. His plan is tried and proven and trading has almost become a repetitive, monotonous calling. This is because his plan works; he has learned to adhere to his plan, and general market conditions are irrelevant.

2. A successful trader knows himself, his strengths and weaknesses. He is a realist who readily accepts an occasional losing trade. He works smart and is in control of his emotions, and possess or has learned patience.

3. A successful trader is not necessarily highly educated - rather, he is shrewd and a good student of human behaviour, as he realises that human emotion is what drives the market.

4. A successful trader is in control of all situations but maintains a degree of flexibility. He does not pay attention to newsletters and tips, and can think for himself and is independent.

5. A successful trader can easily take a break from trading.

Losers are often victims. They tend to be very undisciplined, changing strategies and plans with each trade.

1. A losing trader will make excuses and lay blame everywhere but at their own feet . "My account wasn't big enough. I got bad advice".

2. A losing trader will generally subscribe to various newsletters and seek a "second and third opinion".

3. A losing trader believes that brokers and other experts are more knowledgeable about the future of a stock, and perhaps have inside information.

4. A losing trader will have many of the traits of a gambler, often doubling up on a losing streak, always blaming others and bad luck. He will not accept responsibility for his own actions and decisions.

    If a coin is tossed in the air and heads turn up five times in a row, what is most likely to turn up on the next throw?

    -   Heads? Five heads in a row is a pattern - the trend is likely to continue.
    -   Tails? Six heads in a row is unusual, so tails is more likely.

    The above answers are examples of gambler's logic – the perception of patterns in random data. So which is the correct answer? Neither! Every coin toss has an even chance of turning up heads or tails. It never varies.

5. A losing trader cannot stop trading until he runs out of funds.

6. A losing trader cannot accept losses and will allow a small loss to become a big loss.

Learning a valuable leeson ...

Nick Leeson, the man who spectacularly broke the Baring bank, was a loser. He started by betting that the Nikkei Index would remain close to the 19 000 level.

After the Kobe earthquake, the market began to fall and was below the 17 000 level when his house of cards fell apart.

Leeson was dishonest and undisciplined. His plan failed; he had no risk control and no idea of money management. He added to a losing position, compounding his losses.

Fear, greed and hope brought him and the bank down. He is a classic example of everything you should not be.

Cultivate positive thinking

A losing trader sees a losing trade as failure, whereas the winning trader will take positive steps to rectify their position and learn from the mistake. To overcome negativity and fear of losing, you need to turn your mind around.

Instead of thinking, "What if I'm wrong with this trade?" begin to wonder, "What if I'm right?" Similarly, the thought pattern of, "What if I lose?", becomes one of, "What if I win?"

Now you're getting it! Keep training that brain until, "What if I lose my capital?" becomes, "What if I keep increasing my capital?"

Male and female psychology

Men already know everything. After all, who needs a road map! Men do not take kindly to unsolicited advice. Men need to be right; being wrong is akin to failing. Following a loss, men seek revenge from the market. Men tend to seek short-term trades and find long-term investments. Men initially tend to trade for the short term, but the moment the market dips, they will hold their stock as a long-term investment.

Men tend to be overconfident in assessing their risks and choosing between attack and flight. We could put this down to evolution: down through the ages, when faced with a possibly life-threatening situation, men have tended to attack rather than retreat. We see this in our wars and in men's hunting behaviour. Put it down to testosterone, but it is a characteristic that has been a great strength in men. In stock trading, whilst it is essential to feel confident that you *can* make money, overconfidence is a trap that can soak up all your capital and leave you with nothing.

Male overconfidence tends to work like this: see a stock, make a quick judgement, based on a little information heard on the radio or read in the financial gossip columns, attack with big bucks to buy up the stock, feeling totally confident that the price will rise and make a fortune. If the stock price begins to fall, male attack instincts cause them to hang on ferociously, waiting for the price turn around – after all, they can't be wrong!

Investing in stocks and futures has long been a male dominated domain. This is unfortunate, as it has been my long-held belief that women are better traders than men. At least there is now research to support this observation.

1.   Women tend to seek long-term investments and find short-term trades. Perhaps this is why women are generally better traders than men.
2.   Women seek advice and are willing to discuss problems. This way they learn more.
3.   Women are more patient.
4.   If women have one common problem, it can be a lack of confidence. If this is the case for you, then start small and slowly build up.
5.   Women are more ready to seek advice. (Who uses the street directory in your car?)

Brad Barber and Terrance Odean analysed the stock investments of 35 000 households from a US discount brokerage firm between February 1991 and January 1997. They found that men traded 45% more than women and earned 1.4% per annum less. Single men traded 67% more than single women and earned 2.3% less per annum.

Contrary opinion

Contrary opinion is the idea that when everyone thinks alike, the current trend reverses. In other words, as soon as everyone agrees that the market will rise another 500 points, or the boom will continue for another year, a market top is forming.

For example, in March 1999, when crude oil was trading at $10.00 per barrel, a major economic magazine featured crude as its lead story. There were three pages devoted to why crude was at $10.00 a barrel and why it would go down to $5.00. From that moment, crude began to rally and had nearly doubled in price a mere 2 months later. Following the media is the best way to help form a contrary opinion.

In January 2001, a State election was called in Western Australia. The headline of the local daily Western Australian newspaper on Saturday, 10 February 2001 screamed "CLIFFHANGER". The article said that following many surveys, the result was too tight to call. Voting was to be evenly balanced between the two major parties.

The politicians were unusually reticent in making predictions, as were the media, and the people who conducted various surveys. The following day, Sunday, 11 February, the *Sunday Times* headline was "LANDSLIDE" as the Labor party stormed into office with an enormous majority.

Contrary opinion in practice

In June 1990, I had most of my client base heavily committed to gold call options. (A call option is a derivative that allows you to profit from an upward move in prices). I had "sold" these to my clients as an investment on the basis that there would be problems in South Africa with the great Nelson Mandela being released from a long prison term. I expected major unrest at the time.

Meanwhile, the gold options were doing really well and clients were happy. Again, on a Friday night in September 1990, I was working late, listening to the radio and the latest broadcasts on the 'Kuwait crisis'. I heard that Hussein's troops had surrounded the US embassy, cut the power and the whole situation was very tense. I rang a broker friend in Sydney and asked what their clients were into. He said they were buying more gold that night than in the last two years. Same result from another broker friend in

Brisbane.

This brought out the contrarian in me, so I rang my best broker friend in Adelaide and told her to get out of all gold positions immediately. She laughed. So, back to the phones and I rang my clients and suggested some serious profit taking. A few took my advic,e but many were also listening to the news and watching TV and waiting for gold prices to skyrocket. Gold opened $24 an ounce lower on the Monday night, two days later. Thank you again to the media. I have a collection of newspaper billboards in my office, proving the theory of contrary opinion.

Forming a contrary opinion

Observe the crowd - Have a look around and see what everyone is doing. Go to a hotel or hold a dinner party. If the main topic of conversation is the fantastic trade that your grandmother did last week, the end is nigh.

Check stock values. The "Telco" boom is the greatest example we have ever seen for demonstrating totally unrealistic valuations. Companies that had no more than a blurred vision and a dream suddenly had market capitalisation of hundreds of millions of dollars. It is almost unbelievable to think that people were induced to pay over one million dollars to build web sites. When you think valuations are downright ridiculous, start to think of going against the herd, reducing exposure to the market and tightening your stop-losses. To give you an idea of the ridiculous, let's look at a tiny snapshot of the news that was publicly available during the life of One-tel.

* November 1997. One-tel is floated and publicly listed at $2.00 per share, giving the company a valuation of $208 million.
* August 1998. One-tel reports a profit of $8.8 million dollars, but this was after adding a compensation settlement to the bottom line.
* May 1999. Share split.
* November 1999. The shares traded at a high of $2.84 giving a valuation of $5.3 billion.
* January 2000. The company announces a pre-tax loss of $22 million.

Here we have a company that the "market" values at $5.3 billion dollars, but one month after this valuation announces a pre-tax loss. All this in a little over two years as a public company! GET REAL AUSTRALIA. This is ludicrous!

Form an alternative opinion

Forming an alternative opinion is difficult, as there is a need to go along with the mob.

1. For instance, in a corporate setting there is a need to go along with the boss. He will make decisions that may appear silly, but you dare not state your case for fear of repercussions.

2. You will not want to appear "stupid" in the light of the "obvious" facts. If the front page of the paper says, "The boom will continue", it is very hard to dispute that, let alone be successful in arguing your case.

3. The trend is so well established; it's bound to continue. This is the common fault of people who have not been through similar scenarios in the past.

4. Perhaps you have called for a reversal before, but it was too early, so you are reluctant to repeat the mistake.

5. It's different this time. (I don't know how many times I have heard this one.)

6. It is extremely difficult to form an alternative scenario because:
   - there is a strong need to conform
   - there is a sense of foolishness when you put forward your scenario
   - you will often meet hostility and criticism
   - there is a natural tendency to believe the experts

Question the motives

When anything moves public opinion to an extreme, you need to question the motives of those who shape public opinion. In the case of the stock market, the following questions are relevant -

1. Does the money manager being interviewed own stock?

2. Is the brokerage analyst bullish on a stock because his company is underwriting it?

3. Does the CEO being interviewed have a vested interest in his company and the industry?

4. Government officials usually stick their nose in, claiming credit for something they had nothing to do with, putting a positive spin on the picture, regardless of the facts.

5. There is a natural tendency to feel the establishment has more facts and resources at its disposal.

6. We all feel more comfortable when a successful person reassures us. They must know what they are doing.

7. We also expect that industry experts know what they are talking about.

When enough is enough

There are many events that can be observed that will tell us when a market is moving to an extreme:

1. Unusual events – In 1980, people queued up outside the Perth mint, with various silver heirlooms. Silver reached US$48.00 per ounce and people were selling silver teapots and other heirlooms for the value of the silver. (Silver currently languishes at US4.75 per ounce.)

2. Market commentary rates a three-minute segment rather than a thirty-second overview on television news.

3. Politicians get involved in the market.

4. Float fever develops with an unusually high number of floats generally oversubscribed.

5. Job vacancies in the securities industry with brokers advertising for additional staff.

6. Cover stories are more prevalent in the printed media.

7. New newsletters and magazines promoting stocks emerge.

8. New broking firms emerge.

9. Books on trading are in the best sellers' list.

Top tips for traders

This final section is a collage of the best tips I can possibly pass on to anyone hoping to make their way into the world of the professional trader.

Trading tips

- Always buy stocks that are rising. If in doubt, show a chart to a ten-year-old and ask them. If there is still any doubt, stay out. As a fall back position, use a 100-day moving average.
- Always use a stop-loss: Statistics have proven that traders who use a stop-loss outperform those who don't.
- Always place your stop-loss in the market: A mental stop is not a stop.
- Add to winning positions: This is one of the forgotten keys to real wealth.
- Never average down: Buying more and more as prices fall is not only costly, it becomes incredibly stressful.
- Trade with the trend.
- If trading breakouts, do not pre-empt the break.

Personal tips

- Leave your ego aside. You will have to learn to admit that you are wrong on occasions; the sooner you can do this, the sooner you will be a good trader.

- Do not fall in love with a stock. With Telstra trading down at $4.50 so many people continuously tell me what a great company it is and what a great dividend yield it has. But none of these people have made a profit!

- Be independent, no hot tips, no brokers and no tips sheets.

- Trade to make money, not for fun, not for stimulation.

- Be coachable. You have to listen and learn from people who are successful traders. Preferably those who have been trading a long period of time. Beware the expert who began trading last week or last year.

- Be patient. Wait for a good trade, they don't come along every day.

- Never trade under stress. I have never seen anyone trade for a living with a ten thousand dollar kitty and car and mortgage payments to meet at the end of the month.

- Be comfortable when you research and trade. Whatever that means for you, do it. For me, it is kicking my shoes off, turning the stereo on and being uninterrupted.

- Go with your intuition. I once heard intuition described as experience that resides in the subconscious.

- Maintain a balance – trading is not the only thing in the world. Take time out to have a holiday, walk the dog or play with the kids. The market has been there for over one hundred and fifty years. It will be there when you get back.

- Be consistent. I have seen a lot of "systems" that work, but very few people who can work the system. The moment a losing trade comes along, they change part of the plan.

- Be disciplined. This is the most common trait of all successful traders. It is also one of the attributes that make women, in general, better traders than men.

- Resit the urge to seek a second opinion. If you ring your broker to order a particular stock, don't ever ask what he thinks of it.

- Have confidence. A confident trader knows that in the long run, his plan works.

- Resist the urge to seek advice, particularly advice on a stock that you own.

Risk and money management tips

- Define your risk prior to entering any stock and make sure you can live with that risk.

- Only take trades that comply with your risk management rules.

- Always place your stop-loss at the time of entering the market.

- Don't plunge.

- If you suffer a series of losses, reduce your exposure, always selling losing positions and maintaining winning positions.

- Maximise your gains, not the number of wins.

Planning tips

- Develop a trading plan. Trading without a plan is akin to building a house without a blueprint.
- Write your plan and, if necessary, share it with someone who will make sure you stick to it.
- Plan your daily analysis and stick to a routine.
- The dirtiest four-letter word known to a trader is hope.

A final word from the technicians!

I close this set of trading tips with a quote from Burton G Malkiel, just to remind you of the biggest tip that I can pass on, and the main theme of this book. *Believe in the charts*!

--- **Exploding the Myths** ---

"Curiously, however, the broken technician is never apologetic about his method. If anything, he is more enthusiastic than ever. If you commit the social error of asking him why he is broke, he will tell you quite ingeniously that he made the all too human error of not believing his own charts. To my great embarrassment, I choked conspicuously at the dinner table of a chartist friend of mine when he made such a comment. I have since made it a rule never to eat with a chartist, it's bad for digestion".

13

Darvas box trading

The Darvas story is unique in that there is no mystery as to how he made his fortune. Unlike other theories put forward by so-called market gurus, there is no need to spend years attempting to unravel some mystical form of analysis. You can trade like Darvas today! Simple, practical and logical is the best way to describe "The Darvas Box Theory".

Darvas' story and his trading technique were described in his first book. (*How I Made $2,000,000 in the Stock Market* - 1986, Lyle Stuart Kensington Publishing, New York). His method, like all good systems, is simple and founded in logic. All that is required is the discipline to follow it. Darvas' discipline was remarkable; this, coupled with his ability to analyse himself, as well as the market, was the root of his trading success. Through his self-analysis he came to realise that "his ears were his worst enemy". He amassed his fortune without the help of computers, mobile phones, fax machines or any of the communications technology we have at our disposal today; indeed, he only had access to end-of-day data. All of his trading decisions were made outside trading hours, not sitting watching a live data screen all day. Starting with a purchase of only $3 000 worth of stock, Darvas amassed a fortune of over $2.2 million dollars. This was in 1959 and would be equivalent to over $20 million dollars today.

A truly remarkable aspect of the Nick Darvas story is that he was travelling extensively on a world tour when he developed his trading plan. He was isolated from all external influences, such as telephone, newspapers, brokers and other sources of so-called useful information.

Let's look at how Darvas succeeded.

The Darvas Story - A Synopsis

Darvas the Gambler

Darvas did not set out to be a gambler; in fact, he took his investing very seriously. "Darvas the gambler" is Darvas' own description of himself once he realised that his approach to investing was no better than gambling. His story begins in November 1952, in Canada, when he and his partner were asked to appear in a Canadian nightclub. Rather than pay in the normal fashion, Darvas was offered 6000 shares in a company named Brilund, a stock that was quoted at 50 cents at the time.

Despite not being able to keep to the arrangement, Darvas bought the stock anyway and paid $3 000. Thinking no more about the shares, Darvas was idly skimming the financial press some 2 months later and saw Brilund quoted at $1.92. I believe that Darvas was "hooked" from that moment on. An $8 000 profit in two months would make most people salivate. Working in nightclubs led Darvas to meet various wealthy people whom he asked for advice.

> *"So I asked them, do you know a good stock? Oddly enough, everybody did seem to know one. It was surprising. Apparently, I was the only man in America who did not have his own first hand stock market information. I listened eagerly to what they had to say and religiously followed their tips. What ever I was told to buy, I bought. It took me a long time to discover that this is one method that never works."*

Darvas sought the services of a broker and spent the next year happily buying and selling stocks. In his words he "... jumped in and out of the market like a grasshopper".

No pets Rex

This is not a reference to dogs and cats; rather, a very strong warning for all traders. Darvas developed a special liking for some stocks, some because they were given to him and others because he started making money with them. They became "pets", and he sang their praises, but this mentality lasted until he realised that the pet stocks were causing the biggest losses. As with most people who have traded, Darvas found that he was taking small profits and holding onto large losses. While Darvas was excited by the whole industry, delighted with each small win and overlooking his losses, he was not generally trading profitably.

> *"It was a period of wild foolish gambling with no effort to find the reasons for my operations. I followed hunches. I went by god-sent names, rumours of uranium finds, oil strikes, anything anyone told me. When there were constant losses, an occasional small gain would give me hope, like the carrot before the donkey's nose."*

By the end of 1953, the original stake of $3 000, plus the $8 000 profit from Brilund, had been whittled down to $5 800. Disillusioned, but undaunted, Darvas decided to give up the Canadian market. He moved to the greener pastures of New York and the allure of Wall Street.

Darvas the fundamentalist

Darvas severed all ties with the Canadian market and decided to start afresh. He topped up his account to a nice round $10 000. After doing his homework, Darvas finally decided to dip his toes into the Wall Street market and start trading. His first step was an obvious one and something that no doubt most people have tried without much success. He rang his new broker and:

> *"Trying to be the old financial hand, simply asked what was good. I realise now this enquiry was more suitable for a butcher, but the broker was up to it. He suggested several safe stocks."*

A few of those stocks began to rise immediately and Darvas was sure that he was on the right track with his new broker. Darvas felt that the broker's advice was no longer in the "hot tip" category, but was valid news based on sound logic and current economic events. Darvas continued to trade constantly. Unfortunately, his early success was due primarily to a bull market rather than any wonderful broker research or other insight into the market. It would have been difficult not to choose the odd stock that was rising.

Buoyed by his apparent success, Darvas began to study books on market terminology and how to trade successfully. He subscribed to as many newsletters and tip sheets as he could find. He became a voracious reader of all things financial. Slowly he began to question the validity of these newsletters. They often contradicted each other; a buy in one tip sheet or newsletter was a sell in another.

Compounding his problems, Darvas began to realise that brokerage became a major part of each transaction as he jumped in and out of stocks. This led to the realisation that many of the old market adages were of no relevance, like, "you cannot go broke taking a profit". Of course you can, if your profits are smaller than your losses; or, "buy cheap, sell dear". This was sound logic to Darvas, so off he went to buy "cheap" stocks, or stocks that were a bargain and undervalued. Darvas found that these stocks "stuck to his fingers like tar".

Through all these experiences, Darvas began to reach certain conclusions. Unlike most potential traders, he learned from each series of mistakes. Darvas began to outline some rules that would ultimately be part of the overall plan that led to his great success.

1. I should not follow advisory services. They are not infallible, either in Canada or on Wall Street.
2. I should be cautious with broker's advice. They can be wrong.
3. I should ignore Wall Street sayings, no matter how ancient and revered.
4. I should not trade over-the-counter – only in listed stocks where there is always a buyer when I want to sell.
5. I should not listen to rumours, no matter how well founded they may appear.

6. The fundamental approach worked better for me than gambling. I should study it.   *(How I Made $2 000 000 in the Market, p.34)*

For months, Darvas studied company fundamental information, sifting through dividends, net tangible assets, market capitalisation, assets, liabilities and price-earnings ratios. He developed a "wish list" of what he wanted a company to have. Stocks that the experts liked, stocks with a strong cash position but selling below book value, and companies who had never cut their dividend.

His first crisis

After an enormous amount of research, Darvas decided the steel industry would be the one to make him rich. Playing it safe, he decided to buy a stock in the steel sector and paying a good dividend. Further research led Darvas to the purchase of 1000 Jones and Laughlin shares because:

1. it belonged to a strong industry group
2. it paid almost 6% dividend
3. its price-earning ratio was better than any other stock in that group

Darvas had such faith in his analysis that he mortgaged a block of land, borrowed against an insurance policy and bought on a 70% margin. His cost was $52 652.30 (1000 shares at $52 a quarter). This purchase was made on 23 September 1955.

On 26 September 1955, this fool-proof theory began to unravel as Jones and Laughlin started to drop. Like most traders he was stunned, paralysed, like a rabbit caught in a spotlight. What to do? Based on all the best work Darvas could come up with, J&L was "worth $75.00". Most traders and brokers decide to hang on when a crisis hits. Darvas was no different. He employed the BHP method (Buy, Hold and Pray). As prices continued to slide he was almost too scared to check the latest quote.

Finally, Darvas decided to sell, his loss was over $9 000. At least at this point, Darvas was different from most traders I have seen; he did take a loss, but most importantly, he preserved some of his capital. Many traders wait five, or ten years for some sort of recovery, more often than not, they wait until the company enters bankruptcy. Gambling, tips, research, investigation. Whatever Darvas tried did not work. He became desperate.

Three years had gone by.

Eventually, Darvas noticed a stock, Texas Gulf Producing. He knew nothing about it and had heard no rumours. He simply noticed that the price was rising. Darvas bought Texas Gulf and recouped half the losses from the J&L disaster.

> *"What, I asked myself, was the value of examining company reports, studying the industry outlook, the rating, the price-earnings ratio? The stock that saved me from disaster was one about which I knew nothing. I picked it for one reason only - it seemed to be rising. Was this the answer ... it could be?"*

Darvas the technician

It was time for further reassessment. Darvas admitted that he had tried fundamental analysis without success. However, technical analysis had led to profits. He decided to try the successful approach again. He noticed a stock called M&M Woodturning, none of the financial information services could tell him anything and his broker had never heard of it. He remained interested because the price action reminded him of Texas Gulf Producing.

In December 1955, the stock rose from about $15.00 to $23.50. After a five-week lull in activity, the price began to climb again, accompanied by an increase in volume. Darvas bought at $26.60. The price continued its rise and Darvas sold at $33.00. Again, he knew nothing of the stock, other than the price was rising. Following his sale of M&M Woodturning, Darvas found a newspaper report that a takeover was being secretly negotiated. This was a major breakthrough. Darvas was ecstatic, feeling like an insider without being one. This experience convinced Darvas that a purely technical approach was logical. Studying price action and volume could get positive results.

Darvas began buying stocks solely on the basis of an increase in volume and price. Sometimes this was successful and sometimes not. He found that, on occasions, he would buy a stock only to see it immediately begin to fall, and as soon as he sold, prices would advance. Sounds familiar, doesn't it? As Darvas continued to study books and charts, he realised that price movement was not random; in fact, once stocks had a defined upward or downward trend, that trend tended to continue for some time. Within those trends, stocks moved in a series of patterns, or what Darvas called "boxes". This was the beginning of the "Darvas Box Theory" which was to lead him to millions of dollars.

> *"This is how I applied my theory: When the boxes of a stock in which I was interested stood like a pyramid, on top of each other, and my stock was in the highest box, I started to watch it. It could bounce between the top and bottom of the box and I was perfectly satisfied. Once I had decided on the dimensions of the box, the stock could do what ever it liked, but only within that frame. In fact, if it did not bounce up and down I was worried, no bouncing, no movement meant it was not a lively stock."*

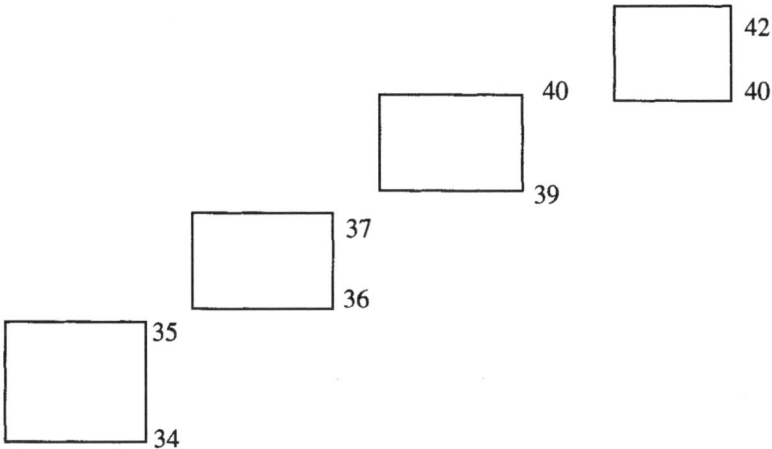

Darvas bought his shares when prices broke out of the top of the box. While this method greatly improved his entry levels, this system still did not lead to each trade being correct and profitable. At this point, Darvas realised that there was no sure thing in the market. He also realised that he could not take chances; he would need to reduce risks as far as possible. With this in mind, Darvas decided to employ an automatic stop-loss system. Further reflection led Darvas to re-define his objectives.

- Right stocks.
- Right time.
- Small losses.
- Big profits.

His best weapons were:

- Price and volume.
- Box theory.
- Automatic buy order.
- Automatic stop-loss sell order.

The world tour

At this stage, Darvas faced a new dilemma; he signed a two-year contract for a world dancing tour. How could he continue to trade? Through discussions with his broker, Darvas agreed on one tool. The broker would airmail the weekly *Barron's* financial publication to Darvas. From this Darvas could study prices and follow any rising stocks. Each day, the broker would send a cable to Darvas with the open, high, low and close of stocks that Darvas was interested in. Darvas felt this was like playing poker but he could not hear the betting, he could not see what was going on; however, he did hold the cards.

Broking terminology

Automatic buy order

The way in which an automatic buy order works is quite simple. In Darvas' case, his entry needed to be at a level when prices burst upwards through the top of a period of consolidation, or the top of the Darvas box. If the top of a box was $35.00, Darvas would give his broker an instruction to buy the stock any time in the future that the stock traded at, say, $35.25 cents. This order may have been transacted weeks later, if at all. If the price did not continue to advance the purchase was not made. This method ensured that at least at the time of entry, prices were rising.

Automatic stop-loss sell order

At the time of entering a stock, Darvas would place an order to sell if prices traded below a certain level. The advantages of this strategy are enormous; it means that all risk is defined **prior** to purchasing any stock.

The theory starts to work

In November 1957, while touring in Saigon, Darvas noticed a stock called Lorillard. There was a bear market at the time but this stock was rising. The stock had risen from $17.00 in the first week of October, then consolidated between \$24 and \$27. Volume had increased from around 10 000 per week to 126 000. Darvas made a series of trades in the stock, finally selling them at \$57.50 for a profit of \$21 052.95. This was clearly the turning point for Darvas. Using the same theory, he made his first "big kill" on a stock called E.L. Bruce, a profit of over \$295 000. In January 1959, Darvas returned to New York with profits totalling more than \$500 000.

The second crisis

Darvas was back in the thick of things, wined and dined by brokers who were amazed at his success, reading everything and listening to hot tips all over again. In the space of a month, he lost \$100 000 and was devastated by this huge setback. Darvas took a short break in Paris to re-group. Once again the human factor had taken over, logic went out the window and emotions ran high. Emotions and ego need to be strictly controlled in order to achieve success in trading.

Making two million dollars

In late February 1959, fresh from a trip to Paris, he returned to New York and made a determined effort to re-use the method that had worked so well. He locked himself away, asked his brokers to send him telegrams as they had in the past. The rest, as they say, is history. By July 1959, Nicolas Darvas had amassed over two million dollars.

Ultimately, the story of Darvas success leaked out. He was interviewed by *Time Magazine* and convinced to write a book that went on to sell over 200,000 copies in eight weeks. I would strongly recommend Darvas' book *"How I Made \$2,000,000 in the Stock Market"* to anyone trading stocks.

"Rediscovering" Darvas

For many years I have tried to teach novice traders about planning, and managing their trades in a disciplined fashion. I consider discipline and timing to be the essence of successful trading; enter and exit at the right time, and always have a plan.

My plan always includes an entry and exit strategy, and a cardinal rule to never, ever, trade without a stop-loss. My own personal trading mantra is simple: "Only own rising stocks". Over the years, I've seen people buy stocks that are clearly in a downward price trend. The reason given for this strategy is usually that they are trying to buy when the stock is cheap to maximise the return when the stock price starts to rise. This is one sure way to lose your trading capital; this method just does not work.

A problem with novice traders has always been maintaining the discipline needed to trade successfully. How could I ensure that my students would trade with a comprehensive plan? To help with this problem, the software package I designed incorporates a "Combo" scan that will find me rising stocks that exhibit certain volume, and price characteristics. My scan solved the entry problem, making it easy to find the right stocks. However, the exit timing and stop-loss setting still proved problematic.

A student brought Nick Darvas' technique to my attention and I quickly realised that this was a solution to the problem. To my amazement, Darvas' entry criteria for his boxes fitted my "Combo" scan so closely that our software developers used it as the entry criteria for a "Darvas Box" scanning program that I quickly commissioned.

Will trading Darvas-style work for you?

My Darvas software was designed to drastically reduce any costly learning experiences. Most people lose thousands of dollars in their early attempts to find financial freedom through the stock market. What is potentially worse than losing thousands of dollars is the wasted time. Darvas served a five-year apprenticeship with no teacher. Traders today have the benefit of computers and software and can be trading successfully in a matter of days.

You need an understanding of why you need a plan. A major obstacle to successful trading is the trader's emotions. Listening to hot tips, blindly following brokers, tipsters' letters and allowing greed to affect a trading decision is the downfall of most new entrants to the market.

Apart from the obvious profits, a trading plan will remove emotion. A good plan -

- will bring **discipline** to your trading

- will help you **manage risk.** Having a system makes you define the risk on each trade. If you don't define the risk then how can you control it?
- will bring you **consistency**
- should **limit your losses** and **let your profits** run
- should allow you to **participate in major moves** and trends

Nicolas Darvas' trading technique fulfils these criteria.

Darvas in practice

A Darvas Box represents a graphical trading plan. Our buy order is placed on a break of the box top with our initial stop-loss set at the price at the box bottom. The height of the box represents our risk level per share (excluding brokerage).

Darvas box construction

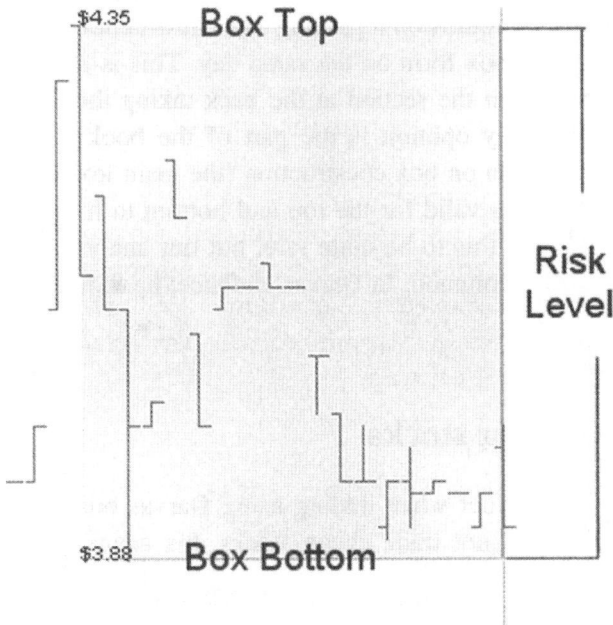

Let me clear up some points of confusion about Darvas boxes. I must admit that when I first read his book, I assumed that Darvas was looking for three points of resistance, and then for some support level; this interpretation is incorrect. The sequence for correct Darvas Box construction is as follows:

1. There must be some volume activity in the stock, i.e. a volume spike of a specified level before the first box forms.

2. The stock must be in an upward trend on entering the first box.

3. The top of the box is found when a price is reached that is an x-day high price (e.g. 200-day high), and then this price is not touched or exceeded for a specified number of days (Darvas usually used three days). This point is important. Darvas was not looking for three days of resistance he was looking for a confirmed top of the trading range.

4. After a box top is confirmed, the bottom is found in the same manner , but in reverse, i.e. once a low has formed and not been exceeded for three days, this becomes the bottom of the box.

5. When the top and bottom are confirmed, we have a box; now we may calculate an initial stop-loss level based on the price at the bottom of the box.

Another source of confusion regarding box construction is where the top and the bottom of the box form on the same day. This is actually referred to in Darvas' book. It's in the section at the back taking the form of a Q and A session. This, in my opinion, is the part of the book containing the most relevant information on box construction (the main text of the book is a bit vague on this). It is valid for the top and bottom to form on the same day. Darvas considered this to be quite rare, but our analysis shows that on the contrary, it's quite common. In Darvas' defence, he didn't have the luxury of scanning software.

Choosing your stocks

Something to consider when trading using Darvas boxes is your choice of stocks. Darvas did not trade cheap stocks; his adage was "buy dear, sell dearer". He was trading stocks priced at over $30 per share in the 1950s; he was not interested in cheap, speculative stocks.

Another characteristic of Darvas' trading was his attention to the price movement behaviour of stocks; this was how he came to develop the box theory. His research led him to look for stocks with a specific signature to their price movement patterns.

His preference was for stocks that made strong definite movements through the box top. Stocks making new price highs incorporating some slight retracements, possibly leading to the creation of a new box. The following figure is an example of such a stock pattern.

Darvas' preference was for stocks in what were then newly emerging hi-tech industries, such as Hewlett-Packard, or for companies with innovative product development, such as filter-tipped cigarettes. Remember this was the mid-1950s.

Do your homework

Darvas' box technique gives us a ready-made trading plan. However, this is only part of the planning process; there are other factors to consider before we enter the trade. Many trades are unsuccessful for the reason that no thought is given to the simple task of calculating a breakeven level for the trade. The breakeven level is the price that must be reached by the stock so that a stop-loss placed at this level will result in a no loss trade. Any price achieved beyond this point must result in a profit for this trade if we exit at this price.

Calculating the breakeven level

The breakeven level is easily calculated, but some traders make the simple mistake of not including all the costs incurred in the trade. It is essential that both the entry **and** exit brokerage fees are included in the cost. The total cost for the trade is then:

Total trade cost = (Parcel size x stock price) + entry brokerage + exit brokerage

For example; suppose we wish to enter a trade at a price level of $1.00, with entry and exit brokerage of $60. If our parcel size is 500, we have a total cost of: total cost = (500 * $1.00) + $120 = $620.

Optimising the breakeven level

The task of optimising the breakeven price level is achieved by finding a minimum breakeven level for the trade. Given that the brokerage costs and the stock price may be taken as fixed for entry to the trade, the breakeven level may only be optimised by carefully adjusting the parcel size. The breakeven level is calculated by dividing the total cost by the parcel size:

Breakeven level = $1 120/1000 = $1.12.

The stock must at least reach this level before we achieve a no loss situation. Any exit price below this level will result in a losing trade. If we increase the parcel size to 1 500 shares the total cost is now:

Total cost = (1 500 * $1.00) + $120 = $1 620.

The breakeven level is now:
Breakeven level = $1 620/1500 = $1.08.

Similarly for 2 000 shares the breakeven price is:
Breakeven level = $2 120/2000 = $1.06.

As can be seen from the preceding examples, an increase in parcel size results in a lower breakeven level. We reach a profitable level sooner, the bigger the parcel size. However, the trade-off is an increase in capital required to fund the trade and a greater capital risk level within the trade. Care must be taken to balance this risk and optimum parcel size for the trade. All of these parameters must take into account our trading rules regarding permitted capital risk per trade and, of course, the size of our trading account.

A common mistake made by novice traders, in the rush to complete their first trade, is to buy a small parcel of "penny dreadful" shares with no realistic possibility of even covering brokerage costs, let alone reaching a breakeven level!

Analysing the trade

Now that we have optimised the parcel size with the maximum size permitted by our trading rules and the limits of our trading account, we are now in a position to estimate the likely success of the trade. We should now stop and ask ourselves some questions, such as:

> *Analysing the past performance of the stock, does a significant rise beyond the breakeven level seem possible?*
> *Is this a realistic possibility, or are we merely gambling on an unlikely event?*

Taking the time to do this simple homework will prevent us entering unrealistic or potentially unprofitable trades.

Managing a successful trade is a balance between good risk management and good money management. A common error is to attempt to reduce the trading cost by using cheaper broking services, such as online brokers, but this is a foolish economy. The benefits provided by broking services offering stop-loss facilities far outweigh the higher brokerage cost. A better strategy is to employ the simple money management technique outlined and optimise the trade.

Placing your order

Once you have found a stock that has formed a Darvas box and your breakeven analysis deems it a viable trade, what next? The Darvas box provides you with a graphical trading plan, an entry level, an exit level, and a risk level. Your first actions should be to place an order to purchase the stock once the stock trades at a price just above the price at the box top, and **at the same time**, place an initial stop-loss to exit the trade when the stock trades at a price just below the price at the bottom of the box.

Do NOT wait for a break of the box top before placing your order. Buying after the break of a box is folly, as you are reacting to the market, not pre-empting it. You will find yourself chasing the stock price and enter at a much higher level than necessary.

Do NOT buy when the stock has not yet penetrated the box top. A comment often made is, *"If I'm going to buy the stock, why not get it at a cheaper price before it breaks the box top?"* The answer is that only the break of the box **proves** that the stock is a worthwhile trade; before the break it is only a possible candidate. It could just as easily drop in price; remember, we only want stocks that are going up.

Managing your trade

A key aspect of Darvas' trades was his use of a trailing stop-loss to manage his trading risk. Using extremely tight stops, Darvas minimised his capital losses. However, this strategy meant he would "stop out" of more trades. He was willing to accept the possibility of brokerage losses, rather than expose an unacceptable level of his trading capital to the market. When trading like Darvas we must accept this risk also.

Let us assume that we are now engaged in a trade. We've placed our order and an initial stop-loss. The stock price has broken through the box top and our order is executed; what next? All we can do now is adjust the stop-loss level. This is done with the caveat that we may NEVER lower the stop-loss level, so all we may do is move it up. Where we move it to is the issue, and this is determined by the price movement.

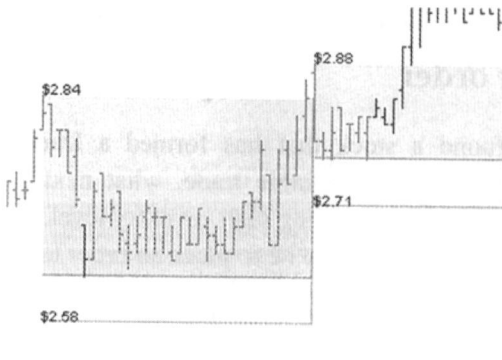

If, as shown above, the stock moves weakly out of the box top without making strong, definite gains, a strategy may be to trail our stop up so as to maintain our maximum risk level. If our initial risk level was 10%, we move our stop up so as to maintain this maximum risk level. Remember, this was the risk level that was acceptable when we formed our trading plan, so we should stick to our plan and maintain this maximum risk level. Our aim is to get our stop-loss up to, and hopefully beyond, our breakeven point. Once the stop reaches the breakeven point, we have a no-lose trade. Always remember that once the price starts to move upwards, if we don't move our stop-loss up also, we are increasing our risk level; all positive price movement is not just changing numbers, it is your money. If the price rises and you don't move your stop, you are exposing more and more of your capital to the market.

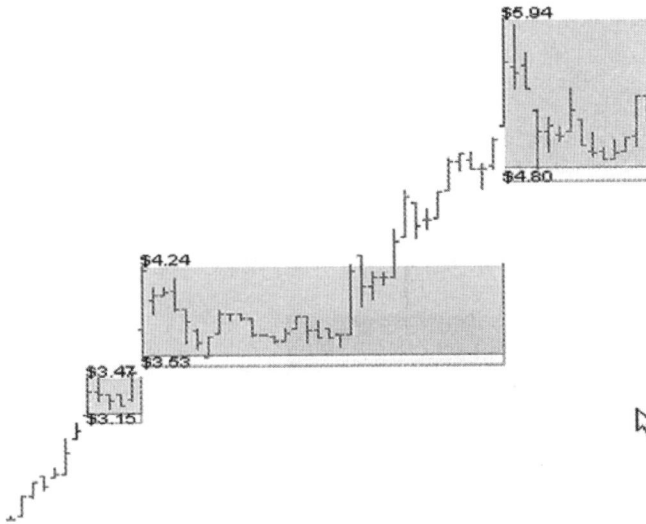

For stock with what I call the "Darvas Signature", we adopt a different approach. We see an example, above. In this case, on the strong breakaway from the box top, we move our stop up to just below the box top. When another box forms we move our stop up to just below the bottom of the new box, waiting for a break of the new box top. When the break occurs, we move our stop again up to just below the box top. If a box does not form quickly as in the third box in our example, don't be afraid to trail your stop up outside the box; remember, we are trying to lock in profits.

Pyramiding the position

Pyramiding the position is a part of Darvas trading that at first may appear unusual. Traditionally, we are taught to diversify our investments to dilute our risk. We may have some high performing stocks, and some stocks that are poor performers, but everything should average out in the long run. In my opinion, this is nonsense. What we are doing is attempting to reduce risk by accepting mediocre performance.

With the risk management provided by the trailing stop, we are refusing to accept poor performance since we will "stop out" of these trades. The stop-loss and market movement will combine to "separate the wheat from the chaff". Darvas' philosophy was to only accept minimal losses. However, when he had a winning trade, he would focus his financial resources, not diversify them in order to maximise his profits.

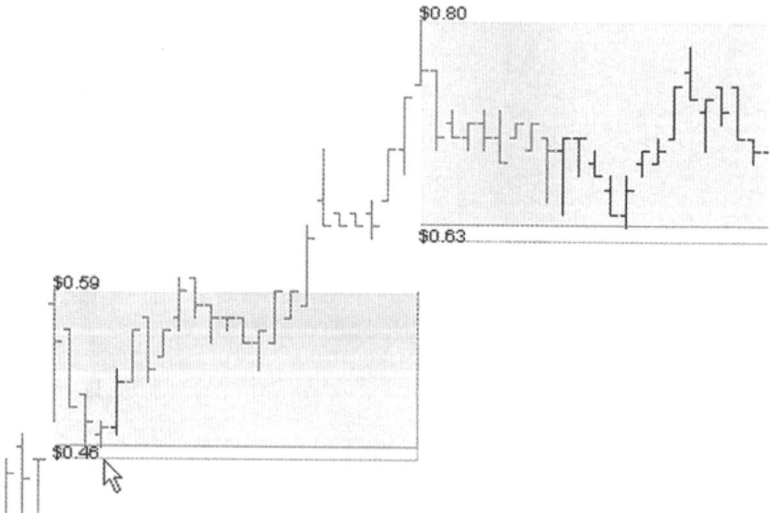

In the figure, above, we see our plan would be to buy a break of 59 cents with an initial stop-loss set at 46 cents. Upon the break of the first box we would quickly trail our stop-loss up to just below the box top at about 58 cents. On the formation of the new box, we trail our stop up to 63 cents, and place an order to buy another parcel of this stock on a break of 80 cents.

If it never breaks the 80-cent level, we never buy the new parcel of shares; but if it does it means the stock is making new high prices so we are attempting to concentrate more of our financial resources into a rising stock. A point to remember, however, is that if we wish to use the pyramiding technique, we must do our homework in terms of breakeven analysis for each individual box trade.

In this current example of a "Darvas Trade", we can clearly see the advantages of a structured trading method. The Darvas method gives the investor a precise entry level, a precise exit level and a precise level at which to add to a winning position. Using the Darvas method of trading covers virtually every component required in a successful and profitable trading plan.

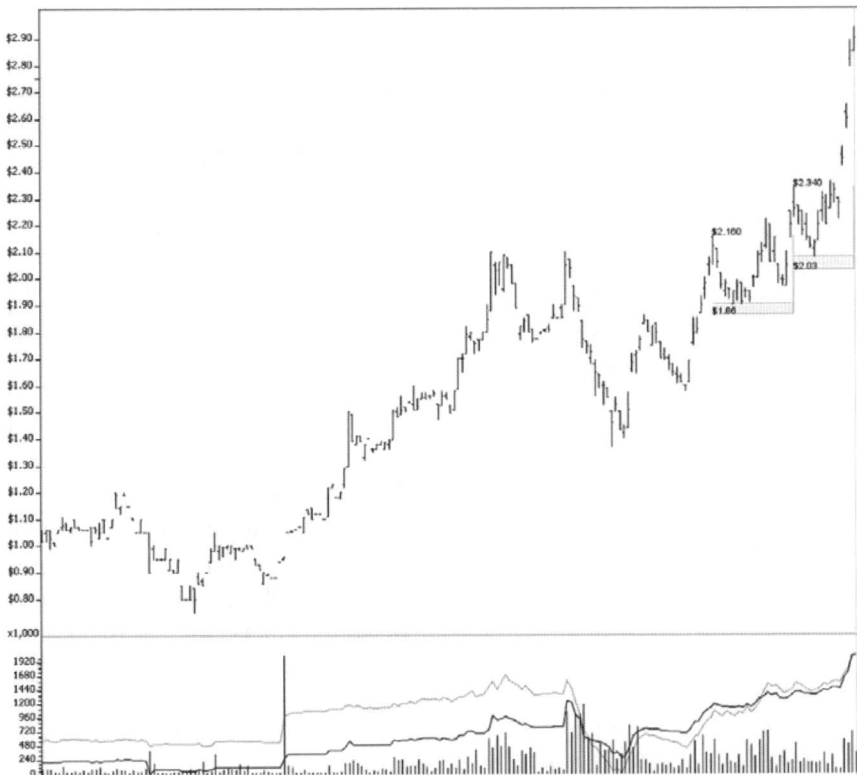

Will it work in today's market?

The first common comment we encounter is;

"The market is far more volatile today, Darvas did not have today's volatility to contend with."

While there is undoubtedly more volatility in today's markets, the methods that Darvas used to define his boxes incorporated the volatility of the day, making his method applicable then, now and in the future.

"Darvas was fortunate that he was trading during an era of great change, the space race was on and the computer age was about to begin."

The facts are that there is always a "new" era of change about to dawn on us. Technology is always advancing. We feel that the Internet has a long way to go, as do most forms of communication, but the real advances have yet to come in the area of health, biotechnology, waste disposal and genetically modified food, just to name a few possibilities.

"Darvas was lucky, he made most of his money in a bull market."

As with most people, the harder Darvas worked the "luckier" he got. The bull market was almost incidental. He would have made his fortune anyway. It may have taken him longer if the bull market did not come along.

The real issue here is that Darvas kept his fortune at the end of the bull market because his unique trailing stop-loss method had him out of stocks when the market duly crashed.

> *The real issue here is that Darvas kept his fortune at the end of the bull market because his unique trailing stop-loss method had him out of stocks when the market duly crashed.*

It is my opinion that with modern software packages, that Darvas trading is as valid today as it was over 40 years ago. Perhaps even more so. Good risk management and trade planning will always be at the heart of successful trading. As an experienced trader, I can't but marvel at the discipline and self-analysis that made Darvas such an exemplary trader. Since discovering Darvas, my first scan every day is for Darvas boxes. I hope you, the reader, embrace Darvas' techniques as I have, I am sure it will be of great benefit in your trading endeavours.

There is ample evidence to show that "Trading like Darvas" will work in any market at any time (given a "Daravs" set-up), provided you have the same discipline as Darvas had.

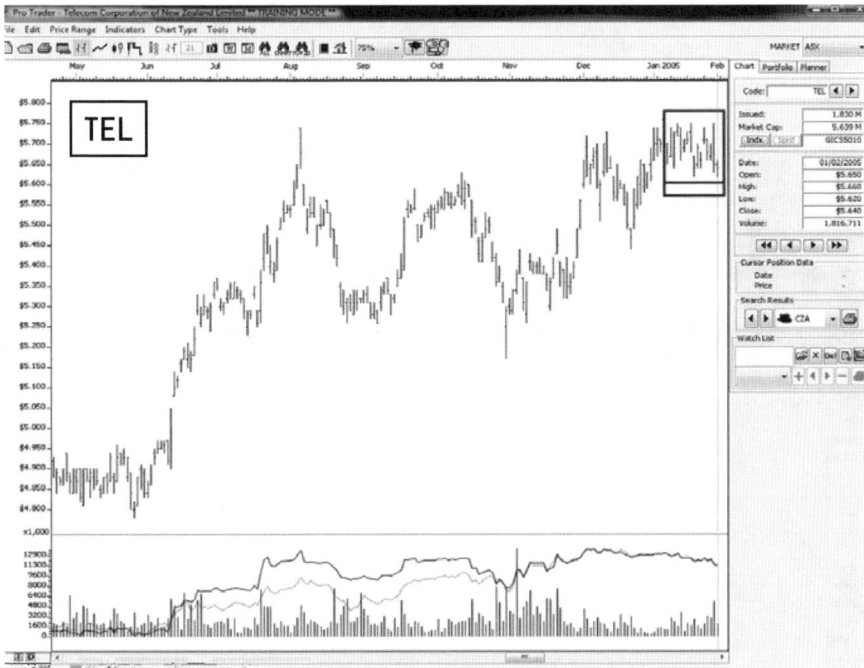

A current example of a Darvas box that has formed on Telecom New Zealand (TEL). The "top of the box" is $5.78 and the "bottom of the box" is at $5.52. To follow the Darvas method, you could place a start gain at $5.79 and your stop-loss at $5.52.

And also, a chart of the ANZ.

"Two of the best tips I can give any trader are; to add to a winning position and always sell the worst performing stock in your portfolio, NOT the best."

14

A few tall tales

People often ask, "What was broking really like." Before I answer, I must point out that most of my broking was in the Futures Industry, not the Stock market. Therefore, we did not have the same boom and bust periods that share brokers had to contend with. There was always something on the move, whether it was coffee, cocoa, orange juice, pork bellies, the precious metals or the grains; opportunities were everywhere.

Futures contracts offer enormous leverage. Generally, a 10% move in a physical commodity gives a 100% return on your investment. This makes trading futures the most exiting, rewarding and frustrating pursuits of all. The futures market is not for the faint-hearted, the undisciplined or the procrastinator. Fortunes are made and lost in a matter of moments; you have discipline or you go broke, that is the choice.

For me, it was a great time; we worked hard and played hard, day traded, position traded and all things in-between. The main benefit for me was being able to observe thousands of traders, learning along the way hundreds of things not to do, and occasionally picking up on someone else's winning habit. It is not the glamorous job that some may have you believe. Never thanked for a winning trade but always blamed for the loss. It can get to you after a while. When I started I was told that I would burn out in two years - I lasted ten. Most of my client-base traded to US markets. This meant some very long working days, often from 7 am to well after midnight.

Before broking

My first story concerning brokers was an event that occurred long before I ever dreamed of being a broker. I was working on a farm near Mount Gambier in South Australia during most of the 1980 gold boom. I traded heavily and paid a lot of brokerage during that time, but had stopped trading during December, as I felt the market was overheated and due to decline for a year or two. One day in January 1981, my Adelaide broker said that he was going to Mount Gambier for the weekend and asked if he could call in to the farm on the Friday night and meet me.

I was naturally flattered and offered him dinner and a nice bottle of Coonawarra red. Well, dinner degenerated into a pretty miserable flop, as we spent the night arguing. I had made a reasonable amount of money on the penny dreadful gold stocks, without any help from the broker, and now he was suddenly full of well-meaning advice once I had stopped trading.

My natural cynicism felt that he did not ring me during the boom, as I was earning him enough brokerage with him making a long-distance phone call. Once the boom was over and I stopped trading, he needed the commission.

Dinner progressed to the tune of, "You've had your fun son, now it's time to get into the blue chips and invest for the long term!" He went on and on, singing the virtues of Howard Smith, great P/E ratio, well diversified, good dividend etc, etc, blah, blah, blah.

After much bickering, I told him to buy me some Howard Smith shares on his return to Adelaide on Monday. They were purchased at $9.10 cents per share and spent most of the next decade trading at about three or four dollars. This was the first and last time I ever turned a short-term investment into a long-term investment. Many many years later, they traded at $9.28. I sold them and still tell everyone how I made a profit from Howard Smith. And every six months they would send me a lousy $5.00 dividend just to remind me how stupid I was. Ah, such is life. (I expect this story to sound familiar to some readers) The moral of the story? Be independent and make your own decisions.

Insider trading?

Inside trading is alive and well, always has been and always will be. My first insight into how this works came in 1988. I was at home enjoying one of those rare quiet evenings when the phone jarred me into action. The boss was on the phone, wildly excited and bursting to share a great opportunity with me and with my clients. David was a good boss, a good leader and generally unflappable.

"Frank, there's a cyclone about to hit the Queensland / New south Wales coast. It a pretty big one and the media is tipping some serious damage to the sugar crop. As you know, Australia is the worlds' fourth largest exporter of sugar. Get onto your clients, get them to buy as many sugar contracts as they can afford on the London exchange. As soon as New York opens, I'll ring the guys on the trading floor and let them know; it'll send sugar through the roof. We can sell in New York and make a killing."

This all sounded great, but I would never ring a client at that time of the night unless they were expecting a call. I ignored the phone call, went to bed and arose very early to rush to the office and see what I had missed.

Checking overnight prices I noticed they were a touch lower. This was strange. I went and checked the Knight Ridder news service for the end of trading session review.

This is the review, I still have it in my possession. "Washington – March 6 KRF – Tropical cyclone Greg brought much needed rains to Australia during the week ended Saturday, helping reverse dry conditions in sugar cane production areas".

I asked David what had happened. He sheepishly told me that he had rung New York and explained the situation, their response was: "What is Queensland?"

The best research

You may have come to the conclusion by now that I am not a strong advocate of other peoples' research. Many years ago I was receiving a weekly newsletter from a particular firm and there was some pretty good stuff in the document. I followed this for several issues and was quite impressed. Then out came a recommendation that was just rubbish, it defied logic and did not fit the mould. I rang the firm, got hold of the author and, after several weeks and a much cajoling, we arranged to meet for a coffee.

I put this particular research on the table and asked what it was about. After a fair bit of embarrassment, the story unfolded. Management had demanded a research document, be produced within 24 hours giving a strong, though speculative buy recommendation on a particular stock.

The reason was simple; the firm was making a placement of a few hundred thousand dollars and needed the price higher. The story was rubbish, but the analyst was told to write it or face the sack.

1986 – the Chernobyl disaster

I had only recently become a broker (or registered representative, as the Sydney Futures Exchange once reminded me) but was gaining the reputation of knowing my stuff when it came to the Agricultural markets. I was playing indoor cricket as the first stories of a nuclear reactor in Russia blowing up began to emerge. My first knowledge was when the boss rang me at about 10.00 PM at the cricket centre.

His first words were, "Chernobyl's blown up!" My response was, "What's Chernobyl?"

Nobody had ever heard of Chernobyl before that day. The boss told me to get into the office, as about ten of my clients had turned up to seek my advice. Great!

I threw the tracksuit on and headed to the office, arriving in a lather of sweat from the cricket match. Sure enough, there they were; doctors, a lawyer, real estate and insurance sales people, all eagerly awaiting the pearls of wisdom from farmer Frank, a broker of some eight weeks experience.

I didn't have a clue what the grains would do, or pork bellies, orange juice, the precious metals nor any other commodity. Nor did anybody else, as this was unchartered water. I recommended to all and sundry that they purchase soybean call options. This worked out well and we tripled our money that night. No doubt it was a fluke, but who cares.

The 1987 crash

The link between the futures market and the stock market came through what we call the SPI, or the Share Price Index contract. In 1987, the SPI was worth $100 per point, so if you were ever listening to the news and heard that the All Ordinaries was up 20 points, the equivalent for us was a $2 000 increase in value for each contract, and only a $2 500 deposit was required. (There are other factors but, it is not necessary to explain all the intricacies of futures trading) From memory, the SPI fell about 80 points on the Monday before the crash in America on the Monday night.

Our client base was holding twenty-one short positions on Monday 19 October 1987. Seventeen of them took profits on the close that day, realising $8 000 profits for the day. Four of our clients carried their winning position overnight. For those four clients, that decision was worth more than $50 000 per contract, as the SPI plunged 500 points following the Wall Street crash.

The best system can go awry

Our firm was at the front of software development in the eighties. A system for trading the SPI had been developed and was showing very good results in the market. I was chasing a particular prospect in an attempt to get his account. (This was the eighties and greed was good.) Finally, one Friday in October 1989, the prospect came into the office with a cheque for $20 000 and opened his account.

We bought a SPI contract based on a buy signal from this wonderful system. By the end of the trading day the SPI had risen 14 points, giving the client a $1 400 paper profit. I sent him a fax at the end of the day congratulating him on his wise decision, and wishing him a great weekend. I arose Saturday morning to hear that the Dow Jones had fallen 200 points in the last 2 hours of trading. Monday was going to be a rough one.

Monday morning I hit the office early, and with some trepidation. The SPI opened about 180 points down and my new client had just lost $18 000. With a trembling finger, I dialled his number and with a quivering voice broke the news. He seemed to take the news very calmly and I wondered why, then he mentioned that he had been in touch with his bank and cancelled the cheque.

I was not a happy chap. I knew the boss would have taken the losses from my commissions, rather than go to the trouble of trying to retrieve the funds from the client. It is always very messy pursuing a client for a debt, as well as bad publicity. The boss was far happier debiting our income.

I excused myself from the office, drove around to the client's surgery and walked in on a meeting. After a brief discussion he agreed to contact his bank and allow payment on the cheque. I remain grateful for his integrity; after all, it was his decision to take my advice.

And the system? It faded into oblivion. My belief is the system worked, would still work and I would be happy to use it, but not on the SPI. The SPI is the most dangerous commodity contract in the world in my opinion, and categorically not to be traded by novices.

Oh, by the way, it was on Friday the 13th that he opened the account.

You can be right and still lose!

Being wrong can obviously be costly, but it is not as bad as being right and losing. The same October '89 correction reminds me of another story. A chap from Melbourne rang us every day for two years, between the '87 crash and October 1989, to get closing quotes on the Dow Jones. He wanted to "short" the market, as he firmly believed that another crash was coming. As time went by it was obvious he was more and more convinced. Finally, in late September, he opened an account with $11 000.

On Monday, 9 October he bought several SP500 put options. (If the Dow fell, SP500 puts would profit from the fall.) By Friday October thirteen 1989, the Dow was up a bit and the client was getting nervous. At 2.00 am Saturday, he closed his positions and took a $3 000 loss.

Two hours later the Dow fell 200 points. Our client missed about $30 000 profit by about two hours.

Whatever it takes

One of my favourite clients was a young man I will call Bill. Apparently, Bill had tried on a couple of occasions to open an account, but when he told potential brokers of his method of analysis they backed off, writing him off as a crackpot. His analysis was unusual, to say the least.

On the odd occasion, Bill's mother would have a dream. Between Bill and his mum they would interpret this into a trading strategy. For instance, one night, Bill's mother dreamt that she was driving around America and everything was brown for as far as the eye could see. The interpretation was drought. Bill bought wheat contracts.

It so happened that this was 1988, the biggest drought since the "dustbowl of the thirties". I saw him trade several times and cannot recollect him being wrong with his analysis. Bill was a thoroughly good bloke and an honest client, he just had a different method of analysis from most other traders.

Appendix

Starting your portfolio

Regardless of the books you have read, the seminars you have attended or the courses you have been to, most people are still confused and all too often ask the question, "But how do I start trading?" This chapter is a step-by-step answer to that question. There are a few basic assumptions that I have to make.

- You own a suitable computer.
- You require software.
- You have funds to trade with.
- You want to do this yourself and not rely on others.
- You have set aside some time each day for your analysis and trading.

1 Step one
Choosing software

Hopefully, you have come to the realisation that it is virtually impossible to do justice to share trading without a suitable piece of software. However, the difficulty for a newcomer is in knowing what he can expect from software. As I have previously mentioned, there is no evidence to suggest that expensive software will produce any greater profits than any other software. At the end of the day, software is a tool. Therefore, the issue becomes, "Can I make this tool work for me?" rather than the perennial question, "Does this software work?"

In 1997, I decided to leave broking and trade professionally. I began searching for software that would best assist me in finding suitable stocks. Despite reviewing more than forty commercially available packages, there was nothing on the market that performed the functions I required.

What do I need from software?

- Functionality - I expect software to be "user-friendly", self-installing, well supported and easy to look at.

- Purpose - The software had to be designed to assist in finding stocks that are rising in price. To fulfil the purpose of finding rising stocks, it is appropriate to define the various ways of determining that a stock is rising.

Determining rising stocks

- Higher highs and higher lows – universally recognised as the first sign of a bull market or a rising stock. To date, this is a subjective feature and not a function performed by software.

- Key reversal bottom – a very early sign that a stock may have changed trend from down to up. This was not available in any software I reviewed, so we had to develop this pattern.

- 30-day high – a method popularised in the futures market in the mid-nineteen eighties, obviously if a stock price trades at a thirty-day high today, it is rising.

- Multiple moving average crossovers – provided prices are above a reasonable set of moving averages, the price is in a general uptrend.

- Breaking above resistance – prices breaking through past resistance levels is perhaps the strongest indication that the price is on the rise. Most of the software I reviewed did not have the ability to find suitable resistance lines.

- Visual - while this is subjective, and up to the trader to determine, it requires a chart to look at.

Scanning functions

The software needed to incorporate a "scanning function", whereby I could enter certain criteria, "click a button", and in a matter of seconds, the software would scan the entire ASX database for stocks that meet my buy and sell criteria.

My "buy" criteria included:

- Buy on support – again, very little software I reviewed had the ability to find suitable support lines.
- Ascending triangles – as with other forms of pattern recognition, I could not find any software designed for this purpose.
- Flags – as above.
- Pennants – as above.
- Key reversal bottom – not available on any software I have seen.
- 30-day high – very few programs had the ability to scan for stocks trading at a 30-day high.
- Volume spikes – very few programs had the ability to scan for stocks that traded huge volume by comparison to the previous day.

My "sell" criteria included:

- Key reversal top – This was not available in any software I reviewed, so we had to develop this pattern.
- Breaking below support.
- Trading below a set of multiple moving averages.

Given that I could not find suitable software, I set about developing my own. While I am obviously biased in this area, there is no doubt that the "Pro Trader" software is specifically designed to find rising stocks, and it is more than a useful tool for both professional and new traders.

Other requirements were that the software:

- would store a list of stocks that I wanted to watch
- would scan the entire ASX database looking for stocks with recognisable patterns
- included a portfolio manager

- loaded the daily data from the exchange very simply and quickly.
- would be a toolbox, not a "black box" (A "Black box" is software that generates buy and sell signals based on mathematical formulae with no input from the user. It is usually expensive, comes with exaggerated historical results and rarely works. In fact, in my last twenty years involvement with software, I have never seen a black box that produces any form of positive return.)
- allowed me to draw trend-lines on a chart and have the software "signal" me anytime prices broke through or crossed any line I may draw
- incorporated on-balance-volume

Obviously, some of these functions were unavailable in software at that time. Over the ensuing years, we have designed several unique "world firsts", such as our proprietary "trend channel indicator", and the "trend channel deviation". The software development is ongoing, as we are dedicated to keeping our software at the cutting edge of analysis and technology.

In the development phase, we included various filters that gave the ability to narrow the search by:

- finding stocks trading between a particular price range

- not finding stocks that traded below a minimum dollar value in the previous five trading days, i.e: the scan will ignore a stock that has not traded at least $500 000 (this is a user choice) in the past five days

- ignoring stocks that do not have a significant history, i.e: the scan will ignore charts that do not have at least 200 (this is a user choice and is designed to keep the trader away from thinly traded stocks) trading days

2 | Step two
Choose a broker

Having chosen and installed your software, the next thing to do is to choose a broker. You have two choices; the traditional broker or the services offered by an "Online broker".

Despite the higher cost, I have always felt that the newcomer should begin his career using a traditional broker. The main reason is that you have enough to learn about trading without needing to learn all about order placement on the Internet. Make sure the broker you choose obeys your requirements. Ask around among your friends and workmates, someone will know a broker they can recommend. Contact the broker and he will give you the necessary documentation to complete.

3 Step three
Trawling for trades

My software allows me to use a "tick box" method to scan all ASX stocks for my buy criteria. For instance, I will "tick" the various boxes looking for stocks that show:

1. an ascending triangle
2. the current closing price trading at a 30-day high
3. 200 days of history
4. any stocks that have a volume spike of 1300% more than the previous day
5. a key reversal bottom
6. a minimum $250 000 traded in the last week
7. a multiple moving average crossover (I use 21,34,55 exponential moving averages)

This scan will typically find around 15 stocks suitable for further analysis. If this scan does not produce a suitable stock for trading, I may move on and perform various other scans with different criteria.

At the time of writing (1 November 2002), the most interesting looking stock was ADA (Adacel Technologies).

This stock intrigues me! The scan bought this stock to my attention due to the large volume spike: over two million traded, compared to 57 000 the previous day; and an average daily volume of less that 100 000 over

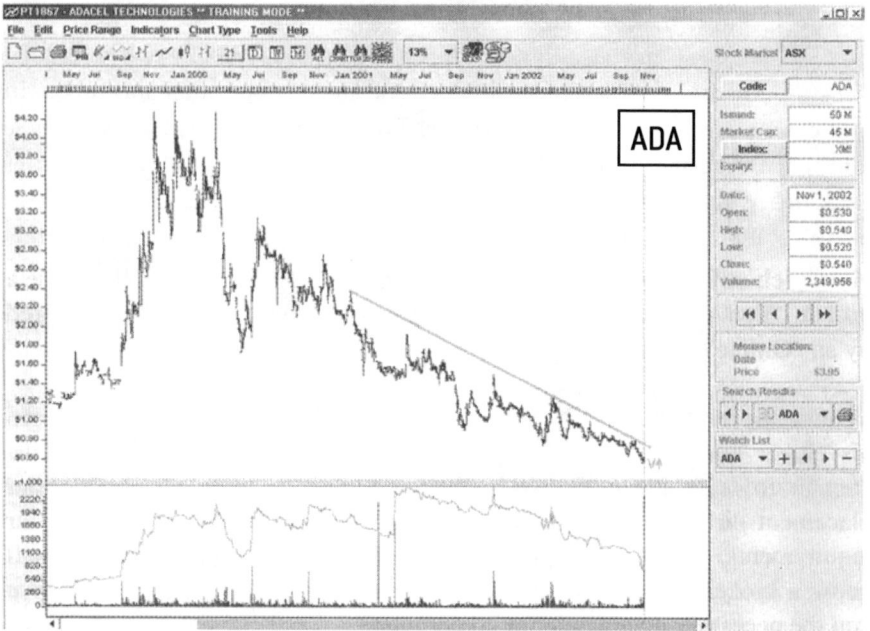

the past couple of months. I can draw a long-term resistance line on this chart. As we can see, it has been a long downward trend since March 2000, falling from $4.20 to current levels of 54 cents.

My thinking tells me that this company needs something to happen, or it may continue its drift into oblivion. The volume spike tells me that it is to happen soon. This stock would certainly enter my "watch list" as a stock to consider for purchase if the resistance line is broken.

If I were commencing a new $50 000 portfolio, ADA would be one of my chosen stocks once it trades above the resistance line. With $50 000 I would look at a portfolio of ten stocks, so I would need to find up to another 13 or 14 stocks and purchase the first 10 that fulfil my buying criteria.

4 Step four
Making the decisions

Having chosen ADA as one of my stocks, I need to work out the following:

- What is my buy signal?
- What are my confirmation factors?
- What is my stop-loss?
- What is my exit level?

Reasons for buying

The signal given was the volume spike, but the real issue is whether the volume spike is a strong enough signal on its own? With the stock clearly falling in price, initiating entry at present would be far too risky. Therefore, my buy signal will be when the price breaks above the resistance line. Given the length of the resistance, I would expect a reasonably strong move when the price breaks out.

Summarising confirmation signals

30-day high
Volume spikes
On-balance-volume
Moving average
Relative strength index
Stochastic
MACD

ADA confirmation

At present, the only confirmation signal that fits is the volume spike. The confirmation factors need to be checked at the time that prices break the resistance. At that point I would expect on-balance-volume to be rising, prices to be above my multiple moving average (21,34,55 exponential) and at, or above, a 30-day high.

Summarising stop-loss protection

Trailing stop-loss
Moving average
Support

ADA stop-loss

If prices break resistance and my confirmation factors are in place, my stop-loss in the early stages of this trade would be at 48 cents. This is below the lowest low on the chart. (51 cents on October 29th 2002)

Summarising exit signals

General philosophy

Split your parcel
Pattern recognition targets
Trailing stops

ADA general philosophy

I would use a trailing stop-loss with ADA and probably split my parcel for the reason given below.

Summarising specific exit signals

Key reversal top
Breaking of support
Pattern recognition target
Multiple moving average cross-over
Prior resistance

ADA specific exit

My thoughts would be to split my parcel on ADA, as there is no pre-determined pattern recognition target. I would intend selling half my holding at $1.37, provided my stop-loss is not activated. (Looking at the chart there is previous support at the $1.40 level. Past support becomes future resistance, so I would be happy to take some profit at this level. It would also be close to a 100% return given, my entry would be close to 70 cents.)

The balance I would follow with a trailing stop-loss and sell on a multiple moving average crossover or a key reversal top, whichever comes first.

5 Step five

Recording your trades

My records would show the following:

DATE	VOLUME	ENTRY	BROKERAGE	TOTAL COST
3/11/02	7000	.70	60.00	4960.00

Buy signal	Confirmation	Stop	Target
Volume spike	On-balance-volume	.48	$1.37 for 1/2
Resistance break	Multiple M. A.	Trailing	
	30-day high		

6 Step six

Placing your orders

The orders for ADA could be placed with a good broker in anticipation. For instanc,e I would have no problem giving a broker the following instructions:

- Buy 7 000 ADA if they trade at 71 cents.
- If this is complete, then sell 7 000 ADA at 48 cents if the stock falls to this level.

Do not be concerned with the correct terminology when placing orders; leave that to the broker, just tell him in simple English precisely what you want to do. Keep a diary note of the time and the course of the conversation. ALWAYS get the broker to repeat your instructions to you.

It may take some time to find ten suitable stocks and to get the orders filled. Remember, there is no rush, as the market has been there for over 150 years, and I daresay it will outlast you and me. One last word; when you find another stock you must buy, always sell the worst performing stock in the portfolio. This ensures your portfolio is being upgraded, not downgraded.

The best of luck with your trading. It will be as profitable as you want to make it.

Index